"This book is a masterpiece. So practical—inspired and inspiring! A dynamic practitioner guidebook that presents a truly remarkable roadmap for unlocking the mysteries of sexual suffering while alchemically transforming our clients' journey toward sexual wholeness."

—**Patti Britton, PhD, MPH**, past president of AASECT, co-founder of SexCoachU.com, author of *The Art of Sex Coaching*

"Gina Ogden has created a sex therapy workbook for clinicians based on her emotional, mental, physical, and spiritual approach. Her unique exercises explore the complexity of sexual desire and intimacy. This will be a valuable resource for body-oriented creative clinicians who advocate breaking barriers so individuals and couples can experience a vital sexuality."

—**Barry McCarthy, PhD**, professor of psychology at American University, author of *Rekindling Desire*

"*Exploring Desire and Intimacy* is a brilliant, action-packed, must-have part of any competent therapist's toolkit!"

—**P. Michele Sugg, MSW, LCSW, CST**, past president of AASECT

"Such a thoughtful, practical resource that enables all of us—layperson and professionals alike—to explore those aspects of sexuality and intimacy that impact our lives in so many complicated ways. Another treasure from Gina Ogden on our bookshelves and in our 'tool kits.'"

—**Judy Norsigian**, past executive director of Our Bodies Ourselves

"In *Exploring Desire and Intimacy*, Dr. Gina Ogden supports her innovations in therapy with the latest neuroscience research findings as she guides practitioners to help clients learn how body, mind, heart, and spirit are all integral parts of sexual experience."

—**Beverly Whipple, PhD, RN, FAAN**, past president of the Society for the Scientific Study of Sexuality (SSSS), co-author of *The G-Spot* and other books

"A treasure! I will definitely be getting it for my students. It will help them see that their job as sexuality educators is to help clients or students find their own vision of sexual life—not intrude into their story but simply offer tools for its construction. The exercises, especially 'Re-Membering,' ensure that they will consult with the dark side as well as the light."

—**Susan Stiritz, PhD**, senior lecturer and coordinator of sexuality studies for the Brown School, Washington University, St. Louis

"WOW! This book is simply brilliant and a wonderful contribution to our field. Dr. Gina Ogden has taken the powerful concept of the Four-Dimensional Wheel and brought it to clinicians in an easy to use, practical format that will be wonderful adjunct therapy for any clinician who works with individuals or couples on matters related to sex, intimacy and relationships."

—**Neil Cannon, PhD, LMFT**, instructor, University of Michigan School of Social Work Sexual Health Certificate Program

"In her most comprehensive volume thus far, Gina Ogden both elucidates theory and offers practical treatment tools that transcend standard sex therapy treatment models. Drawing on her original 4-Dimensional Wheel paradigm, and introducing original intervention strategies from actual sessions with clients and supervisees, Ogden's wisdom will surely inspire and enhance your practice."

—**Talli Y. Rosenbaum, MSc, CST**, academic advisor,
The Yahel Center for Jewish Intimacy

"Reading this workbook made me feel I had just spent the weekend with a mentor and friend, and I cannot imagine teaching her work without including this book. As you read *Exploring Desire and Intimacy*, you'll be guided by a master as she gives you specific ideas and practices for integrating the Wheel into your particular setting."

—**Tina Schermer Sellers, PhD**, founder of the Northwest
Institute on Intimacy, Seattle, WA

"*Exploring Desire and Intimacy* is a bit of magic that interweaves the processes of learning, experiencing, teaching, listening, and interacting. Gina Ogden has more than just authored this workbook, she also stands within the text, mirroring the journey we wish our clients to take: coaching, inviting, challenging readers to better understand themselves, their clients, and the field of sex therapy itself."

—**Daniel Rosen, LCSW-R**, sex therapist,
neurofeedback therapist, EMDR practitioner

"After 20 years of practicing gynecology, I have discovered that introducing women to the 4-Dimensional Wheel makes pelvic exams more informative and empowering. This workbook provides a consistent, reproducible framework to help clinicians communicate efficiently and powerfully about reproductive anatomy, sexual function, and the lifelong effects of a woman's sexual experience."

—**Debra S. Wickman, MD, FACOG**

"This workbook is filled with vast wisdom about how all kinds of people can regain sexual health and wholeness. It's presented so that even a busy doctor can use it to engage patients in their own healing—physical, emotional, mental, and spiritual."

—**Pebble Kranz, MD**, family physician,
University of Rochester Medical Center

"Once again, Dr. Ogden provides a rich resource full of tools and insightful guidance on how to bring the four dimensions alive. I will be providing copies of this workbook for all members of my staff and introducing it to my students."

—**Elliott Kronenfeld, LICSW, CST**, owner
of Insight Psychotherapy, Brookline, MA

"Award-winning Gina Ogden is recognized by her peers as a thought leader and top expert in sex therapy."

—**Bill Taverner**, editor-in-chief,
American Journal of Sexuality Education

Exploring Desire and Intimacy

This integrative book is like having a wise supervisor in the room with you. Stop "fixing" your clients—engage them in their own healing through the Four-Dimensional Wheel of Sexual Experience. Gina Ogden guides you in helping your clients explore the full range of their sexual issues and challenges—including couple communication, erectile dysfunction, vaginismus, low desire, affairs, trauma, religious proscriptions, pornography use, and more. Part I offers strategies that correspond to the core knowledge areas required for certification as a sexuality professional, while Part II puts these innovative approaches into action through following five case examples from seasoned practitioners. The numerous user-friendly elements, such as quizzes, worksheets, and "hot tips," will help you see the larger picture of an issue, become fluent with a diversity of sexual identities and behaviors, and expand your ability to offer safe, ethical, evidence-based therapy.

Gina Ogden, PhD, LMFT, is an adjunct professor at the California Institute of Integral Studies, an award-winning sex therapist, supervisor, researcher, and founder of the 4-D Network for Body, Mind, Heart, and Spirit. She conducts retreats, trainings, and online courses in how to use the Four-Dimensional Wheel. She lives in Cambridge, Massachusetts (www.GinaOgden.com and www. 4-DNetwork.com).

Other Books by Gina Ogden

The ABCs of Love and Sex

Extraordinary Sex Therapy (Ed.)

Expanding the Practice of Sex Therapy

The Return of Desire

The Heart and Soul of Sex

Women Who Love Sex

Safe Encounters (with Beverly Whipple)

Food for Body and Soul

Sexual Recovery

When a Family Needs Therapy (with Anne Zevin)

Exploring Desire and Intimacy
A Workbook for Creative Clinicians

Gina Ogden

Innovative Approaches
Practical Applications

A Companion to *Expanding the Practice of Sex Therapy:*
An Integrative Approach for Exploring Desire and Intimacy

Routledge
Taylor & Francis Group

NEW YORK AND LONDON

First published 2017
by Routledge
711 Third Avenue, New York, NY 10017

and by Routledge
2 Park Square, Milton Park, Abingdon, Oxon, OX14 4RN

Routledge is an imprint of the Taylor & Francis Group, an informa business

ISBN: 978-1-138-93376-7 (hbk)
ISBN: 978-1-138-93377-4 (pbk)
ISBN: 978-1-315-67836-8 (ebk)

Typeset in Frutiger
by Apex CoVantage, LLC

Printed and bound in the United States of America by Publishers Graphics,
LLC on sustainably sourced paper.

A portion of the author's proceeds will be donated to organizations promoting women's health.

The author and Routledge/Taylor & Francis thank Shambhala Publications for permission to adapt the template and descriptions of the Four-Dimensional Wheel from Gina Ogden's books *The Heart and Soul of Sex* and *The Return of Desire*.

Disclaimer

This book is intended as an educational volume only, not as a prescriptive manual. The information provided here is designed to help readers make informed, evidence-based decisions about their clients and themselves, not to substitute for therapeutic or medical treatment. While professional attributions are acknowledged throughout, all identifying details of a personal nature that appear in the case examples have been substantively altered to honor anonymity and confidentiality.

Whatever else we do as sex therapists, we must first of all do no harm. *Primum non nocere* is the oath of medical ethics, and is the underlying ethic of sex therapy, whether our primary mode is psychology, sociology, or neurobiology, whether we are psychotherapists, teachers, bodyworkers, or coaches; no matter where we look for information and inspiration—in the literature, in the spirit world, in our own experience.

To do no harm requires that we clear ourselves of whatever keeps us mired in our own dramas so that we can focus always and steadily on the well-being of our clients, not on how much we know (or fear we don't know) as therapists. The core of extraordinary sex therapy is relatively ordinary after all, although it is not always simple to practice. It is that we listen to our clients, create safe space, encourage movement—physical, emotional, mental, and spiritual—and trust our clients to do their own work so we are not working harder in their therapy than they are.

—*Gina Ogden,* from the Introduction to
Extraordinary Sex Therapy

About the Acronym ISIS

In 2004, I began using ISIS as an acronym for my nationwide survey "Integrating Sexuality and Spirituality." Eventually, ISIS also stood for the four-dimensional clinical approach that developed from the survey findings that sexual experience is multidimensional, once you factor in thoughts, emotions, and meanings as well as physical sensations. Three of my books feature the ISIS survey, the ISIS approach, and the ISIS Wheel of Sexual Experience, along with references to the "ISIS Network": the growing international group of clinicians who practice and teach this approach. A major reason I resonated to the name ISIS is that it placed this work directly in the lineage of the Egyptian goddess Isis, famously known as "Initiator into the Sexual Mysteries," which lent a mythic relevance to our deeply nuanced and integrative approach to sexual issues.

Enter the ISIS jihadists, who began wreaking havoc in 2014. At first, it seemed crucial not to capitulate by giving up our treasured name. But it's become increasingly misleading to speak to colleagues and clients of ISIS methods, and the ISIS Wheel, and particularly the ISIS Network, because the acronym links our healing work to a political movement focused on violence and destruction. At this writing, I am opting to retire the name ISIS, or at least send it securely underground. This workbook represents a transition to renaming the ISIS Wheel as the "Four-Dimensional Wheel," or "4-D Wheel." You'll still see ISIS written in my earlier books, and hear it referred to by colleagues—it's the same approach, just a different name. The truth is, the power of the ancient Isis mysteries lives on, and I have every hope that the name ISIS will again be recognized as a transformative force for integrating sexuality and spirituality.

Contents

Activities and Exercises for Practitioners and Clients

* Activities and exercises with asterisks are available to photocopy for clients as well as practitioners

Informational Sections for Practitioners and Clients

* Informational sections with asterisks are available to photocopy for clients as well as practitioners

Preface
"Help! Who Can I Talk with about Sex?"

"I know there's something wrong with me but I didn't want to go to my family doctor—is it low testosterone?" Sondra had come for help with low sexual desire. Pleasurable sex had stopped 12 years ago, after her daughter was born. Now she was in perimenopause and felt numb. She spoke in spurts, barely above a whisper. She perched on the sofa, her eyes avoiding mine. Her arms crossed her heart as if she could protect it from onslaught.

The very first moments of Sondra's story revealed numerous clues, but none of them pointed to medical or pharmaceutical intervention—at least not right away. What were these clues? What did they indicate about her sexual desire or lack of it? What had finally moved her to seek help? Sondra's husband had said he was going to leave unless she "shaped up in bed."

By 15 minutes into our session I found myself at a major choice point. Choice #1 was to continue listening empathically to Sondra's story of what was so wrong with her. Choice #2 was to divert her story and focus on taking a detailed sex history. Either of these choices would fit into standard sex-therapy practice for an initial session.

But there was a third therapeutic choice, and this was the one I opted for: I could set the stage for Sondra to expand her story beyond numbness and self-blame. I could invite her to take steps to inhabit her numbness consciously, so that she could begin to be aware of exactly what she was doing to close herself off from desire—for sex and perhaps other aspects of her life. I could invite her to discover for herself the multiple factors involved in her longing for intimacy with a partner who was threatening to leave her—to validate why it may have been necessary for her to shut herself down by stages year after year. With her permission, I could engage her in conceptualizing new scenarios for herself and her relationship. I could help her visualize a sea of possibilities—physical, emotional, mental, and spiritual—and encourage her to move toward that compelling sea.

For over four decades as a sex therapist and supervisor, I've consistently opted for the choice of expansion—helping clients of all genders and orientations open up their stories until they can find positive directions that lead beyond numbness, pain, blame, self-blame, fear, rage, and despair. My teachers in this choice of expansion have always been my clients, and more recently my supervisees. I've learned to listen closely to all of them, invite them to explore nuances of their stories, and collaborate with them rather than taking the role of Ultimate Expert.

What would such expansive sessions look like? How do these sessions compare with professional standards of "best practices"? How might expanding the practice of sex therapy affect your clients? And what might be the effects on you, the therapist, clinician, counselor, educator, guide?

The approaches and applications in the pages that follow address these questions. They are time-tested with both clients and practitioners. How effective they will be for you depends largely on your willingness to engage in the activities offered in each chapter, because this is a "workbook" in the true sense of the word. So I invite you to work it as well as read it so that you can make the practice your own.

Gina Ogden
Cambridge, Massachusetts
Gina@GinaOgden.com

Expanding the Title of This Book
Some Operational Definitions

Exploring—Active seeking. In this workbook, it means being open to surprise, adventure, and discovery as each client's story unfolds—as distinct from routinely following set protocols for diagnosing and treating pathology, or interpreting clients' behaviors. This degree of exploration requires courage, self-knowledge, and enough ego strength to invite collaboration with a client rather than maintain the role of Expert.

Desire—Passion. The "I want" of every synapse and energy center; activating physical pleasures, creative power, connection of hearts, open communication, clear understanding, and spiritual union.

Intimacy—Connection. Energy exchange between partners—body, mind, heart, and spirit. The "intima" is the innermost lining of the blood vessels and organs: the closest you can get to heart, brain, bone, memory, and other keepers of energy.

Innovative Approaches—Ways of expanding therapeutic interactions beyond clinical orthodoxy—as long as these ways are within your expertise and in the best interest of your clients. In this workbook, these approaches are centered on the template of the Four-Dimensional Wheel of Sexual Experience.

Practical Applications—Explicit examples, questions, activities, resources, and worksheets that enable you to incorporate innovative elements into your own practice.

Workbook—A personal arena that invites you to continually question, reconceptualize, write, create. An interactive forum that asks thought-provoking questions, offers inspiring quotes, illustrative examples, charts, and links to help you expand your practice.

Creative—Willing to tap your own resources, move beyond conventional definitions and dogmatic protocols in responsible ways for the well-being of clients. To paraphrase a quote attributed to Albert Einstein: "Creativity is contagious; pass it on."

Clinicians—Professionals who help clients expand their awareness and change their lives. Because clinical change is so entwined with open and active information, this workbook includes educators as well as therapists and other health professionals. A moving example of a professional who expanded awareness is Annie Sullivan, the "Teacher" who opened the world to the deaf and blind Helen Keller.

Introduction
The Four-Dimensional Wheel of Sexual Experience: A Guide to Creative Practice

Helping our clients on their quest for sexual desire and intimacy can be one of the most fascinating and rewarding journeys on the planet. Yet most therapists are not trained to talk about sex, and most sex therapists are trained to focus only on performance goals and behavioral treatments for dysfunction.

Exploring Desire and Intimacy offers the Four-Dimensional Wheel of Sexual Experience as a creative structure through which to help your clients explore their core sexual issues. The focus is on guiding you to expand your clients' capacity for health and pleasure, rather than on diagnosing and fixing symptoms.

The approaches offered are consistent with the latest neuroscience. The protocols are clear and interactive. Quizzes and worksheets highlight basic skills that are too often left out of our training. Case examples detail how you can apply the 4-D Wheel to address trauma, hormone imbalance, couple communication, religious proscriptions, and a range of other issues. You are encouraged to think intersectionally, to consider sexual issues through multiple lenses—gender, orientation, age, cultural differences, and more, and to recognize where past, present, and future intersect in your clients' lives.

WHAT IS IN THIS WORKBOOK?
AND HOW WILL IT HELP YOU HELP YOUR CLIENTS AND GROW YOUR PRACTICE?

Part I offers 4-D strategies that correspond to the core knowledge areas required for certification as a sexuality professional. The 4-D Wheel provides a structure for taking sex histories that explore physical, emotional, mental, and spiritual aspects of your clients' life spans. The Wheel also provides structure for creating a safe and powerful arena for change, inviting clients out of their chairs to access body intelligence, and encouraging clients to concretize abstract concepts to particularize the issues that overwhelm them. Activities for helping clients move from "No" to "Yes" fully acknowledge the "shadow" dimensions of their sexual stories while encouraging them to open themselves to what excites them and nurtures their relationships. You are guided to create your own Wheel and adapt it to fit your clients and your unique strengths.

Part II offers practical applications of the innovative approaches outlined in Part I, with cases, questions, activities, resources, and worksheets that help you incorporate the 4-D Wheel into your own practice. Five case examples from seasoned practitioners illustrate the collaborative nature of this work. Most importantly, they demonstrate how you can use the Wheel in sessions with challenging clients who present with a range of issues and problems, including erectile dysfunction, vaginismus, low desire, affairs, trauma, and self-diagnosed addiction to pornography. Therapeutic approaches these practitioners use with the Wheel include cognitive behavioral therapy (CBT), mindfulness, sex therapy, sensorimotor therapy, Jungian archetypes, EMDR, brainspotting, and more. Each case is accompanied by supervisory commentary—with invitations for you to comment on the process as it evolves.

It has been my experience that to use the 4-D approach most gracefully and effectively with clients, practitioners also need to have experienced it themselves. Almost every page presents opportunities to expand your own therapeutic wisdom, expertise, compassion, and presence. I invite you to work the pages that call out to you, walk the Wheel yourself, and trust in the possibilities of transformation.

Are You New to Sex Therapy?
Four Ways You Can Open a Conversation about Sexual Desire and Intimacy

Each of the questions below focuses on an area of sexual experience: physical, emotional, mental, or spiritual. Each area is distinct, yet related to all the others. You can ask these questions (or variations of them) during intakes and evaluations with your clients, or at any time you suspect that sexual issues may underlie your clients' relationship dynamics. You can ask them in any order. Asking them can be effective whether or not your clients bring up the subject of sex as a presenting problem.

1) **What are some of the *sexual messages* you received when you were growing up—and how do they affect your attitudes about sexual desire and intimacy now?**

This question focuses on the mental and cultural aspects of sexual experience that impact all the other aspects—physical, emotional, and spiritual. When you ask this question of clients, you present an opportunity for them to put sexual issues into context for themselves. You also present an opportunity for them to understand that much of our present sexual experience is shaped by the past—by culture, family, media, religious teaching, and more. Reviewing details of clients' sexual messages with them can also help couples understand each other at a new level, especially if their attitudes about sex differ.

2) **What is (or was) your *physical experience* of sexual desire and intimacy?**

This is an opportunity to help your clients explore all the sensations of touch, taste, smell, sight, and hearing—including pleasure and pain. Here, you can guide your clients to recognize the sensual patterns that are unique to each one of them. In addition, you can help them discover the intelligence of their bodies—how their physical sensations connect with their thoughts, emotions, and meanings. Such an exploration may reveal crucial nuances about desire. For instance, you may help a client understand that avoidance of sex may relate to physical pain rather than to a wish to reject a partner.

3) **What are (or were) your *emotional feelings* regarding sexual desire and intimacy?**

This is an opportunity to elicit the heart of the matter, quite literally. How do your clients open or close their hearts? Give and receive love? Express fear, sadness, disappointment, rage, hope, joy, comfort? Withhold their feelings? Exert control? Exploring the sexual emotions is fertile ground for helping clients relate their present blocks to early negative experiences, family patterns, sexual assault, or abusive relationships—and to explore positive experiences of comfort, acceptance, and love.

4) **What do (or did) sexual desire and intimacy *mean to your life*?**

This question focuses on the spiritual aspects of sex, which relate to connection and meaning. Note that for some clients (but not all), spirituality strongly includes religious beliefs. In this dimension, you can help your clients see the large picture—to explore the significance of sex in their lives. It's a further opportunity to explore discrepancies of desire in couples, when sex may be more crucial for one partner than the other.

You can use any or all of these questions to invite your clients to explore issues of sexual orientation, gender identity, cultural and ethnic differences, sexual compatibility, recovery from affairs, and much more. What's important is that you encourage your clients to explore their experience of sexual health and pleasure as well as what's wrong. When you frame these questions as part of overall relational patterning, your openness and curiosity transmit a message to your clients that can guide them to communicate more clearly with you—and, most importantly, with themselves and their partners.

Are You a Seasoned Sex Therapist?
Four Ways You Can Address Desire and Intimacy
—Beyond Performance Issues

These are the same questions, about physical, emotional, mental, and spiritual dimensions of your clients' sexual stories. As a seasoned sex therapist you can use your education and skills to deepen your clients' experience of the intrinsic complexity of desire and intimacy—to help them understand that there's more to sex than intercourse and other goals, and that sexual desire and intimacy often begin with self-esteem—the kind that allows for both excitement and close connection.

1) **What are some of the *sexual messages* you received when you were growing up—and how do they affect your attitudes about sexual desire and intimacy now?**
This question opens a prime opportunity for you to educate clients about how events can reach up from the past to control the present—everything from childhood abuse to questions about sexual identity: what does it mean to be a man, a woman, a transperson, a sexual being? What about lesbian, gay, bisexual issues? Poly relationships? Kinky sex? And more. Here also is an opportunity to encourage clients to re-examine specific messages for themselves, updating them, and making crucial decisions about which ones to keep and which to move beyond.

2) **What is (or was) your *physical experience* of sexual desire and intimacy?**
Here is an opening for you to help clients explore numerous approaches to the specific sexual dysfunctions that may affect desire and intimacy. You can apply your skills to helping them relieve vulval pain, erection difficulties, and other physical issues that affect their experience of sex. Equally important for some clients, you can help them "connect the dots" so they understand which of their physical issues affect desire (what they want) and intimacy (their sense of closeness in sexual relationships)—for instance, when addressing body image and/or sensate focus, how are physical sensations connected to emotional, mental, and spiritual issues?

3) **What are (or were) your *emotional feelings* regarding sexual desire and intimacy?**
Exploring your clients' sexual emotions is an opportunity to delve as deeply as your expertise allows into anger, fear, grief—and also excitement, joy, love—to help your clients differentiate between what they feel and what they *think* about what they feel (the mental dimension), to identify what they want and do not want, to take responsibility for their desires rather than expecting their partners to provide all the stimulation, and to discover when and how they concede their own desires in reactivity to their partners' real or imagined wishes. Here is an opportunity to encourage clients to move beyond blame and self-blame when sex is not working according to their preconceived goals.

4) **What do (or did) sexual desire and intimacy *mean to your life*?**
This question is about spirituality—the sense of connection and meaning. For some clients this can include transcendent experiences, which may be difficult for them to articulate. Here is an opportunity to help your clients deepen their explorations of desire—what is it they truly want? Is it bigger, better, more frequent orgasms—with more risk and play and possibly kinky adventures? Here also you can help your clients explore intimacy: Is it heart-to-heart connection with a partner—with more honesty and commitment? Always, you can encourage your clients to listen to their soul's voice as they honor body, mind, and heart.

"OUR OTHER THERAPIST NEVER GOT AROUND TO TALKING ABOUT SEX"

This is a comment I've heard from too many clients. Many clinicians avoid sexual issues because they are not trained as sex therapists. Their reticence to introduce the subject ranges from embarrassment, to concern that they don't know enough, to fear that initiating a conversation about sexuality may be unethical or even abusive to their clients.

It doesn't have to be this way. Opening the conversation about sexual issues can be a huge relief to clients. The Four-Dimensional Wheel on which this workbook is based offers safe, effective ways to introduce sexual issues into your clinical work with individuals and couples—even if you're not an expert in sex-therapy techniques and pharmaceutical interventions. If the conversation goes beyond your depth, you can always refer to a certified sex therapist or seek sex-therapy training. An excellent place to begin the search for either a referral or training is the American Association of Sexuality Educators, Counselors, and Therapists: www.AASECT.org.

Part I

Innovative Approaches

Strategies for Change and Transformation
through the Four-Dimensional
Wheel of Sexual Experience

1

Asking New Questions of Our Clients—and Ourselves

Exploring Body, Mind, Heart, and Spirit

"As you go the way of your life
you will come to a great chasm.
Jump! It is not as wide as you think."
—*Traditional Native American Wisdom*

OPENING QUIZ:
YOUR ATTITUDES ABOUT EXPLORING CLIENTS' ISSUES
WITH DESIRE AND INTIMACY

This quiz is not a test! It is to help you recognize your own opinions and consider new ones. There are no right or wrong answers—interpret them as you wish, and write other questions on this page as they occur to you.

Circle the number that most closely reflects your views on the questions below:

1 always true; 2 sometimes true; 3 seldom true; 4 never true

Sex is mainly about intercourse	1 2 3 ④
Sex is connected with every aspect of our lives	1 ② ·3 4
Sexual desire exists mainly in relationship with a partner	1 2 ③ 4
If a couple resolves their differences, the sex will take care of itself	1 2 ③ 4
Too much intimacy can dull sexual desire	1 2 3 4 ?
Sexual desire and intimacy can enhance each other	① 2 3 4
Sexual desire can be scientifically measured	1 2 3 ④
Sexual intimacy can be scientifically measured	1 2 3 ④
Gay, lesbian, and trans clients have different desires than heterosexual clients	1 2 3 4 ?
Clients with histories of abuse can never have satisfying sex	1 2 ③ 4
I don't know enough to help clients with sexual issues	1 ② 3 4
Pharmaceutical intervention is the most effective way to cure sexual dysfunction	1 2 ③ 4
Evidence-based treatments are the only responsible way to practice sex therapy	1 2 3 ④
Effective sex therapy involves body, mind, heart, and spirit	① 2 3 4
Effective sex therapy may mean reframing dysfunction rather than curing it	① 2 3 4
Sharing personal information with a client is always therapeutic	1 2 ③ 4
Other issues _____	1 2 3 4
Other issues _____	1 2 3 4
Other issues _____	1 2 3 4

There are many effective ways of taking a sex history—which ways do you use? (Check all that apply)

___ A written questionnaire before or after the initial session with a client
___ One or more intensive sessions dedicated to sex-history issues
___ A sexual genogram to explore generational issues about sexual attitudes and behaviors
___ Relevant sex-history issues gathered over time during sessions
___ Questions organized around 4-D Wheel explorations of body, mind, heart, and spirit
___ Other ways _____
___ Other ways _____
___ Other ways _____

What can we learn from our clients? Often, an uncanny combination of humility and resilience regarding ourselves. And an understanding that in order to help certain clients you may have to exercise creativity. There are seldom truly resistant clients, only uncreative therapists.

This workbook is designed as a companion for *Expanding the Practice of Sex Therapy*. Chapter 1 is based on *Expanding* Chapters 3–8, which detail the Four-Dimensional Wheel of Sexual Experience.

EXPANDING YOUR TAKE ON SEX-HISTORY TAKING: A FOUR-DIMENSIONAL APPROACH

What questions are you asking your clients about sexual desire and intimacy? Unless you're specifically trained in sex therapy or counseling, you may be avoiding the issue almost entirely. If you're a seasoned sex therapist, you have probably been taught to lead with inquiries about performance, such as: "How many times have you had intercourse in the last week/month/year?" This is a question considered primary to most sex-therapy training—and most of us are taught to follow it closely with: "How often do you achieve orgasm?" These and other performance-focused questions are rooted in the notions that it is possible to quantify sexual response and that effective sex therapy is based on behavioral goals and outcomes. They are basic tenets pioneered by Alfred Kinsey et al. in the 1940s and 1950s and William Masters and Virginia Johnson in the 1960s and 1970s.

This workbook expands sex counseling and therapy beyond performance behaviors to address desire and intimacy—both infinitely complex issues that cannot be counted and measured, much less "cured." Here, you will find a four-dimensional approach to help you help your clients. This approach is based on a truth that has emerged for me over my years of clinical practice and sex-survey research:

Sexual experience is multidimensional.
Desire and intimacy involve our bodies, minds, hearts, and spirits.

This workbook offers step-by-step practices that walk you through helping clients identify what they want, investigate how they may be preventing themselves from having what they want, and discover multiple ways to experience more of what they want—in right relationship to their partners, if they have partners.

This workbook also expands beyond the notion that therapists have to be fully formed experts. Another emergent truth is that none of us can be expert in everything. Our clients are our teachers, sometimes fully as much as we are theirs. Moreover, our clients' issues may strike resonant chords in us—the official name is "countertransference." The profound lesson here is that the professional is personal, often deeply so. My hope is that the practices in this workbook inspire you to participate in them personally, so that you can experience them for yourself before you ask your clients to engage in them.

To conduct "expanded" sex therapy means that we actively and continually participate in our own awareness and growth as human beings and clinicians.

That said, each of us is expert in something important that opens us to this work. So let's begin this work with your own expertise, as a marker to which you can always return. Please complete the sentence stems below:

I am an expert in _____

_____

My expertise leads me to this work because _____

_____

_____

My hope is that participating in this workbook will enable me to_____

_____

_____

EXPLORING DESIRE AND INTIMACY: STARTING YOUR 4-D PRACTICE

At the heart of the expanding practice is the Four-Dimensional Wheel of Sexual Experience (4-D Wheel).

The 4-D Wheel includes the mental, physical, emotional, and spiritual dimensions that are always present in our sexual experience, whether or not we are aware of all of them. The Wheel can be used to help clients map all sorts of sexual responses—past, present, and even future. Note that each dimension includes both positive components (such as excitement, joy, and love) and shadow components (such as pain, dysfunction, and rage). Most often it is the shadow that clients bring into our offices. But shadows cannot exist without light. It is crucial to help clients bear in mind the wished-for positives so that their stories are not constantly mired in pathology.

The point of diagramming the Wheel is to help both therapists and clients see at a glance that the picture of sexual desire and intimacy is more than just genital, or even just physical. Seeing the large picture can encourage clients to expand their stories of desire and intimacy beyond habitual narratives, which are often self-defeating. Using the Four-Dimensional Wheel as an organizing principle for exploring these stories can help clients describe their unique experiences from the perspective of each dimension—sensations, feelings, thoughts, and meanings—rather than focusing only on frequencies of intercourse or orgasm or on what is wrong with themselves or their partners.

When you help clients organize their descriptions in this differentiated way, you encourage them to provide both verbal and nonverbal clues about what they really want—from therapy and from their lives. These clues always inform the therapy, and they can surprise clients. For instance, a woman may present with a physical dysfunction such as vaginismus, yet her expanded story may reveal that her major issues are primarily emotional (e.g., rage at her partner), or mental (e.g., stuck in the "shoulds" and "oughts" of a repressive childhood), or spiritual (e.g., longing for connection and meaning). Any or all of these issues may reside in unexplored parts of her history, trapped, like proverbial flies in amber. You'll find much more about the revelatory aspects of working with the Wheel in chapters that follow.

> **???** **Did You Know—Some 700 sex surveys were conducted in the US during the 20th century.** They primarily investigated quantifiable questions about behaviors, such as: "How many times did you have intercourse in the last week/month/year?" This limited focus has resulted in misinformation about the wide range of ways Americans of all ages, genders, and other diversities may actually experience sex.

Facts and trends from sex surveys that I use to inform myself and my clients _____

_____

_____

Facts and trends from other sources that I use to inform muself and my clients _____

_____

_____

_____

**THE FOUR-DIMENSIONAL WHEEL OF SEXUAL EXPERIENCE:
AN ORGANIZING PRINCIPLE FOR SEXUAL AWARENESS AND GROWTH**

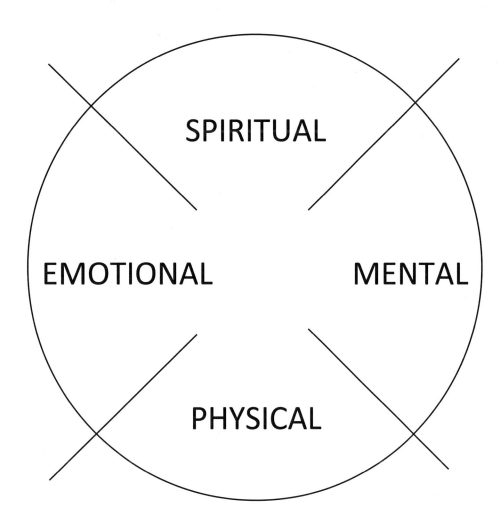

SPIRITUAL

EMOTIONAL   MENTAL

PHYSICAL

THE PHYSICAL DIMENSION OF THE 4-D WHEEL

The physical dimension of the 4-D Wheel is the arena where clients can locate and explore a full range of sensory experiences, sometimes in ways they have never considered before. Exploring this dimension in depth allows them to experience basic sensations of their identity as sexual beings— as fully male or female, as intersex, or as trans. It also allows them to reflect on the kinds of stimulation they find most erotic, and on their sexual orientation—as heterosexual, lesbian, gay, bisexual, queer, questioning, or other. The physical dimension includes:

- Smell
- Taste
- Touch
- Sight

- Hearing
- Interior sensations—gut
- Interior sensations—heart
- More/other_____

Positive aspects of the physical dimension are characterized by:

- Heightened sensations
- Awareness of how all the senses connect to all parts of the body

- Awareness of how all the senses connect through attraction, excitement, arousal, and orgasm
- More/other_____

Shadow aspects of the physical dimension are characterized by:

- Pain
- Distaste
- Disgust

- Lack of feeling: numbness
- Dysfunctions of intercourse and orgasm
- More/other_____

> **???** **Did You Know**—"Numb" is a marvelously descriptive word from the Middle English, meaning "taken"—that is, having your sensations literally seized and taken away.

YOUR OBSERVATIONS ABOUT THE PHYSICAL DIMENSION OF THE 4-D WHEEL

Physical issues clients bring into my office include_____

_____

Physical issues I feel able to help clients with include_____

_____

Physical issues I find difficult to help clients with include _____

_____

Clients' physical issues that may raise countertransference for me include_____

_____

My own physical issues that may affect my work with clients include_____

_____

What I know about sexual anatomy and how it functions includes_____

_____

What I need to learn about sexual anatomy and how it functions includes_____

_____

© 2017, *Exploring Desire and Intimacy: A Workbook for Creative Clinicians*, Gina Ogden, Routledge

THE EMOTIONAL DIMENSION OF THE 4-D WHEEL

The emotional dimension is the arena where clients can locate and explore a full range of their emotional feelings, including how they experience their sexual identity and orientation, how they relate to themselves, their partners, and others, and how their present emotions may be affected by past and possibly the future. Issues in the emotional dimension include:

- Love
- Passion
- Compassion
- Empathy
- Longing

- Anger
- Fear
- Grief
- More/other_____

Positive aspects of the emotional dimension are characterized by:

- Open-heartedness
- Heightened emotions
- Nuanced emotions

- Trust, ability to let go of control
- Empathy, ability to feel what others feel
- More/other_____

Shadow aspects of the emotional dimension are characterized by:

- Constriction
- Anxiety
- Disappointment
- A closed or broken heart
- Distrust, the inability to let go of control
- Depression

- Conflict
- Rage
- Boredom
- Shame
- More/other_____

> 🔆 **Hot Tip—The emotional dimension is where clients often reveal issues of post-traumatic stress disorder (PTSD).** It is in this dimension that I most often see time literally collapse, as a client suddenly begins to speak in a child-voice and exhibit child-like body language (especially notice fingers, toes, positioning of head, and facial expressions). The therapeutic dialogue might begin like this:
>
> **Therapist:** "How old do you feel right now?"
> **Client:** "I'm three years old—and I'm so small, and my brothers are so big and so mean . . ."

YOUR OBSERVATIONS ABOUT THE EMOTIONAL DIMENSION OF THE 4-D WHEEL

Emotional issues clients bring into my office include_____

_____

Emotional issues I feel able to help clients with include_____

_____

Emotional issues I find difficult to help clients with include _____

_____

Clients' emotional issues that may raise countertransference for me include_____

_____

My own emotional issues that may affect my work with clients include _____

_____

I create safety for clients to open up emotionally by_____

_____

I inhibit clients opening up emotionally by_____

_____

THE MENTAL DIMENSION OF THE 4-D WHEEL

The mental dimension is the arena where clients can seek understanding about the many issues that affect their sexual identity and emotions, along with their beliefs and messages about sex, intimacy, and love, and messages from family, religion, medicine, the media, and the overall culture, especially the culture they were raised in. Also inhabiting the mental dimension are issues that include:

- Imagination
- Intuition
- Memory
- Dreams
- Fantasies
- Wishes
- Intentions
- Anticipations and expectations
- More/other_____

Positive aspects of the mental dimension are characterized by:

- Curiosity
- Discernment
- Expanded beliefs
- Increased understanding
- Illumination
- Problem-solving
- Capacity to seek positive alternatives
- More/other_____

Shadow aspects of the mental dimension are characterized by:

- Self-limiting messages
- Negative memories
- "Shoulds" and "oughts"
- Rigid judgments about the right way to have sex
- Rigid judgments about how, what, and with whom one is supposed to be sexual
- Lack of curiosity
- More/other_____

> ☀ **Hot Tip—The mental dimension is where many clients automatically gravitate to as a "safe place"**—an escape from both physical senses and emotional feelings. It is also where clients often reveal learned and habitual responses about domination, control, and violence, especially regarding gender roles, orientation, race, and other sexual differences.

YOUR OBSERVATIONS ABOUT THE MENTAL DIMENSION OF THE 4-D WHEEL

Mental issues clients bring into my office include_____

_____

Mental issues I feel able to help clients with include _____

_____

Mental issues I find difficult to help clients with include _____

_____

Clients' mental issues that may arouse countertransference in me include _____

_____

My own mental issues that may affect my work with clients include _____

_____

I allow my clients to define themselves when I_____

_____

I may impose my values and constructs onto my clients when I _____

_____

THE SPIRITUAL DIMENSION OF THE 4-D WHEEL

The spiritual dimension is the arena where clients can explore what sex, love, and intimacy mean in the context of their sexual identity and their whole lives; how these may connect them to themselves, their partners, and a power beyond themselves: nature, or a universal energy, by whatever name. For some clients, the spiritual dimension is intimately connected with religious experience; for others it is not. Issues in the spiritual dimension may include:

- Inner visions
- Extraordinary communication—with a partner, with nature, with divine beings
- Experiences that are "beyond words"
- Oneness, a sense of being part of "all that is"
- More/other_____

> 🔆 **Hot Tip—When clients interpret the concept of "spiritual" as "religious" it can be helpful to validate this, then to differentiate between these terms.** Short form: "spiritual" refers to personal connection with a power greater than you; "religious" refers to cultural traditions that connect you to that power. To elaborate, you can ask clients to bring their attention to the line between the spiritual and mental dimensions. This is often the most accurate place from which clients can explore the difference between their spiritual teachings and beliefs and their religious teachings and beliefs.

Positive aspects of the spiritual dimension are characterized by:

- Connection
- Expanded meaning
- Increased energy
- Transcendence
- Ecstasy
- More/other_____

Shadow aspects of the spiritual dimension are characterized by:

- Disconnection
- Depression
- Immobilization
- More/other_____

> 🔆 **Another Hot Tip—When you ask direct questions about sex and spirit, the answers may surprise you.** In my survey "Integrating Sexuality and Spirituality," I received thousands of responses about how women and men all over the US define spiritual sex. One of my favorites is from a 32-year-old journalist: "Sacred sex is not just found in intercourse. It's all around, in everything we see, hear, smell, touch, taste. Honey is sex. A fresh warm strawberry is sex. Living is a sacred sexual experience."

YOUR OBSERVATIONS ABOUT THE SPIRITUAL DIMENSION OF THE 4-D WHEEL

Spiritual issues clients bring into my office include _____

Spiritual issues I feel able to help clients with include _____

Spiritual issues I find difficult to help clients with include _____

Clients' spiritual issues that may arouse countertransference in me include _____

My own spiritual issues that may affect my work with clients include _____

My beliefs about organized religion include_____

THE CENTER OF THE 4-D WHEEL

The center of the Wheel is a place of integration and transformation, where all the other dimensions meet and merge—body, mind, heart, and spirit. In this book, the center is represented as white space—unlabeled in the 4-D diagram because it is not differentiated in the same way that the physical, emotional, mental, and spiritual dimensions are. The center is the indefinable "All." I call it the place of "O God!"—because that is what people cry out in bedrooms across the world in a moment of orgasm or ecstasy. The shadow side of "O God" is a cry for light in the darkness, a cry of despair uttered by so many of our clients. Issues in the center of the Wheel may include:

- A sense of entering the uncharted territory of the sexual mysteries
- Extraordinary vibrancy and significance
- Spontaneous life changes and healing—of body, mind, heart, spirit
- Uncanny merging of opposites
- Sexual ecstasy—beyond pleasure or orgasm
- More/other_____

Positive aspects of the center of the Wheel are characterized by:

- Oneness
- Integration
- Timelessness
- Extraordinary lightness of being
- Profound ability to communicate
- Mental clarity
- Unconditional love
- More/other_____

Shadow aspects of the center of the Wheel are characterized by:

- Fragmentation
- Hopelessness
- Dissociation
- Despair
- Existential heaviness
- More/other_____

> ⚡ **Hot Tip—When clients are totally immersed in either ecstasy or despair, it can be helpful to acknowledge that they may be in the center of the Wheel.** You can then guide them from this place to explore each dimension of body, mind, heart, and spirit as they seek the most helpful routes to begin to differentiate their issues.

YOUR OBSERVATIONS ABOUT THE CENTER OF THE 4-D WHEEL

Center-of-the-Wheel issues that clients bring into my office include_____

_____

Center-of-the-Wheel issues I feel able to help clients with include_____

_____

Center-of-the-Wheel issues I find difficult to help clients with include _____

_____

Clients' center-of-the-Wheel issues that may arouse countertransference in me include_____

_____

My own center-of-the-Wheel issues that may affect my work with clients include_____

_____

OPENING THE CONVERSATION ABOUT DESIRE AND INTIMACY: HELPING YOUR CLIENTS EXPAND THEIR STORIES

Sex therapists the world over have developed diverse ways of gathering information about their clients' sex histories. Some ask clients to fill out a preliminary questionnaire—often a chronology of events and behaviors, starting from birth or early childhood and on into the present. (If you work in an agency, a preliminary questionnaire may be standard procedure, but it may not include much relevant information about sexual issues.) Other sex therapists systematically ask questions during the first few sessions, sometimes via structured interviews on a clipboard. Others elicit relevant sex histories more organically, over time. What ultimately works for you will depend on your own style as well as the specific client and situation—for instance, a need for crisis intervention involves a sex history that's different from gathering information from partners who come for help in enhancing pleasure.

THE 4-D WHEEL AS A GUIDE FOR SEX-HISTORY TAKING

The Wheel has become the primary organizing principle through which I gather information about clients—whatever their problems and however complex their life journeys.

I may simply keep the 4-D template in mind during our initial interviews, making sure to ask clients about their physical, emotional, mental, and spiritual experiences as they relate their stories. Or I may ask clients to speak significant parts of their stories from various dimensions—as I suggested you do in the activities on the previous page. Or I may ask clients to embody their stories by standing up and "walking the Wheel." This offers both you and your clients a sense of their body language. Most important, walking the Wheel offers an opportunity for clients to access their own body intelligence as they move from mental to emotional to physical, and so on, back and forth during their journey on the Wheel. Details of these techniques are spelled out in following chapters.

When clients come into therapy, they invariably carry with them a basic story that is attached to their presenting problem. If you listen deeply, this story almost always loops around to some predetermined conclusion of pain or dysfunction—such as: "My alcoholic mother never formed healthy attachments, and now that I'm 48 (or 36, or 73 . . .) I'm a person who can never commit to a partner." Or: "I was abused as a child, and now my life is a constant search for someone who'll take care of me."

Clients may not verbalize their core issues this succinctly because every story has its own compelling details, detours, side roads, dramas, special effects, and dead ends. But the bottom line is the same: most clients are stuck in pain or dysfunction because of some degree of trauma, and the story, repeated over and over through the years, has become part of the glue. Using the Wheel can help you help your clients recognize that glue, and practice ways to dissolve it—instantly, or over time.

When you ask clients to tell their stories from the perspective of each dimension of the Wheel, those stories inevitably expand to more than their predetermined conclusion. In my experience, once a story is told in that multidimensional way, it changes, and also changes its impact. The old story is like a black-and-white snapshot, crinkled and smudged with handling. The expanded story is more like a vibrantly colored video with titles, music, and constantly available links and updates. The old picture of the past loses its fascination and much of its power. The new picture is compelling—and often hopeful as well.

4-D HISTORY TAKING: CREATIVE WAYS YOU CAN USE THE WHEEL

Note: Guidelines for confidentiality and other safety issues are in Chapter 2.
Before you begin, make one or more copies of the Wheel diagram on p. 7 or p. 175.

EXPLORING YOUR OWN SEX HISTORY VIA THE 4-D WHEEL

Do this activity yourself first before you use it with clients
Beside each of the dimensions, write comments, dates, memories, questions about your own sex history—your sensations, feelings, thoughts, and dreams. Use pencil, pen, crayons, whatever moves you. Use extra paper if you run out of room. One colleague recorded her sex history starting with her year of birth—and used a roll of shelf paper to register her events and thoughts and drawings. Another colleague recorded her sex history as a series of self-portraits from various times in her life. She started in the present and moved backward in time. What is your way?

TALK ABOUT YOUR OWN SEX HISTORY VIA THE 4-D WHEEL

Do this activity with your partner or a friend
- Each of you take at least 20 minutes (decide on more or less time if you like—just be sure each of you has equal time). Set a timer to keep yourselves honest.
- When you are speaking, be as clear as possible about locating yourself in a particular dimension (body, mind, heart, spirit) and also in time (then, now, recently, "When I was a little kid . . ." "Right now . . ." "Yesterday . . ." etc.).
- When your partner or friend is speaking, listen. Stay open and allow them to have their space. Make eye contact. No interrupting, arguing, advice-giving, grunts, gestures, or finishing sentences. No rescue measures if they cry. Have Kleenex nearby just in case.
- To conclude the activity, thank each other, and each of you say what you learned about yourself from this activity—then say what you learned about each other. Decide if you want to continue the conversation—and how.

HELP YOUR CLIENTS EXPLORE THEIR SEX HISTORIES VIA THE 4-D WHEEL

- Show a copy of the Wheel diagram to your client(s). Allow 10 or 20 minutes (or whatever it takes) to clarify for them that sexual experience is more than just physical or just performance oriented, and allow for questions and explanations. This can be a time for sex education where it is warranted. To structure your explanation of the Wheel, draw from what you learned by doing the activity yourself.
- Ask client(s) to take a copy home. Suggest they write in each dimension—their comments, memories, questions about their sex histories, in terms of sensations, feelings, thoughts, and connections—as you did in the activity on the previous page.
- Ask client(s) to take a copy home to share with their partners—to open a discussion of their sexual desire and intimacy—and to facilitate the discussion. Use or adapt from the guidelines on this page.
- To deepen parts of the sex-history taking, ask clients to get out of their chairs and explore the Wheel with you. This powerful and empowering activity is outlined in Chapter 3.

© 2017, Exploring Desire and Intimacy: A Workbook for Creative Clinicians, Gina Ogden, Routledge

Three Activities to Open Awareness about Sexual Desire and Intimacy

Part I: Practice These Activities Yourself

Before you ask your clients to explore the Wheel, use these activities to begin your own exploration of each dimension of the Wheel, past, present, and possibly future

Part II: Ask Your Clients to Practice These Activities—in Your Office or as Homework

Once you have explored your own stories, use these activities to ask your clients to begin exploring the Wheel

A Mindfulness Practice:

Imagine describing your own experience of desire and intimacy from each dimension
As you read the descriptions of the Wheel dimensions on the previous pages, *imagine yourself* speaking from each dimension of the Wheel: physical, emotional, mental, and spiritual. Feel free to alter any of these descriptors or add new ones. Jot down any changes you notice to the descriptions as you engage your imagination in this way_____

_____

_____

_____

_____

An Embodiment Practice:

Physically step into each dimension and describe your own experience of desire and intimacy
Place a template of the Wheel on the floor, and *actually stand* in each dimension as you describe your experiences of desire and intimacy: physical, emotional, mental, and spiritual (in any order). Jot down your felt sense of these descriptions as you engage your story in this embodied way_____

_____

_____

_____

_____

_____

An Integration Practice:

Explore each dimension of your experience of desire and intimacy in terms of time
As you journey around the Wheel, speak from each dimension about your experiences of desire and intimacy in your *remembered past, in your present, and in your imagined future.* Jot down any changes you notice to the descriptions as you "time travel" in this way _____

_____

_____

_____

_____

HELP YOUR CLIENTS CLARIFY AND INTENSIFY THEIR SEX HISTORIES BY MOVING BETWEEN THE DIMENSIONS OF THE 4-D WHEEL

Clients give you distinct clues as to which dimension will help them locate their stories. When a client is telling a story via the Wheel, suggest that s/he move to the following dimensions:

- **Physical dimension**: if you notice exaggerated or repeated body movement or twisting, placing hands on body parts; also no movement and/or constricted breathing—**Ask: "What is your body saying?"**
- **Emotional dimension**: if you notice tears, angry words, or changes in breathing patterns—**Ask: "What is your heart saying?"**
- **Mental dimension**: if you notice words like "should" and "ought," or retelling the same story as if by rote—**Ask: "What is your head saying?"**
- **Spiritual dimension**: if you notice a sudden shift, eye-movement denoting contemplation, change of tone, or speechlessness—**Ask: "What kind of meaning are you making of all this?"**

THE 4-D WHEEL: LETTING THE DIMENSIONS SPEAK FOR THEMSELVES

Write any other phrases here that will help you describe the Wheel to yourself or your clients.

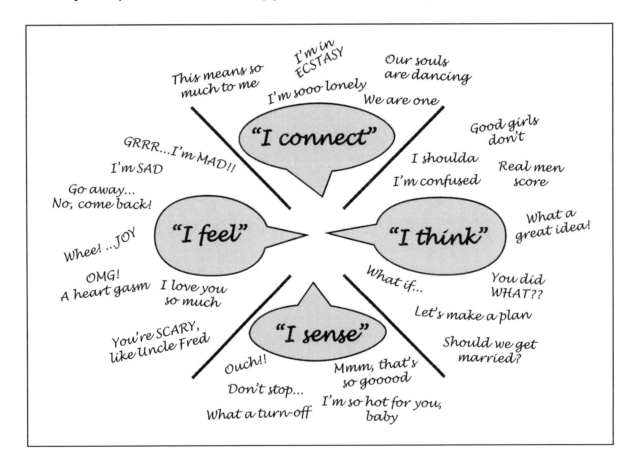

HOW ARE RESULTS OF SEX-HISTORY TAKING VIA THE WHEEL DIFFERENT FROM JUST TALKING ABOUT OUR SEXUAL STORIES?

In the physical dimension: A sense of embodiment may spontaneously replace numbness and pain ("For the first time I can feel my heart connected with my body and my genitals. No wonder I've had low desire—most of what I've ever experienced until now has been out-of-body sex.").

In the emotional dimension: Feelings may emerge where a client had formerly been unable to express any emotions at all ("I'm so f-u-r-i-o-u-s at my mother for drinking her life away instead of paying attention to me!"). The feelings may not be warm and fuzzy at first (or ever), but they spell release, and can clear blocks between present and past so clients can feel more alive in their present partnerships.

In the mental dimension: A bolt of illumination may suddenly reframe old, repeated messages ("Wait! My mother was a drunk—but that doesn't have to mean I can't bond with my partner now!").

In the spiritual dimension: An acknowledgment that past pain is, and even was, meaningful ("I had a totally lousy deal as a kid. But I sure learned a lot about taking care of myself—thanks, Mom!").

What Has Happened?

By telling the story from a variety of different perspectives (and especially if they walk the Wheel), clients spontaneously interrupt the rote story they brought into therapy. They are encouraged to explore and expand it to where they actually experience positive options emerging. These options may include a broader range of emotions, or increased self-esteem, or a vision of the kinds of desire and intimacy clients want, and do not want. Or all of the above. Or something else.

What makes four-dimensional sex-history taking different from linear, talk-therapy sex-history taking is that clients are making these discoveries for themselves—often beyond where talking chronologically about their situation could lead them. Clients effectively take their own histories by showing (and sometimes re-experiencing) feelings and events rather than only telling us about them. Moreover, clients may make organic, self-generated connections between events (e.g., ". . . my stepfather's abuse and my partner's touch—I never got the connection before! No wonder I have to smoke pot and zone out before we have sex.").

What Does This Mean for Therapists?

Four-dimensional history taking involves engaging our clients in fully exploring their own stories, often in layers and often back and forth in time. This means the therapist's job is to hold space and encourage clients without offering interpretation or advice, or being bound to specific diagnoses. It means we give up the role of expert question-asker and diagnostician and take on the role of active listener and holder of safe space. In shifting roles like this, many practitioners who have trained in the 4-D approach report that they suddenly learn more about their clients without having to work so hard.

In following chapters: look for activities on the whats/whys/whens/hows of creating safe space, eliciting your clients' stories, practicing active listening, and offering education where relevant.

THE NEUROSCIENCE OF 4-D SEX-HISTORY TAKING

Describing desire and intimacy in four dimensions activates multiple areas of the brain and involves moving between the left and right hemispheres—from linear and rational to imaginative and poetic. Encouraging clients to tell their stories in this multidimensional way reorganizes their neural pathways—opening up new landscapes to explore, both for healing old patterns and exploring new avenues for erotic pleasure.

Guiding clients to differentiate their experience via the dimensions—physical, emotional, mental, and spiritual—sets the stage for integration and healing by helping them link separate aspects of their sexual stories: physical desires and emotional desires; what they want in their heads and what they want in their hearts; and so forth. This process of differentiation and integration is basic to neuroscientist Dan Siegel's "Mindsight" approach; he calls it the core mechanism in the cultivation of well-being. To see the complexities of brain interactions during desire, see the animated tour narrated by anthropologist Helen Fisher and neuroscientist Lucy Brown: TheAnatomyofLove.com.

As Part I continues, short guidelines on neuroscience will highlight how using the 4-D Wheel activates new neuronal connections to enrich the therapeutic experience for you and your clients.

HOW CAN INFORMATION ABOUT NEUROSCIENCE HELP US HELP OUR CLIENTS?

"Am I normal?" This is a basic question many clients bring into sex therapy, whether or not they say this phrase out loud. These clients need reassurance that there's not something inherently wrong with them, especially early in therapy, before they've learned some mindful ways of assessing their own desires and behaviors in the harsh light of post-traumatic stress, cultural messages, media hype, criticism from their partners, and on and on.

Increasingly, our clients place enormous value on evidence-based information. These clients may be greatly relieved to know you have access to neuroscientific "proof" that their actions, reactions, and sometimes quirky responses to desire and intimacy are entirely "normal," in that they are rooted in mammalian biology and largely dictated by how human neural pathways have evolved over eons. Freedom from this bit of existential anxiety can free up clients' receptiveness to seeking solutions to their issues with desire and intimacy and learning new ways to view their behaviors; perhaps even to learning new behaviors that feel less furtive and more satisfying, nurturing, and fulfilling.

Bottom line: evidence-based information used in tandem with 4-D Wheel consciousness and the activities in following chapters is an integrative way of helping clients become aware of their responses, and ultimately more in charge of them—in the bedroom, and beyond.

💡 Hot Tip—Each dimension of the Wheel may hold special keys for helping clients move toward their wished-for experiences of desire and intimacy—starting with a sense of intimacy with themselves.

Sex-History Taking 101: A Brief (and Biased) History

Human beings have always been fascinated by sex, and even by sex research. In 1886, in Germany, Richard von Krafft-Ebing published his first edition of *Psychopathia Sexualis*. The book was addressed to physicians, to describe a range of pathological sexual behaviors—in lurid detail. Even though some of it was written in Latin, it was read avidly by the public as well as the medical community, and went into 12 editions, each a best seller.

The six-volume *Studies in the Psychology of Sex* by British physician Henry Havelock Ellis was published beginning in 1897. These volumes are remarkable for their non-judgmental curiosity about the wide range of sexual behaviors Ellis observed, from masturbation and sado-masochism to homosexuality, cross-dressing, and "the transgender phenomenon." They are not sex surveys, sex histories, or medical case reports; they are detailed stories depicting sexual attitudes and behaviors that bridge Victorian Britain into the early 20th century. Ellis's intent was to move sex research beyond the age of morality. His work influences all subsequent sex research.

The first known sex survey was a study of "45 Wives," conducted in the US between 1892 and 1912 by Clelia Mosher, a Stamford, CA physician. This survey was never published or publicized during Mosher's lifetime. In 1999, when I read microfiche copies of the survey responses in their crabbed Victorian handwriting, I was astounded to find that many narratives from Mosher's women included issues markedly similar to narratives my survey respondents had sent to me in the late 1990s. These were the emotional and spiritual dimensions of sex, such as love, passion, oneness, connection, and extraordinary communication. Mosher's narrative responses and mine diverged so widely from the quantified data of researchers such as Kinsey et al. that I was moved to ask: "What got lost during the last 100 years of sex research?" This question was a major motivation for my creating the integrative 4-D Wheel approach—to raise awareness for both clients and clinicians that there's more to sex than researchers can possibly count and measure.

America's ultimate sex-history takers were Alfred Charles Kinsey and his co-investigators who created a scientific method for quantifying information about sex, to counteract mid-20th-century moral attitudes toward homosexuality, extramarital affairs, and other sexual "outlets." They authored the two massive *Kinsey Reports*: 1948, on male sexual behavior, and 1953, on female sexual behavior, asking hundreds of questions of some ten thousand respondents (the story is depicted in the film *Kinsey*). To see their complex method of sex-history taking, you can download *The Kinsey Interview Kit,* direct from the Kinsey Institute in Bloomington, IN.

Other nationwide sex surveys explore other sexual attitudes and behaviors in different populations. A sampling includes: *The Hite Report* in 1976, the first large survey to investigate women's sexual attitudes and experiences; *The Gay Report* in 1979, the first to investigate gay and lesbian attitudes and experiences; and *The Social Organization of Sexuality* in 1994, the first to investigate sexual behavior related to HIV-AIDS. My survey "Integrating Sexuality and Spirituality" was conducted between 1997 and 1999. It is the only large-scale survey to investigate the spiritual dimensions of sexual experience. Results were reported in *The Heart & Soul of Sex* (2006).

Specialized sex-history questions for investigating clients' attitudes and behaviors can be found in:
William Masters and Virginia Johnson (1970) *Human Sexual Inadequacy*, pp. 34–51.
William Hartman and Marilyn Fithian (1972) *Treatment of Sexual Dysfunction*, pp. 21–67.
Julia Heiman and Joseph LoPiccolo (1987) *Becoming Orgasmic*, pp. 19–21.

FOOD FOR THOUGHT

Notice whose benefit your sex-history questions are for—the client or you, the therapist? It may not really matter how many details you amass. What matters are the life changes your client takes home.

SELF-EVALUATION:
WORKING WITH A FOUR-DIMENSIONAL CONCEPT OF SEX-HISTORY TAKING TO HELP CLIENTS EXPLORE DESIRE AND INTIMACY

Special gifts I bring to this practice_____

_____

Ways I prevent myself from being my most effective_____

_____

What I need to learn in order to optimize my gifts_____

_____

An action step I will take_____

_____

An affirmation I offer myself_____

REFERENCES AND SUGGESTED RESOURCES FOR SEX HISTORIES, SURVEYS, AND MORE

Bancroft, J. (Ed.) (1999). *Researching sexual behavior: Methodological issues*. Bloomington, IN: Indiana University Press.

Brower, J.S. (Ed.) (1985–2001). *The Kinsey interview kit*. Bloomington, IN: The Kinsey Institute for Research in Sex, Gender, and Reproduction, Inc.

Davis, C., and Yarber, W. (1998). *The handbook of sexually related measures*. Thousand Oaks, CA: Sage.

Ellis, H.H. (1913). *Studies in the psychology of sex* (3rd ed.). Philadelphia: F.A. Davis Company.

Eriksen, J.A. (1999). *Kiss and tell: Surveying sex in the twentieth century*. Cambridge, MA: Harvard University Press.

Fisher, H., and Brown, L. (2015). Animated Brain Tour: https://theanatomyoflove.com/3d-brain-tour/.

Hartman, W., and Fithian, M. (1972). *Treatment of sexual dysfunction: A bio-psycho-social approach*. Long Beach, CA: The Center for Marital and Sexual Studies.

Heiman, J., and LoPiccolo, J. (1987). *Becoming orgasmic: A sexual and personal growth program for women* (rev. ed.). New York: Fireside.

Jay, K. (1979). *The gay report: Lesbians and gay men speak out about sexual experiences and lifestyles*. New York: Summit Books.

Kaplan, H.S. (1974). *The new sex therapy: Active treatment of sexual dysfunctions*. New York: Brunner-Mazel.

Kinsey, A.C., Pomeroy, W.B., and Martin, C.E. (1948). *Sexual behavior in the human male*. Philadelphia: W.B. Saunders Co.

Kinsey, A.C., Pomeroy, W.B., Martin, C.E., and Gebhard, P.H. (1953). *Sexual behavior in the human female*. Philadelphia: W.B. Saunders Co.

Kort, J. (2008). *Gay affirmative therapy for the straight clinician: The essential guide*. New York: W.W. Norton.

Laumann, E.O., Gagnon, J., Michael, R., and Michaels, S. (1994). *The social organization of sexuality: Sexual practices in the United States*. Chicago: University of Chicago Press.

MaHood, J., and Wenburg, K. (Eds.) (1980). *The Mosher survey: Sexual attitudes of 45 Victorian women*. New York: Arno Press.

Masters, W., and Johnson, V. (1970). *Human sexual inadequacy*. Boston: Little, Brown & Company.

Mutrux, G. (producer) and Condon, B. (director) (2004). *Kinsey* [Motion Picture]. United States: Fox Searchlight Pictures.

Ogden, G. (2002). Sexuality and spirituality in women's relationships: Preliminary results of an exploratory survey. Working Paper 405. Wellesley College Center for Research on Women, Wellesley, MA.

Ogden, G. (2006). *The heart and soul of sex: Keys to the sexual mysteries*. Boston: Trumpeter.

Platoni, K. (2010, March/April). "The sex scholar." Alumni.Stanford.edu.

Rosenbaum, T. (2011, August). "How well is the multidisciplinary model working?" *Journal of Sexual Medicine*. 2957–2958.

Siegel, D. (2010). *Mindsight: The new science of personal transformation*. New York: Bantam.

2

Creating Safe Space and Effective Rituals for Clients

"This is what rituals are for . . . to create a safe resting place for our most complicated feelings of joy or trauma, so that we don't have to haul those feelings around with us forever, weighing us down."
—*Elizabeth Gilbert*

OPENING QUIZ:
YOUR ATTITUDES ABOUT CREATING SAFE SPACE AND RITUAL

This quiz is not a test! It is to help you recognize your own opinions and consider new ones. There are no right or wrong answers—interpret them as you wish, and write other questions on this page as they occur to you.

Circle the number that most closely reflects your views on the questions below:

1 always true; 2 sometimes true; 3 seldom true; 4 never true

Creating safety is crucial for the well-being of clients 1 2 3 4
It's important to keep my office clean and welcoming for clients......................................1 2 3 4
Healthy boundaries are essential for effective sex therapy..1 2 3 4
It's OK to be Facebook friends with our clients...1 2 3 4
Clarity about fees and cancellations is just logistics, not an important part of therapy...........1 2 3 4
It's beneficial to include some kind of ritual elements in sex therapy...............................1 2 3 4
Rituals are religious and have no place in sex therapy...1 2 3 4
Rituals are contraindicated as they can restimulate clients' experiences of abuse...........1 2 3 4
My practice is evidence based, so I don't consider space or ritual to be important..........1 2 3 4
It's OK to bend boundaries when a client is especially needy...1 2 3 4
I find myself working harder than some of my clients..1 2 3 4
Hugging clients is always unethical behavior for a sex therapist......................................1 2 3 4
Demonstrating that I'm an expert is what helps clients feel safe......................................1 2 3 4
Other issues _____1 2 3 4
Other issues _____1 2 3 4
Other issues _____1 2 3 4

There are many ways to create safe space and effective ritual for clients. Which ones do you use? (Check all that apply)
___ Before I see clients I visualize them and their issues
___ I greet my clients in a friendly open manner
___ I make sure my office and waiting space are private and soundproof
___ I am transparent about my confidentiality policies
___ I guide anxious clients to breathe and ground themselves
___ My treatment plan for clients often includes meditation as part of their homework
___ When it's relevant, I invite clients to explore their issues on the 4-D Wheel
___ Other ways _____
___ Other ways _____
___ Other ways _____

> "How each clinician chooses to create and hold space will be shaped by the inclination of the therapist, the nature of the therapy, and the needs of the client. [4-D] Wheel practice can be as simple as creating welcoming space in an office and using the Wheel as a mental construct only. However, an actual Wheel invests [the] practice with increased meaning and power."
> —*Expanding the Practice of Sex Therapy*, p. 92

This workbook is designed as a companion for *Expanding the Practice of Sex Therapy*. Chapter 2 is based on *Expanding* Chapter 9, which details the core dynamics of the 4-D Wheel approach.

CREATING SAFE SPACE AND USING RITUAL: CORE DYNAMICS AND SKILL SETS FOR EXPLORING DESIRE AND INTIMACY

Of all the therapeutic attributes a sex therapist may possess, perhaps the most fundamental is the ability to create and hold safe space for clients. The importance of safety is often in direct proportion to how dangerous, and sometimes how taboo, our clients' sexual desires and behaviors are treated in the public narrative, within their cultural neighborhoods, and by their intimate others. Specific dangers vary among different regions and cultures, but the bottom line is that too many clients of all genders and orientations come to us filled with anxiety and despair because they feel shamed about their sexual actions and interactions and uninformed about how to pursue their deepest desires for sexual health and pleasure. They have been diagnosed or self-diagnosed with sexual dysfunctions. Many have been violated physically, emotionally, mentally and/or spiritually. A perennial opening statement is often, "There must be something wrong with me."

Holding safe space for clients means that we establish an arena in which we can acknowledge their pain and dysfunction while also encouraging them to expand their options for desire and intimacy. Optimally, such space is clear, comfortable, confidential, protected from intrusion, and focused absolutely on the clients' well-being. I think of it as a kind of therapeutic feng shui, which encourages a flow of connection between us and our clients; a resonance that generates growth and change. Creating safe space is part of what scientists call placebo effect, which helps clients shift from fear and pain to an expectation of healing and health, and which can actually change our neurochemistry.

An integral part of creating that space is ritual. Each time we invite clients into our offices, we enact a kind of ritual, whether we name it that or not: how we greet each other, who sits in what chair, and so forth. Ritual can also be an elegant way to help clients expand their concepts of desire and intimacy beyond performance, when that's appropriate. Later in this chapter you'll see some ritual activities you can use for clearing, relaxation, mindfulness, and focus.

THERAPEUTIC PRESENCE

Practitioners who hold safe space and create effective rituals have a common attribute: an indefinable bearing called "presence." Other descriptors for presence include poise, authority, self-assurance, and quality of being. I would add groundedness and also a sense of connection to an energetic power beyond ourselves—call that nature, God, Goddess, universal energy, or any other name we choose. Some practitioners lead with the mind, others with the heart. Some are body-centered, others are gently or outspokenly spiritual. What is most likely to help our clients overall is how we are, not what we say. In my experience, our therapeutic orientations may often be secondary to our presence.

Crucial to presence is knowing when to back off and let clients do their own work, and when to step in, even occasionally to act "in loco parentis"—No! Not act like an actual parent (or non-parent), but encourage clients to re-parent themselves so they can grow themselves up to become sexually mature and consenting adults. We can take a hint from nature. Have you ever observed a hawk or robin raising a family? Mama bird soars off to find food for her ravenous chicks, and once she's fed them, she's simply there. Not so much *doing* as *being*—a presence. Emitting confidence that her chicks will go about their own serious business of eating, sleeping, pooping, and flexing their own wings.

WHY IS OUR PRESENCE SO IMPORTANT TO OUR CLIENTS? A 4-D APPROACH

When clinicians are connected with our own energies, body, mind, heart, and spirit, clients are apt to intuit this as permission to become connected with themselves. When we're disconnected, our clients can lose out. I'm thinking of a colleague who has an off-the-charts IQ; a brilliant author of several books, she can outsmart even her smartest clients. But she complains about burn-out. She's always exhausted and frequently sick. She's anxious about paying for two kids in college, so she schedules clients back-to-back with no breaks. But now she's finding referrals are down, and she's depressed as well as anxious.

Do any parts of this story resonate for you—about yourself or any of your colleagues?

In 4-D Wheel terms, she's so locked into the mental part of her Wheel that her ability to be fully present during therapy appointments is limited. This means that her clients' explorations are limited too—to investigating only the ideas about their issues, not the actual issues themselves. The question is: when (and how) will she start listening to her heart, spirit, and body as well as her mind?

Take a moment to note how you assess your own presence with your clients (Use the 4-D Wheel as a guide) _____

_____

Are there changes you want to make? If so, what might these be? (Use the 4-D Wheel as a guide)

_____

_____

THE NEUROSCIENCE OF THERAPEUTIC PRESENCE: CAPITALIZING ON OUR MIRROR NEURONS

Evidence from neuroscience shows that therapy (and sex therapy) is likely to stimulate brain synapses that affect all four dimensions of experience—physical, emotional, mental, and spiritual. Neuroscientists speak of the functional value of mirror neurons, those brain cells that cause us to grin in response to a baby's smile and cringe when someone falls on an icy sidewalk. Some degree of mirroring is what good therapists instinctively do—to reflect the joy, sorrow, and other states our clients experience.

The science of mirror neurons offers evidence-based substantiation that our natural instincts can intensify a sense of safety for clients as we reflect openhearted acceptance of their deepest stories, and also inspire positive action as we invite them to repeat, and even ritualize, actions that affirm their own goals for desire and intimacy. Neuroscience also helps us understand that when our clients respond to us by imitating our affect or doing exactly what we suggest, it's not necessarily about transferential motives or pathological projection issues. It may simply be human nature.

For a dramatic film on mirroring (and parent–child attachment), see the "Still Face Experiment" (2:49 on YouTube). A mother smiles and plays with her baby, then suddenly stops responding, which triggers a tantrum from baby. This film can be effective in initiating conversations with clients, especially couples seeking information about how crucial emotional responsiveness is to building desire and intimacy.

CREATING AND HOLDING SAFE SPACE FOR CHALLENGING CLIENTS

There are clients who energize us and sometimes make us feel like geniuses. There are also clients who present ongoing challenges—often because their particular rigidities, disregulations, or neediness hook our own at some level and throw us out of whack. Beware of biting that hook! It's not helpful for us or our clients if we become reactive or overly protective in the face of incoherence. In fact, it's called countertransference, and it may constitute a hazard for us as well as for our clients. An alternative is: Know your own ground and hold it, firmly. That way, you're activating your own positive presence instead of resonating to your clients. Better their mirror neurons respond to yours than your mirror neurons respond to theirs. For details on helping you pinpoint where you may be stuck with a client (and yourself), see Chapter 17 of *Expanding the Practice of Sex Therapy*.

The kinds of clients who challenge me are_____

_____

THE WHEEL CAN CREATE SAFE SPACE FOR THERAPISTS AS WELL AS CLIENTS

You can use the Wheel to help you address your clients' challenging issues—in nonjudgmental ways that open up layers of information about their behaviors and attitudes, and how these affect you. Here's one way you might use the Wheel to approach countertransference issues, with thanks to Grace, a supervisee who talked with me about the agitation she felt about her sudden terror-response to a client:

> His judgmental harangues were so like my abusive father. And he sneered at his wife. Ugh! I felt like crying. Then I felt like running out of the room and hiding.

I didn't have to remind Grace that as a therapist she had a responsibility to her client to stay in the room. I did have to remind her, though, that her very first responsibility was to prepare herself, so she didn't get knocked so far off base. I asked if she'd used the kind of self-preparation outlined on the following pages. "No," she admitted, "though I've used energy clearing in the past—and I know that once you've practiced a few thousand times, you can do it in seconds . . . even in the middle of a session."

My further suggestion was that she step into the Wheel again, to revisit the issues that arose for her in that session—in all four dimensions: physical, emotional, mental, and spiritual. Grace was already adept at Wheel work, and quickly identified that during that session she'd found herself waffling between the mental and emotional dimensions, unable to root herself solidly in either one. Consequently, she had been unable to take a strong mental stance to reason cogently with that client, or a strong emotional stance to connect honestly with her feelings so that she could help the client begin to connect with his.

What happened for Grace on the Wheel: "Once I located myself on the Wheel, I found I was literally running back and forth between messages about how I *should* be GOOD (meaning I should let my father mess with me when I was eight), and heart-pounding fear that said 'get me *out* of here!' Running back and forth like this between mental and emotional, I totally got it *in my body* why I felt like running from that toxic client. In his presence, I'd literally stepped out of my power and into his. Whew!"

Her learning: "I can instantly pull the Wheel around me to feel safe when panic mode is coming on."

Your reflections on Grace's story_____

Creating Therapeutic Presence through Ritual and Holding Space—Clearing Yourself: Body, Mind, Heart, and Spirit

These are basic practices you can learn yourself and teach to your clients when they need to develop the kind of presence that gives them power to know what they truly desire, power in their intimate relationships, and power to say a definitive "Yes!" and "No!"—so that they mean it, and others get it and respect it.

Breathing, grounding, and opening the heart are ancient and universal practices basic to mindfulness and deep spiritual transformation. Using them will help you connect with your own essential presence, and help you maintain it when you are with clients. There are a great many ways to do these practices. The adaptations below are just a taste for those of you who may be new to these practices, and a gentle reminder to those who are already familiar with them.

Breathing—for your body's awareness:
Allow your inhale breath to flow all the way into your body—and follow its course. How far down can you feel the air? In your mouth, throat, lungs? Fill up the bottom of your lungs as well as the top.

On your next inhale, let your breath expand your diaphragm . . . your belly . . . and more . . . Imagine you can expand all the way down into your genitals. To intensify the sensations, imagine you can pull your inhale breath in from your vagina and/or anus—up from the very earth. (We will weave an erotic scenario about this later in the book. But for now, simply focus on the sensations of your inhale breath.)

Now, concentrate on your exhale breath, the breath of pleasure. With each exhale, feel your body letting go. Letting go of tension. Letting go of that which is not wanted. Let go of the burdens you're carrying around today, the burdens you carried around yesterday . . . and from w-a-a-y back. This is a letting-go breath I use with Kegels; you may find that you're activating genital sensations as you let go.

Now, notice that transitional moment between breathing in and breathing out. This is the place of energy exchange, of transformation. Where insight happens. Where choice happens. What's happening for you? When you inhale, is the exchange of energy different than when you exhale? Just notice.

Focusing—for your mind's awareness:
As you continue to breathe, allow your thoughts to focus on whatever comes. With each breath, expand each piece of that thought—until it is as diaphanous as mist. Notice what happens.

Grounding—to connect you with spirit:
As you continue to breathe, plant your feet firmly on the ground. Know without a doubt that the earth is strong enough to hold you. Plant yourself deeply in the earth. Feel your energetic self expand and grow with magical leaves that can fill the room you're in, and connect the center of the earth with the sun and the stars.

Opening your heart—this is where the real action is:
When you are fully connected and expanded, you're also energetically protected; you've created safe space for yourself. When you're fully in this space, you can safely open your heart to your clients. Continue breathing and notice what's happening inside now. You can intensify your heart opening by chanting the sound that tunes your heart chakra: "Ahhhhh." Feel it in your heart. Now gently open your eyes, wiggle your fingers and toes, and come back, feeling the power of your presence.

Clearing Your Office—and Your Clients

Using the activities and rituals below will help you enhance the powerful presence you have, and help you transmit a sense of safety and power to your clients.

Clearing your office to create a safe and welcoming arena for change:
For the most part, our offices provide safe space.
Can you do even more to make yours safe and clear?
- **Make sure your office is accessible** for the kinds of clients you see, and that your waiting area suits your particular clients. For example, offering information about desire and intimacy is great, but if you see families and kids, be sure to put the kids' toys in the waiting room and keep the adult toys and sex books on a high shelf.
- **Pick up clutter and place office seating** so clients can easily see and hear each other—and you.
- **Between clients, open a window or run a fan** to air the place out.
- **Put appropriate and uplifting artwork** on the walls—clients really do notice these.
- **Water your plants.** Nothing says "This isn't working" like a dead spider plant.

Helping your clients clear themselves:
Suggestions for clearing are throughout this book. If the notion of clearing energy is new to your clients, you may have to offer them a rationale for it—engaging their mental dimension to help them move their attention into the subtleties of their bodies, hearts, and spirits. You can adapt the sequence on the previous page to guide your clients into clearing and grounding with breath and visualization.

Use your own visualization skills to answer the questions:
- **Might some kind of clearing help your client today?**
- **Specifically what kind of clearing might your client need for today?**
- **How might clearing help you and your client work together more effectively today?**

Clearing anxious clients:
Encouraging clients to notice minute sensations during breathing and grounding will help them let go of tension so they can actually feel sensations of "here and now" as distinct from past or future, which is where anxiety resides. Ask them to notice those sensations and expand them with each breath.

Clearing depressed clients:
Deep clearing breaths help open the diaphragm so clients can access feelings and memories they may be literally "depressing." Encourage them to be mindful of any openings they notice. Be aware that long-held emotions may surface—and may surface explosively. Encourage your clients to release those feelings if it's appropriate. If not, help them relate these feelings to other dimensions of the Wheel, so they have an organized container, otherwise these feelings can become free-floating projectiles, like rogue missiles.

Clearing toxic clients:
Routinely begin sessions with breathing exercises, focusing on "letting go of that which is not wanted"—asking them to name their toxicities ("anger," "fear," "my ex," "my abusive uncle," whatever poison they are harboring). Breathing exercises are also helpful to practice with partners who are projecting toxicity onto one another.

THE WHEEL AS HOLDER OF SAFE SPACE AND RITUAL

The template of the Wheel holds four dimensions of therapeutic space: physical, emotional, mental, and spiritual. The space it contains is infinite; enough for every aspect of our clients' stories—past, present, and future, along with all their relevant metaphors, myths, archetypes, "parts," and more. When we ask clients to step into the Wheel, we're inviting them into a potent and evocative arena for whatever they bring, from pain and trauma to a longing for sexual experience that's interesting, juicy, and fun. Although the Wheel holds infinite possibilities, clients aren't doomed to stay there if the session feels too intense. They can step in and out. To help them become aware of their choices, see especially the "Re-Membering" activities in Chapter 5.

> "The Wheel provides a defining boundary for clients, a safety net so they do not fall off the edge of their known world no matter how far their therapeutic journey may take them. For some clients this space can feel like stepping over a threshold into another world—a world of insight, inspiration, fluidity, and sometimes fear of the unknown . . . For others . . . it can serve as a harbor that takes the wind out of fear and suffering."
> —*Expanding the Practice of Sex Therapy*, p. 77

The Therapeutic Role of Ceremony

Ceremonies can enhance sexual desire, punctuate the beginning or end of an intimate union, relieve pain and constriction, and open partners to pleasure. They can include elaborate rituals, with singing, dancing, and feasting. Or they can simply bring a sense of full acknowledgment to everyday activities. What makes them special is that they focus attention, and connect to a larger reality—body, mind. heart, and spirit. Basic elements of all ceremony are some kind of invocation, offering, and closing.

For some clients, it can be life-changing to create ceremonies that focus their energies, declare their presence, express their desires, and expand their intimacy. Areas you might explore include:

Celebrations—to proclaim significance. Encourage clients to mark meaningful dates and events for themselves and their partners.

Invitations and Initiations—to let your partner know what you want. Sometimes desire can be heightened by novelty, whether that's kinky power play or sit-by-the-fire-and-read-poetry together. For instance, a couple seeking relief from fundamentalist religious restrictions bought sexy underwear, put on sensual music, and exchanged bondage fantasies to invite each other into playful moods.

Closures—to truly end an unwanted relationship. A woman who felt haunted by her ex-husband ceremonially invited three close friends to witness her burying her wedding ring in a patch of wet cement recently poured on her sidewalk. The ring never resurfaced, and he didn't either.

Exorcisms—to remove unwanted spirits. A young couple grappling with low libido helped energize themselves by sending the spirit of their disapproving homophobic parents out of their bedroom. They banged on metal pots, yelled, laughed, cried, flung open the windows and threw each one of the parents out. By the time they finished, they found they'd worked up a gigantic appetite for sizzling sex. Now they periodically revisit that exorcism as a form of foreplay.

RITUAL AND CEREMONY: WHERE DOES RELIGION FIT?

When clients are introduced to the idea of ritual or ceremony, their first thought may be *religion*, which is a usual context for both of these. It can be helpful to point out the differences between spirituality and religion. Here is my understanding, culled from thousands of definitions shared by respondents to my survey on sexuality and spirituality, and mentioned on p. 11:

Spirituality—usually refers to one's personal relationship with a Higher Power—by whatever name.

Religion—usually refers to specific teachings, traditions, and laws that define and mediate one's relationship with a Higher Power.

The truth is, rituals exist in all aspects of our lives, including desire and intimacy. When we use the 4-D Wheel with clients, spiritual issues are an essential element of that exploration. The truth is also that many traditions of religious worship and sexual romance have a spectrum of rituals in common, such as dancing, laying on of hands, anointing with oil, making a joyful noise and . . . well, ask your clients to think of a few more—it can be a mind-opening exploration of terms.

If your clients are committed to observing strict religious laws around sex, you can offer a brief activity to further articulate the idea that sex and religion share many rituals. This will appeal to their mental dimension, and hopefully the discussions it generates will expand their context for desire and intimacy. Suggest they answer the short questionnaire below, which is part of my nationwide survey "Integrating Sexuality and Spirituality." Ponder the questions for yourself before you ask your clients to ponder them.

RITUALS COMMON TO RELIGIOUS WORSHIP AND SEXUAL ROMANCE

Check all that you associate with both sexual and spiritual experience.

1 ☐ Candles		7 ☐ Special foods
2 ☐ Incense		8 ☐ Words of comfort
3 ☐ Flowers		9 ☐ Words of love
4 ☐ Wine		10 ☐ Laying on of hands
5 ☐ Music		11 ☐ None of the above
6 ☐ Dancing		12 ☐ Other (please specify)

If and when it's appropriate for your clients, there is a wealth of information you can explore with them about sexuality and spirituality. References in *The Heart & Soul of Sex* include information on Tantra, the chakra system of energy centers, and the relationship of brain research to integrating sexuality and spirituality. Beyond this, a vast literature exists on sex and the various organized religions. Specific teachings about sex differ according to different faith traditions: Roman Catholic, Jewish, Hindu, Muslim, Buddhist, Taoist, Mormon, and more.

What issues regarding sexuality, spirituality, and religion do your clients bring to therapy?_____
_____

What issues regarding sexuality, spirituality, and religion can you safely and productively help your clients with? _____
_____

What issues regarding sexuality, spirituality, and religion do you need to understand more fully?
_____
_____

HOW YOU CREATE AND HOLD SAFE SPACE FOR CLIENTS TO EXPLORE DESIRE AND INTIMACY

Assess how you hold space for your clients regarding desire and intimacy. Place a number in the blank before each item, using the key below. The point is not to attain a certain score, but to find out where you feel comfortable and competent, and where you feel you may need to focus attention.

Key: 1 = I do this routinely; 2 = I need to remind myself to do this more; 3 = I'd like to do this, but am not sure how and need guidance; 4 = I never do this, but will remind myself in the future

How You Create and Hold Safe Physical Space for Clients

___ I begin and end our sessions on time
___ I make sure my office is accessible, clean, and welcoming
___ I clear my office before and after each client session
___ I intentionally breathe and move my body before and after each client visit
___ Other_____

What I do best to create safe *physical* space for clients_____
_____

How You Create and Hold Safe Emotional Space for Clients

___ I honor strict confidentiality (except in life-threatening instances)
___ I clearly define the therapy relationship for my clients from the very beginning
___ I create mutual agreements, when necessary, so I can challenge clients on certain behaviors
___ I refrain from "biting the hook" when clients project their negative or positive feelings onto me
___ I observe my own reactivity and then work with my own issues
___ I respect my clients' boundaries regarding how deeply they want to dig into their pain
___ If I share personal information with clients, I make sure it's relevant to helping them toward their stated goals
___ I intentionally clear my own emotions before and after each client visit
___ Other_____

What I do best to create safe *emotional* space for clients_____
_____

How You Create and Hold Safe Mental Space for Clients

___ I clearly communicate and discuss fees and relevant financial arrangements with clients
___ I examine any assumptions I may have about clients and their situations
___ I hold no cherished outcomes for my clients
___ I don't impose my own values and constructs on clients, even when their sexual or spiritual lifestyles differ from mine
___ I clear my own thoughts before and after each client visit
___ Other_____

What I do best to create safe *mental* space for clients_____
_____

How You Create and Hold Safe Spiritual Space for Clients

___ I honor my clients' religious and spiritual belief systems (unless they involve life-threatening situations)

___ I introduce spirituality as an aspect of relational connection and meaning

___ I introduce the template of the Wheel as a spiritual container for clients' sexual stories

___ I clear my own spiritual energy before and after each client visit

___ Other_____

What I do best to create safe *spiritual* space for clients_____

_____

HOW YOU CREATE SAFETY (OR LACK OF SAFETY) FOR CLIENTS: PHYSICALLY, EMOTIONALLY, MENTALLY, SPIRITUALLY

Use the blank spaces around the Wheel below to note how you create safety (or lack of safety) in each dimension: physical, emotional, mental, spiritual.

Safety   Lack of Safety

Safety   Safety

Lack of Safety   Lack of Safety

SPIRITUAL

EMOTIONAL   MENTAL

PHYSICAL

Safety   Lack of Safety

SELF-EVALUATION:
WORKING WITH A 4-D CONCEPT OF SPACE AND RITUAL
TO HELP CLIENTS EXPLORE SEXUAL DESIRE AND INTIMACY

Special gifts I bring to this practice_____

_____

Ways I prevent myself from being my most effective_____

_____

What I need to learn in order to optimize my gifts_____

_____

An action step I will take_____

_____

An affirmation I offer myself_____

_____

FOOD FOR THOUGHT

"[In 4-D Wheel practice], it is possible to introduce a variety of rituals designed to underscore and heighten therapeutic experience for clients. But, to remove the mystery factor, most of these . . . are actually exercises about awareness, mindfulness, and reminding clients to notice where they are, where they are going and who is around them."

—*Expanding the Practice of Sex Therapy*, p. 87

REFERENCES AND SUGGESTED RESOURCES FOR CREATING SAFE SPACE AND THERAPEUTIC RITUAL

Beattie-Jung, P., Hunt, M.E., and Balakrishnan, R. (2001). *Good sex: Feminist perspectives from the world's religions.* New Brunswick, N.J.: Rutgers University Press.

Bonheim, J. (1997). *Aphrodite's daughters: Women's sexual stories and the journey of the soul.* New York: Fireside.

Gilbert, E. (2006). *Eat, pray, love: One woman's search for everything across Italy, India, and Indonesia.* New York: Penguin.

Kaptchuk, T.J. (2002, June 4). The placebo effect in alternative medicine: Can the performance of a healing ritual have clinical significance? *Annals of Internal Medicine*, 136 (11): 817–825.

Kaptchuk, T.J., and Miller, F.G. (2015, July 2). Placebo effects in medicine. *New England Journal of Medicine*, 373: 8–9.

Maltz, W. (2012). *The sexual healing journey: A guide for survivors of sexual abuse* (3rd ed.). New York: William Morrow.

Najavits, L. (2001). *Seeking safety: A treatment manual for PTSD and substance abuse.* New York: Guilford Press.

Ogden, G. (2006). *The heart & soul of sex: Keys to the sexual mysteries.* Boston: Trumpeter.

Ogden, G. (2012). Are you working harder than your clients? Audio presentation: www. GinaOgden.com.

Scurlock-Durana, S. (2010). *Full body presence: Learning to listen to your body's wisdom.* Novato, CA: North Atlantic Books.

Siegel, D. (2010). *Mindsight: The new science of personal transformation.* New York: Bantam.

van der Kolk, B. (2015). *The body keeps the score: Brain, mind, and body in the healing of trauma.* New York: Penguin.

Film: "The Still Face Experiment" (2009). University of Massachusetts Infant-Parent Mental Health Program: https://www.youtube.com/watch?v=apzXGEbZht0.

3

Inviting Clients Out of Their Chairs to Access Body Intelligence

"Our bodies are the containers for our spirits.
They are incredible navigational systems that
inform us constantly, from our gut instincts
to our heart's deepest yearnings."
—*Suzanne Scurlock-Durana*

"Movement is what we are,
not something we *do*."
—*Emilie Conrad*

OPENING QUIZ:
YOUR ATTITUDES ABOUT USING MOVEMENT IN SESSIONS WITH CLIENTS

This quiz is not a test! It is to help you recognize your own opinions and consider new ones. There are no right or wrong answers—interpret them as you wish, and write other questions on this page as they occur to you.

Circle the number that most closely reflects your views on the questions below:

1 always true; 2 sometimes true; 3 seldom true; 4 never true

Physical movement during sessions can help open clients to deeper emotional work............1 2 3 4
Sitting in chairs and talking is more professional than asking clients to move.........................1 2 3 4
My training in sex therapy or other therapy included movement...1 2 3 4
I have suggested yoga as homework for some clients...1 2 3 4
I have used family sculpture with clients 1 2 3 4
I have used relaxation exercises with clients..1 2 3 4
The effects of movement in therapy can't be scientifically measured....................................1 2 3 4
I'm afraid to ask my clients to move..1 2 3 4
I feel stuck with certain kinds of clients 1 2 3 4
Some of my clients are totally stuck and cannot seem to change..1 2 3 4
Therapists should be the acknowledged experts in therapy sessions......................................1 2 3 4
I doubt I can change the way I approach therapy with clients...1 2 3 4
Other issues _____ 1 2 3 4
Other issues _____ 1 2 3 4
Other issues _____ 1 2 3 4

There are many effective ways of creating movement, or a sense of movement, during therapy sessions—which ways do you use? (Check all that apply)
___ Mindfulness exercises to help clients become more aware of their issues
___ Breathing exercises to help clients be more aware of their bodies
___ Hypnosis to help clients shift levels of consciousness
___ Asking couples to change positions so they can relate to each other differently
___ Asking couples to reverse roles
___ Questions organized around 4-D Wheel explorations of body, mind, heart, and spirit
___ Other issues _____
___ Other issues _____
___ Other issues _____

> "In [4-D] work, physical movement around and within the Wheel initiates emotional, mental, and spiritual movement among the concrete and imaginal layers of clients' sexual stories. It also suggests the kind of intention and fluidity that makes for optimal sexual experience."
> —*Expanding the Practice of Sex Therapy*, p. 84

This workbook is designed as a companion for *Expanding the Practice of Sex Therapy*. Chapter 3 is based on *Expanding* Chapter 9, which details the core dynamics of the 4-D Wheel approach.

MOVEMENT AS A WAY TO ACCESS BODY INTELLIGENCE: ANOTHER CORE DYNAMIC AND SKILL SET

Movement is one of the four core dynamics and skill sets of the 4-D Wheel approach; a primary way to help you help your clients expand their stories of desire and intimacy. When you invite your clients to get up out of their chairs to physically walk their issues in the container of the 4-D Wheel, you are offering them an opportunity to engage their body's intelligence. This widens their sphere of information beyond cognitive thinking as they work through their issues with you, and allows them to notice more than is possible if they remain seated and not moving their bodies in intentional ways. You are asking them to literally "walk their talk" in safe four-dimensional space. For some clients this is an inspiration to open up to a new depth of honesty—with themselves, and their partners.

Research is clear that children learn more effectively when they are active, not tied to their desks. The same is true for adults. Moving our bodies generates emotional, mental, and spiritual movement as well. It increases respiration and blood flow. It engages multiple areas of our brains and activates neuroplacity. Movement is also integral to all sorts of sexual activities, and therefore integral to desire and intimacy.

MOVEMENT, SEXUALITY, AND RELATIONSHIP

The therapeutic power of movement burst on me early in my sex therapy career. My supervisor had trained with Wilhelm Reich, the radical and controversial psychoanalyst who broke with Freud to pioneer bioenergetic therapy, a body-centered approach to what he called "character analysis." In Reich's universe, sexual issues were primary, and emotions were quite literally "feeling in movement"—to activate a client's "bio-electric charge" and access the orgasm reflex. Reich's practices included therapeutic stress exercises such as beating pillows and applying pressure to contact points in the neck, back, and chest to help clients discharge blocked anger, sadness, and fear. His theory was that once clients broke through their muscular armor, they could melt into the "charged" state of orgasm.

A subtler and even deeper truth emerged for me during more recent years of bodywork training with Emilie Conrad, who pioneered the process of Continuum Movement. Continuum helps people, including those with spinal cord injuries, extend their range of movement. In Conrad's universe, chronic pain, dysfunction, and paralysis are patterned responses of incoherence. When we can find ways to bring these patterns into coherence, we open up new physical and neural pathways to connection and healing. The Continuum approach teaches focused consciousness and specific breaths that dissolve constraint, access our fluid systems, and connect us with the fluid biorhythms of the universe itself.

But wait—there's more! From my family therapy training in the 1970s, I learned from another innovator, Virginia Satir, who pioneered the technique of family sculpture: reenacting key scenes through role-playing to dramatize the complex dynamics embedded in the family system. In one of our trainings she offered a series of activities to demonstrate the diagnostic and therapeutic value of movement in couples' relationships. Most importantly for me, it demonstrated how fast, and how indelibly, awareness and change can occur when we invite body movement into the therapeutic conversation. On the next page, find my adaptation of three specific activities, direct from Satir.

Moving Activities for Couples (Adapted from Virginia Satir)

Using all three activities as a set takes about 10–15 minutes (allow additional time for processing). See illustrations on the next page.

"We Rely on Each Other *Totally* . . ."

Partners face each other, standing about three feet apart, with arms raised above their heads. Partners lean forward onto each other's hands, and balance their full weight against each other. When they find their point of balance, ask them to bend their arms and let go.
Result: The couple falls into disorganized lack of balance. Notice how they respond to this.
Teachable moment: "Practice ways to stand on your own two feet and connect with your partner from your own center—with freedom for either partner to move away and return."
Relation to desire and intimacy: Erotic connection between partners (paradoxically) begins with self-connection and self-esteem. From this stance desire and intimacy can flow between partners.

"We Go *Everywhere* Together . . ."

Partners stand back to back and link arms—so that each partner is facing an opposite direction. Allow partners to stumble around this way for a while, then give them a compelling directive to start walking in the direction that each one is facing—one heads north, the other south.
Result: Partners struggle against each other to get where each wants to go. Neither reaches their objective unless one partner submits totally.
Teachable moment: "If you want to get somewhere together, let go and/or face the same direction."
Relation to desire and intimacy: Erotic attraction and connection mean (paradoxically) giving each other enough freedom of movement to make choices about what each of you wants and how you get there. Eye contact also helps. For couples who are erotically stimulated by playing dominance and submission games, a more complex relational message may emerge about who is top and who is bottom. Cooperation is still essential, however, and it is crucial that partners pay attention to each other's desires.

"Hand Dance . . ."

Partners stand facing each other, making eye contact, hands held up at heart-level with palms toward one another. Slowly, partners begin to move their hands and bodies, following each other's hand movements, without touching and without talking. After a few minutes, ask couples to feel the pulsing ball of energy between their own hands, and to pass it back and forth with their partner.
Result: Ideally the couple creates a flowing dance with their hands simultaneously following and leading one another—increasingly experimental and joyous as they begin to feel the energy they generate together. When couples feel stuck and immobilized in this activity, it is usually because one or both partners are trying to control the movement, or else are frozen—unable to move freely or feel energy. Therapist (and couple) can see where intervention might help free the energy blocks. (See next page for caveats.)
Teachable moment: "It's possible to connect with your partner and also remain in your center—but first you have to know where you are yourself, which is a learnable skill."
Relation to desire and intimacy: The ability to be fully in your own energy while also being aware of your partner's energy is the basis of great sex and great relationships. Learning how to do the hand dance, and practicing it, can be, well, fabulous foreplay—a preamble to both desire and intimacy.

MOVING ACTIVITIES FOR COUPLES

"We Rely on Each Other *Totally* . . ."
(Codependent Relationship)

"We Go *Everywhere* Together"
(Controlling Relationship)

"Hand Dance"
(Fluid Relationship)

> 🔆 **Hot Tip**—Ask couples to practice the hand dance in each of the Wheel dimensions—body, mind, heart, and spirit. See what happens.

When inviting couples into the Wheel, I may use some version of these activities to illustrate the difference between needy/controlling codependency and fluid connection where each individual has a solid base of self-responsibility while also being mindful of the other. The information these activities can yield about desire and intimacy may generate endless material for discussion, for clients—and their therapists. These activities are informed by my experience with bioenergetics, Continuum, and family sculpture. In turn, they inform a spectrum of movement generated by walking the Wheel.

What body-centered influences inform your therapeutic approaches to issues of desire and intimacy?_____

_____

How have you used them with clients?_____

_____

How might you use them with the 4-D Wheel? _____

_____

> 🔆 **Hot Caveat—The point of the moving activities for clients is not to complete the directions perfectly.** It's to evoke crucial information clients might not access without placing physical stress on energetic awareness, power and control, regulation of closeness and distance. For instance, you might find a client-couple laughing, arguing, pushing, shoving, or otherwise distracting. Don't despair. This is golden information and grist for the mill. It's your signal to call a halt to the activity and address what's going on. These couples are showing you how they interact around desire and intimacy. If their dynamic in the therapy room is similar to their dynamic in the bedroom, you may have hit therapeutic pay dirt!

LOCATION! LOCATION! LOCATION!
HELPING YOUR CLIENTS MOVE THROUGH TIME AS WELL AS SPACE

When you invite clients into the 4-D Wheel to explore desire and intimacy, you offer them opportunities to step directly into their own experience rather than filter it through a rote kind of narrative *about* their experience, or through definitions that come from experts, partners, and other sources outside themselves. As you encourage them to move freely among the dimensions of their stories—physical, emotional, mental, and spiritual—you'll find lateral movement, often back and forth between mental and emotional (see especially the story of Curtis and Elsa on pages 117–119 of *Expanding the Practice of Sex Therapy*).

Be aware also of the dimension of time. Your clients' movements may become vertical as well as lateral as their stories shift back and forth between time present and time past. You see it in their body language, hear it in their voices, discern it in details of their stories.

> **???** Did You Know—Movement in the Wheel moves the whole story—past, present, and even future. Just as clients move back and forth laterally between mental, emotional, physical, and spiritual dimensions, they may move back and forth vertically in the dimension of time.

For some therapists, time shifting can be disconcerting. Are your clients dissociating or otherwise "losing it"? My experience is that this kind of movement signals a lowering of defenses, and the very good news that barriers and blocks are melting and that your clients are instantly accessing new information. Either way, it's a strong cue for you to inquire what they are experiencing. Is it in their present life or in the remembered past? "Is that a here-and-now thought/feeling/sensation? Or does that come from earlier in your life?"

To help clients clarify present or past, you can ask them to use phrases such as:

"I feel/I think/I am"

or:

"I felt/I thought/I was."

You can also inquire if their sexual and relational desires are focused on the future rather than the present ("I wish my partner would make eye contact with me"; "I don't want any more abuse"; "I want us to have a baby").

The truth is, many clients have not yet learned to locate themselves in time in a way that helps them make useful connections about desire and intimacy. As a result, they find themselves in a kind of limbo between now (the present) and then (the past or future). This limbo may be a place of free-floating worry and/or distraction that inhibits both desire and intimacy. Perhaps it's that very limbo that's brought them to your office for help. It's imperative that you continually help them clarify exactly where they are—on the Wheel and in their lives—so their time in your office doesn't become part of that limbo.

Fluidity in Time: Dissociative Disorder or Uncharted Lacuna?

Dissociative disorder is a serious diagnosis. Addressing its complexities is beyond the scope of most sex and relationship therapy, and beyond the scope of this book. But not all dissociation is "disordered," and I believe it's crucial to let clients hear that it's not, especially those who come for sexual healing—because fear of sex is so often a trigger for dissociation, and because both sex and dissociation have a common stigma: We're not supposed to talk about them, so they become our "dirty secrets."

Call it denial, fantasy, or spacing out, most of us use our imaginations at some point to escape what we perceive to be intolerable situations and take ourselves to a temporary place of safety and/or pleasure. This is not pathological. It is life-affirming—a survival mechanism that's built into our neurological systems, and that involves body, mind, heart, and spirit (see "Polyvagal Theory" in Chapter 5).

The problem is that our patterns of seeking safety in this way may begin early, often in infancy, before we have cognitive understanding of how the world works—including sex, our complex families, and other scary things to flee. We don't receive Dissociative Skills Training as we grow up, so when we need to flee to safety as adults, we may still be using infant methods, which may not work well for us—in fact they may work against us, especially during the relational aspects of sex. My experience is that acknowledging our particular skills for dissociation, and updating them to present time, can be a crucial part of exploring the sometimes scary adult world of desire and intimacy.

The subject of dissociation almost always surfaces during the retreats I offer, and is almost always connected with shame or some other negative self-judgment. To remove the stigma and secrecy, I normalize it as a survival mechanism, and pose the following questions—asking for a show of hands, and raising mine as I ask. You can "raise your hand" (or not) by answering below (check all that apply):

____ **Have you ever dissociated?**
____ **When you dissociate, do you leave your body, fly out of the room?**
____ **When you dissociate, do you burrow deep inside yourself where nobody can find you?**
____ **Are there other methods you use to leave intolerable situations to find safety or pleasure?**

Addressing dissociation directly is relieving for participants, because it brings into the open a dynamic around keeping secrets, especially around issues such as gender identity, sexual abuse, or kinky fantasies and behaviors. And, importantly, it allows group members to see beyond a doubt that they are not the only ones who respond to intolerable stress by seeking a safe place to go. And that they are not alone in still using infant methods. And that they're not going to die if they tell other people where they go, or divulge what their escape routes are.

If we think of dissociation in terms of movement, it very simply means leaving one (scary) place or state of being and moving to another (supposedly safe) one. We can help our clients chart their movements on the Wheel. The basic questions become focused on tracking rather than pathology:

Where do you go when you feel threatened, stressed, or scared—(body, mind, heart, spirit)?
What's happening there? (feelings, sensations, judgments, "Aha's!")
How do you come back?

Tracking where clients go, and following them, can reveal important parts of the journey to reclaim desire and intimacy. It can also reveal that the safe place we find in childhood may become a prison by the time we become adults—as Zahira's journey on the Wheel illustrates (next).

TRACKING THE STORY IS EXPANDING THE STORY: STEPPING INTO THE PAST TO HELP A CLIENT RECLAIM DESIRE

Allowing your sessions to encompass fluidity about time can offer a surprising amount of information. Below is an example of how moving through time can play out on the Wheel.

Forty-three-year-old Zahira presented with low desire. She is outraged that her husband is "a controlling beast" when it comes to sex. Bubbling up through her anger are smart insights. She's aware that her husband is really a good (though sometimes clueless) guy whom she loves, and that her outrage energy must stem from her history of trauma. But in three years of cognitive therapy, insight alone hasn't helped change her situation. In our second meeting, I introduce her to the concept of the Wheel, saying that I think working with this model can help her "move out of her head" to make some essential connections between her past and her present, and she agrees to explore her story: body, mind, heart, and spirit.

- Zahira begins by stepping into the mental dimension, acknowledging that she is outspokenly judgmental about how her husband treats her: "He shouldn't push me around like that . . ."
- Noticing the tears and anger that accompany her many "shoulds," I ask her to move to the emotional dimension. Here she yells "I'm soooo M-A-D!" After the initial outburst, she sinks into herself and looks more like a helpless rag doll than the powerfully put-together executive who walked into my office. As she stands in the place of emotions, she seems to diminish in size. She is giving me two distinct clues to follow: her present rage, and time-shifting into her traumatic past.

> **▓▓ Choice Point—Do I encourage Zahira to express her rage right now?** This would be the Reichian choice—to encourage her to physically discharge her blocked emotions so she can melt into a more fluid and powerful bioenergetic state. In fact, I am curious about Zahira's dramatic time shift—and curious to meet the "helpless" manifestation of her anger. What information might this helpless one offer about the lack of warmth, fluidity, play, and nurture in her life now? **I decide on a more subtle intervention, suggesting that Zahira revisit the past, and the suspected roots of her low desire.**

- I ask: "How old do you feel right now?"
- Time instantly telescopes for Zahira. "I'm five. That's when my mother got sick. I want my mom. And Daddy keeps pulling me away." Through sobs, she relates the story of her mother's drawn-out illness and her father's doing what he can to keep the family farm going. The picture is of rural poverty and constant work, where a little girl had to grow up fast and do her share with no time out for love or fun.

> **▓▓ Choice Point—Do I encourage Zahira to stay five years old and plunge deeply into her past trauma or invite her back to the here and now?** The reason for asking Zahira to journey on the Wheel is to help her make a connection between past and present that will shed light on how she experiences desire and intimacy with her partner now. I am convinced of her strength and commitment to her relationship and to her therapy. **I trust the 4-D Wheel process and decide simply to hold space and track her story, letting Zahira be the guide as to where, and how, she needs to be right now.**

Zahira stays in the emotional dimension relating pieces of her story. Her body, voice, and vocabulary return by stages from childlike to more adult. I repeatedly offer prompts: "What's happening now?" "How old are you right now?" She answers "I'm eight years old," then "14," then eventually, "43." I can see that she is moving at her own pace through what Sue Johnson, founder of Emotionally Focused Therapy, calls the "emotional raw spots."

When Zahira reaches age 43, I see her literally reinhabit her adult body. She says she can feel herself carrying the five-year-old sense of "I want so much to be held and know it's never going to happen" into interactions with her husband.

When she has grown herself fully back to the here and now, I ask her what part of the Wheel she wants to explore next.

- She steps into the mental dimension again. Here, she acknowledges that her husband's intentions are always kind, but that his communication is not always mindful—sometimes downright klutzy.
- I ask her to explore the physical: "My gut is churning—I don't want to stay in the physical right now."

⫶⫶⫶ Choice Point—Do I push Zahira to explore what's going on in her gut? Here's a compelling chance to learn more about her family drama (as in Satir's approach), and help her explore the patterns of pain she laid down so long ago and has been holding inside (as in Conrad's philosophy). It's also a chance to help her bioenergetically discharge her blocks to desire (as in my Reichian training). **Instead I take my cues directly from Zahira** (noting to myself that she's worked intensely, experienced several transformational moments, and that we have only 20 minutes left in our session). **I acknowledge her wish not to stay in the physical, and invite her to move into the spiritual dimension.**

- I take care to name the spiritual dimension "the dimension of connection and meaning," and ask Zahira to say what she's learned from her journey on the Wheel so far:
- "As long as I hang on to that old story about Dad, I'll always experience my husband as controlling. Standing here right now, I can literally feel the separation. My father on the one hand, husband on the other. I can feel it in my body here and here"—she places her hand on her heart and throat. Then she steps briefly into the physical dimension. Finally, she nods and steps out of the Wheel.

Time elapsed in the Wheel session so far: about 20 minutes.

Immediate result: Zahira receives a spontaneous "download" of multidimensional information about how she collapses and gives over power when she wants close contact or sexual stimulation. She has experienced when and how this process began, and how it translates now into her relationship with her husband.

Result after reflection in the remainder of the session: Zahira says she's gained a more informed way of communicating with her husband about sex and many other issues. She feels it in her body as well as understanding it in her mind and emotions. She can reproduce the sensations, and remember them. She's also identified places she needs to focus on (the churning in her gut, for one).

Long-term result: After four months of weekly sessions, Zahira eventually translates her spontaneous information into skills in taking care of her sad unnurtured "inner child" and as a byproduct becoming more responsive to the needs her two young daughters have for attention, affection, and play. In terms of sexual desire and intimacy, she explores her gut-churning on the Wheel, and finally allows herself curiosity about what she wants sexually and in all aspects of her life—and a commitment to "go for it." She is still working on being clear with her husband about asking for what she wants. She no longer experiences him as trying to control her through sex.

REFLECTING ON ZAHIRA'S CASE

Do you have clients with issues similar to Zahira's? (If yes, please describe.) _____
_____

How do you usually address those issues with them? _____
_____

How do you see that this 4-D Wheel approach was effective with Zahira? _____
_____

How might it have been more effective? _____
_____

How might cognitive behavioral therapy (CBT) or other talk therapies have been more (or less) effective for helping Zahira address her low desire? _____
_____

How do you assess the Wheel approach to Zahira's "emotional raw spots"? _____
_____

Do you consider Zahira's "time travel" to be healthy or unhealthy dissociation? _____
_____

What further questions would you ask Zahira? _____
_____

What other issues might you address with Zahira? _____
_____

What countertransference issues does Zahira's case evoke for you? (Check yourself out using each dimension of the 4-D Wheel as a guide.) _____
_____

INVITING CLIENTS OUT OF THEIR CHAIRS: CREATING A "YES!" RESPONSE

To make sure that your invitation for physical movement is relevant to your clients' situation, follow it with an opening statement that spells out exactly how you think this exploration can help them. Some sample opening statements are below with actual words you might say. Of course tailor any of these statements to fit the issues and personalities presented by your particular clients. Of course use your own words. Also, of course, use any of the other relevant approaches and techniques you know.

Inviting Clients Out of Their Chairs: Sample Opening Statements

For a woman with low desire:
"I'm suggesting we explore each dimension of the Wheel because desire has so many different facets. It's important that you be able to relate to your whole story—physical, emotional, mental, and spiritual—so we can assess how much of your low desire has to do with your body, how much has to do with your present relationship with your partner, and how much is hooked to the abuse you suffered as a kid. Maybe other factors, too. Are you with me ...?"

For a man with problems maintaining erections:
"Physical erections are clearly biological. But there may be other factors involved, too—which is why pharmaceutical approaches might not always be a permanent solution. I'm suggesting we help you explore all the dimensions of the Wheel to find out all the factors in your story that might affect your erections—physical, emotional, mental, spiritual—so that you can have more control over your sexual encounters. Ready to start ...?"

For a couple recovering from an affair:
"It's important for you both to see this diagram of the Wheel, because it shows that there are many different elements involved as you try to understand where each of you is in terms of the affair. Working with this Wheel offers us a structure to discuss in detail what's going on for each of you—and allows each of you to show the other clearly where you are at any given time, and what you might want and need in the future. Most importantly, this structure allows each of you to validate your feelings and your differences without blame. Are you open to beginning ...?"

For a man who self-identifies as a porn addict:
"When anyone develops a pattern of behavior that disturbs them or their partners, there are a bunch of factors involved in how the reward system actually works—physical, emotional, mental, and spiritual. We can use the Wheel to explore what you really want sexually and how best you can move toward what satisfies you most—without judgment. Are you interested in finding out more ...?"

For a client with questions about gender-identity:
"There are so many factors involved in our true identity as sexual beings that there's often no one right 'either–or' answer. We can use this Wheel to explore all the issues that play a part in your story—biological, emotional, spiritual, cultural, social—and more—so you can have the space to identify who you are, who you want to be, and how to get there. It really is a journey of discovery. Ready to step into the Wheel ...?"

You can see that all of the invitations described on the previous page are designed to elicit a "Yes!" response. Here are some quick opening lines you can adapt to your clients' situations:

- "Would you like to find a way to move much faster toward knowing what you want?"
- "What if you could step into that story about your childhood and change your relation to it so that it didn't have such a grip on you?"
- "Did you know that moving our bodies activates neuroplasticity—enabling us to make complex connections we can't make just by talking?"
- "Research shows that kids learn best through activities, not just sitting behind a desk."
- "Let's stand up and move together into the Wheel, so we can discover various layers of the template. We'll explore how to use it, and how using it might lead to deeper healing for you."

PRACTICE ELICITING A "YES!" RESPONSE: REMEMBER "WIFM"

Before you begin inviting your clients to engage in an activity they may resist at first, practice eliciting "Yes!" from those you contact on a daily basis—your co-workers, your partner, your four-year-old, even your dog. Since it is human (and animal) nature to be most interested in something that holds immediate reward, step into their shoes to think "What's in it for me?" (This is an honored term in the world of advertising. The acronym is WIFM.) Once you understand what it takes to lead your daily familiars to "Yes!" you can start developing engaging techniques to interest your clients in getting out of their chairs and taking their first steps into their own healing journey.

> 🔆 **Hot Tip—Make an offer they can't refuse.** A veterinarian friend once said, "If you want to get the attention of that horse in the field, hold an apple or carrot in your hand." What are you offering clients that will tempt them to become curious enough to look up from their routines?

There are countless ways you can invite clients to get out of their chairs and step into exploring the Wheel. Think of three clients you have, or had, or might have in the future. Jot down an invitation you imagine will elicit a "Yes!" response to explore the 4-D Wheel of Sexual Experience.

Client #1 (describe client) _____
How I might elicit a "Yes!" response to work with the Wheel? _____

_____

How I might address my own inhibitions about asking that client to move? _____

_____

Client #2 (describe client) _____
How I might elicit a "Yes!" response to work with the Wheel?_____

_____

How I might address my own inhibitions about asking that client to move? _____

_____

Client #3 (describe client) _____
How I might elicit a "Yes!" response to work with the Wheel? _____

_____

How I might address my own inhibitions about asking that client to move? _____

_____

SO YOU GET A "YES!" RESPONSE: WHAT DO YOU DO NOW?

"Yes!" responses to explore the Wheel exist on a spectrum, depending on you, your clients, and the situation. So first, you need to know how to recognize when you've gotten to "Yes!"

What are indications of a "Yes!" response?
- **Clear Indication:** A resounding, "OK let's go!"
- **Less convincing indication:** A nod, a shrug, "Well ... OK—do you think it'll help?"
- **A chink in the armor:** A subtle change in facial expression or body language, a glint in the eye, perhaps a momentary sense of openness that signals a willing suspension of disbelief.

What now . . . how do you invite clients to begin?
If you feel moved to do so, engage clients at the slightest indication of "Yes." Begin by acknowledging where the client is right now and in the course of therapy, and offer a hopeful outcome—both verbally and with your own body language. As always, it's crucial for you to tailor your response specifically to your client, to the situation, and to what feels comfortable and natural for you to say.

Here are a couple of phrases you can adapt:
- "Wonderful! Let's begin our exploration right now. I think it will help clarify how you close yourself down when you really want to open up . . ." Rise from your chair offering an invitational gesture for your client to rise with you.
- "I can see you may still have some doubts—so let's both stand up and let's see how we can make it work for you. I think approaching your issues in this way will show you some new options for responding to your partner . . ." Rise from your chair offering an invitational gesture for your client to rise with you.

SUPPOSE YOU GET A "NO!" RESPONSE? AND WHEN DOES NO MEAN NO?

It can be as powerful to acknowledge a client's "No!" as to acknowledge a "Yes!" I find that "Yes!" is generally a statement of power, while "No!" tends to be a statement of control. A fluid combination of both is necessary to activate and maintain desire and intimacy. But when "No!" becomes a chronic pattern instead of a conscious statement of desire, it becomes a tyrannical gatekeeper, preventing us from discovering what we want.

The "No!" reflex may be tied to developmental issues. It typically develops during the "terrible twos." If "No!" is negated then, it can become frozen, resulting in an inability to set boundaries. Or it can manifest in a tendency to erect walls so rigid that no warmth or pleasure can seep through. Helping clients break through the "No!" of exploring the Wheel can be a concrete way of helping them break through a chronic "No!" about exploring their sexual issues. You can use the Wheel to guide your clients to find exactly where and when "No!" is stuck, then practice releasing it in this safe venue so that it can become an intentional, adult, empowering, effective "No!" It can be deeply therapeutic for clients to differentiate between a power "No!" and a powerless "no" that's stuck somewhere in the murky past.

> 💡 **Hot Tip—Not every client will be willing to walk the Wheel** no matter how enticing you are, or how therapeutic you think it would be for them. To ease them into 4-D work, try giving them a diagram of the Wheel to take home. Ask them to write something about their issues in each quadrant of the Wheel ("quadrant" might be a friendlier word for them than "dimension"). A colleague who works with lots of brainy engineers gets almost 100% engagement when she asks them to see if they can *improve* the model to fit their own situations. One wrote an entire instruction manual that changed his life.

Re-cap: When Clients Respond to Your Invitation to Explore the Wheel

If your client indicates . . .	You respond . . .
"Let's go!"	"Wonderful!"
"Well, maybe . . ."	"Let's see if we can make it work for you—we'll do it together . . ."
Total resistance: arms crossed and jaw set.	"Perhaps we'll try this another time—meanwhile, it's important for you to know that your story contains all four elements: body, mind, heart, spirit. So where would you like to begin right now?"

WHAT IF I DON'T HAVE ROOM IN MY OFFICE?

If your office is too small to allow clients to walk around the Wheel, you can still create effective movement. Here's how four creative Wheel practitioners do it.

Sherri Aikin, MSN is a Fellow of Integrative Medicine, nurse practitioner, and certified sex counselor in Reno, Nevada. Her office is sized to accommodate two chairs and an exam table—no room for patients to walk the Wheel. She keeps a lightweight poster of the Wheel on her wall and hands it to patients as an interactive, quick, effective, and space-efficient awareness activity. She asks them to point to each of the four dimensions of their experience as they describe their vaginismus, vulvadinia, and low libido. She hears responses like: "Ohhhh! Maybe my avoidance of sex isn't all about my testosterone levels, it's about my relationship with my husband," or "Maybe my vaginismus has something to do with anger. Could my tightening up like that be connected to how I was date-raped in college?"

Elliott Kronenfeld, LICSW is an infertility specialist with a focus on LGBTQQIA issues in Brookline, Massachusetts. He engages client interaction by drawing the Wheel on a whiteboard and recording his clients' responses. He reports breakthroughs, even though his clients are still sitting in their chairs . . . but note that *he* is up and moving.

Claudia Thompson, LMFT, LPC is a certified sex therapist and supervisor in Austin, Texas. Her office has just enough room for four chairs around a coffee table. When using the Wheel, she places a diagram on the table and asks clients to move from chair to chair as they speak their story.

Debra Wickman, MD is an OBGYN in Phoenix, Arizona. (Meet her again in Chapter 7.) Debra uses the 4-D Wheel as part of her pelvic exam protocol for women with histories of pain and trauma. She creates her Wheel on her desk by criss-crossing two ribbons and placing a plush velvet vulva puppet in the center. Though her patients do not physically walk the Wheel during an office visit, their movement to the pelvic exam is greatly enhanced by discussing the four dimensions, which provides a common language that Debra and her patients can use during the pelvic exam to locate areas of pain, and discuss the release and pleasure they both anticipate in the future.

WHAT YOUR CLIENTS MIGHT LEARN WHEN THEY MOVE OUT OF THEIR CHAIRS AND WALK THE WHEEL

Write your ideas in the blank spaces next to each dimension.

HOW MIGHT YOU ADAPT YOUR OFFICE TO INCORPORATE THE 4-D WHEEL APPROACH?

I have room to set up a permanent Wheel (describe how you might do this) _____
_____

I can create space in my office to put a Wheel when I feel it can help clients (describe how you might do this) _____
_____

I don't have space for clients to walk around the Wheel, so I can be creative by (describe) _____
_____

SELF-EVALUATION: WORKING WITH MOVEMENT TO HELP CLIENTS ACCESS BODY INTELLIGENCE

Special gifts I bring to this practice _____
_____

Ways I prevent myself from being my most effective _____
_____

What I need to learn in order to optimize my gifts _____
_____

An action step I will take _____
_____

An affirmation I offer myself _____

FOOD FOR THOUGHT

When clients get out of their chairs and tell their story on the Wheel they are literally "walking their talk." This degree of active participation can jumpstart a therapy session. Kind of like unplugging your frozen computer and rebooting it.

REFERENCES AND SUGGESTED RESOURCES FOR HELPING CLIENTS ACCESS BODY INTELLIGENCE

Conrad, E. (2007). *Life on land: The story of Continuum*. Berkeley, CA: North Atlantic Books.

Johnson, S.M. (2004). *The practice of emotionally focused couple therapy: Creating connections* (2nd Ed.). New York: Routledge.

Levine, P.A. (1997). *Waking the tiger: Healing trauma*. Berkeley, CA: North Atlantic Books.

Ogden, G. (2006). *The heart and soul of sex: Keys to the sexual mysteries*. Boston: Trumpeter.

Ogden, P., Minton, K., and Pain, C. (2006). *Trauma and the body: A sensorimotor approach to psychotherapy*. New York: W.W. Norton.

Reich, W. (1942). *The function of orgasm*. New York: Orgone Institute Press. Reprint: Cafagno, V.R. (1973). New York: Farrar, Straus and Giroux.

Satir, V. (1983). *Conjoint family therapy* (3rd. rev. ed.). Palo Alto, CA: Science and Behavior Books.

Scaer, R. (2014). *The body bears the burden: Trauma, dissociation, and disease* (3rd ed.). New York: Routledge.

Scurlock-Durana, S. (2010.) *Full body presence: Learning to listen to your body's wisdom*. Novato, CA: New World Library.

Van der Kolk, B. (2015). *The body keeps the score: Brain, mind, and body in the healing of trauma*. New York: Penguin.

4

Helping Clients Concretize Abstract Concepts to Expand Awareness

"To see a World in a Grain of Sand
And a Heaven in a Wild Flower
Hold Infinity in the palm of your hand
And Eternity in an hour."
—*William Blake*

OPENING QUIZ:
YOUR ATTITUDES ABOUT CONCRETIZING ABSTRACT CONCEPTS

This quiz is not a test! It is to help you recognize your own opinions and consider new ones. There are no right or wrong answers—interpret them as you wish, and write other questions on this page as they occur to you.

Circle the number that most closely reflects your views on the questions below:

1 always true; 2 sometimes true; 3 seldom true; 4 never true

Clients are good at saying what they don't want, not so good at saying what they do want.. 1   2   3   4
Intimacy means being able to ask directly for what you want... 1   2   3   4
When a client says "I want more emotional contact," I know exactly what that means......... 1   2   3   4
It's impossible to help clients who can't define their own issues.. 1   2   3   4
I spend too much of my time interpreting clients' thoughts and feelings.................................. 1   2   3   4
Sex therapy is serious—asking my clients to use objects would make me feel silly.................. 1   2   3   4
I wish I could get a really clear picture of what my clients mean by "love" or even "sex"...... 1   2   3   4
Engaging clients in doing their own work is a secret of successful sex therapy........................ 1   2   3   4
Clients who are stuck in defensive patterns wear me out.. 1   2   3   4
Clients' problems hold major clues to their healing.. 1   2   3   4
Sometimes clients' issues are beyond words and we need to look beyond words.................... 1   2   3   4
It's always moving when clients initiate their own steps to changing their lives...................... 1   2   3   4
Other issues _____ 1   2   3   4
Other issues _____ 1   2   3   4
Other issues _____ 1   2   3   4

There are many effective ways of helping clients make abstract concepts concrete during therapy sessions—which ways do you use? (Check all that apply)
___ I encourage clients to be as descriptive as possible
___ I listen closely to clients' language, especially their metaphors
___ I observe how clients use their hands—and ask them to repeat certain gestures
___ I ask clients to use art to express their issues
___ I use guided imagery, to help clients relax enough to come up with their own solutions
___ I use a sand tray to help them outwardly play out their inner feelings about their relationships
___ I ask clients to bring in objects that represent different aspects of their sexual stories
___ Other ways _____
___ Other ways _____
___ Other ways _____

> "It is supremely important to guide clients to speak from the heart and not from what they think you want to hear. Even in [Wheel] work, which focuses so intently on collaboration between client and therapist, a power gap sometimes surfaces. It is essential to help clients be aware that they are speaking from their own desires and on their own behalf [and] not just to please you."
> —*Expanding the Practice of Sex Therapy*, p. 141

This workbook is designed as a companion for *Expanding the Practice of Sex Therapy*. Chapter 4 is based on *Expanding* Chapter 9, which details the core dynamics of the 4-D Wheel approach.

USING TANGIBLE OBJECTS TO ENGAGE CLIENTS: CORE DYNAMIC AND SKILL SET #4

When we invite clients to give tangible form to their thoughts, feelings, and ideas about desire and intimacy, we give them an opportunity to bring to life significant events that inform their sexual experience. Tangible objects can engage clients and help them recognize the differences between stuck relationships and satisfying ones—with their partners and also themselves. In art therapy, clients concretize their thoughts and emotions by creating paintings and sculptures. In psychodrama, they concretize an old story by acting it out with words and gestures. In mindfulness, hypnosis, or guided imagery, clients cue in to images and messages they can use as guides. As a core dynamic in the 4-D Wheel approach, we ask clients to choose tangible objects that represent and embody certain aspects of their sexual stories. Clients work with these objects throughout the session, and take the objects home to continue the work themselves.

Asking clients to bring objects to sessions serves several purposes, some all at once. If you're willing to try a quick experiment right now, let me demonstrate. I'm hoping for a "Yes!" response, but if not, skip to where it says "end of experiment."

Put this book down and go find two objects that represent the sexual desire and intimacy you experience in your own life:

- **One object is to represent a part of your sexual story you want to keep, nurture, and expand.**
- **The other object is to represent a part of your sexual story you want to release and move beyond.**

What is your immediate response to this request? (Check all that apply)
___ **Curiosity**
___ **Confusion**
___ **Resistance**
___ **Imagining which two objects you might choose**
___ **Engagement in starting to differentiate some parts of your story from other parts**
___ **Physical movement toward finding your objects**
___ **Other**

In which dimensions of the Wheel would you place your response(s)—physical, emotional, mental, spiritual? _____

End of experiment. And no, you don't have to go find your two objects right now (I'll suggest that later). The point is, when you read the request to search out your objects, some kind of gut response probably occurred for you. At the very least, the request got your attention—yes?

When you ask clients to bring objects to a therapy session or to a group, you can expect a similar constellation of initial responses. Be prepared to offer explicit directions and rationale (see pp. 52–53) and to field some questions—with the kinds of answers you can give only if you have experienced working with your own objects in each dimension of the Wheel.

WORKING WITH OBJECTS: FAQS

When clients bring objects to therapy sessions, you'll find that they have done a great deal of their work before they ever get to your office. The process of choosing their objects may involve all dimensions of the Wheel: thinking, feeling, meaning, action steps, and often an "Aha!" of recognition or surprise. Be ready for recognition and surprises yourself when clients bring their objects to you.

What kinds of objects do clients bring? There are no right or wrong objects, and what clients bring varies greatly—from luscious fruits that represent juicy love, to a knitting needle that represented what a client's mother tried to abort her with 50 years earlier. Clients bring mirrors, lipsticks, musical instruments, watches, stuffed animals, stones, scarves, cell phones, bibles, rulers, running shoes, lacy underwear, gym towels . . . and much more.

Is two a magic number for objects? Is it OK to have more? What about using just one object? The reason for asking clients to bring two objects is to highlight both sides of their issues in any or all dimensions—the light and the shadow, as outlined in Chapter 1, and in the "Re-Membering" activities in Chapter 5. Some clients bring more objects, which is fine as long as all the objects are meaningful. Sometimes a single object is what does the job (see the example on p. 56). Be attentive to the situation so you can be creative in how many objects will work best for particular clients.

Suppose clients forget their objects? "Forgetting" a therapy assignment is grist for the mill, and opens up possibilities for addressing issues which may range from anxiety all the way to dissociative disorders. If clients arrive at a group without objects, I ask them to dig in their pockets or pocketbooks to find objects they can use to introduce themselves.

Suppose clients ask if they can use objects from your office instead of bringing their own? It's essential to determine clients' motives if they ask to use your objects. Clients who have worked with the Jungian sand tray expect to use objects provided by the therapist. But if you suspect that a client is avoiding the choice process, then that becomes another "grist" issue to address directly with that client.

Suppose partners bring objects that focus on each other, not themselves? A colleague reported that the "objects" brought by a battling couple were lists of complaints about each other. She asked them to reverse roles as they read the lists—so that Carl's list of complaints were addressed to Carl, and Maria's complaints were addressed to Maria. This was one of the spontaneous interventions that working with objects can inspire. The surprise element scrambled this couple's pattern of projection and blaming, enabling both Carl and Maria finally to understand the term "owning your own feelings." It was the beginning of their ability to have honest, meaningful conversations.

Do you always work with objects in the context of the Wheel? "Bring in two objects . . ." can be a powerful exercise in itself for some individuals and couples. Walking each dimension of the Wheel with one or both objects can be just right for others. You need to take into account your clients' needs, the therapeutic context, and the amount of time available. The approach is flexible, so be inventive. Above all, stay curious, and let the client do all the interpretation of what the objects signify. Neo Freudians, take heed.

WORKING WITH OBJECTS

"[The objects clients bring to therapy] take on the aura of 'power objects' or 'medicine pieces' that contain potent seeds of a whole story—memories, myths, 'irrational facts,' and most significantly, possibilities for transformation. Concretizing in this way allows multiple layers of a story to emerge at once, visibly and clearly, calling up events, reactions to events, the history of events, even the projected events of the future. It offers a unique way for clients to focus their stories, reconceptualize them, and try out various scenarios until they find ones that work for them."

—*Expanding the Practice of Sex Therapy*, p. 91

Working with Objects: How You Can Introduce the Concept to Clients

"Bring two objects that represent your experience of desire and intimacy. One object is to represent a part of your sexual story you want to keep and nurture and expand. The other object is to represent a part of your sexual story you want to release and move beyond."

"Working with tangible objects can help give life to concepts like love and hate, pleasure and pain. It can also be a positive and imaginative way to help you Interrupt a story that's been haunting you, or help disrupt old patterns so you can try new conversations, scenarios, and behaviors."

Using objects incorporates the other 4-D Wheel dynamics and skills:
Creating Safe Space—Using the Wheel as a container for clients' objects creates permission to explore, guidance for exploration, and also a defining boundary to offer context for the work.
Ritual—Intentional repetition is built in to presenting both positive and negative objects.
Movement—Physical activity is built in to clients moving their objects. Emotional, mental, and spiritual movement occurs as clients explore their objects from each dimension.

Using objects is not rocket science, and yet . . .
. . . The implications can be both dramatic and nuanced. Each object holds a story with multiple layers of information that can enrich your sessions. For some clients, the act of choosing their objects is inspiring and freeing. Some clients find their objects immediately and recognize their messages and the lessons they generate. Other clients discover the power of their objects only as you facilitate their working with these objects in the Wheel. The process is akin to energy work in that the objects reveal layers of clients' stories that may be difficult or impossible to articulate in words or other linear forms.

Further uses of objects:
Ask your clients to:
- Hold one or both objects as they speak (see pp. 56, 66).
- Speak as their object(s) (see p. 56).
- Hold one or both objects as they practice the "Re-Membering" exercise (see Chapter 5).
- Place objects in the Wheel to explore physical, emotional, mental, spiritual messages (see *Expanding the Practice of Sex Therapy*, Chapters 10 and 11).
- Bring objects to a group and introduce themselves with these objects (see *Expanding the Practice of Sex Therapy*, Chapters 10 and 11).

THE NEUROSCIENCE OF CONCRETIZING: BILATERAL STIMULATION OF THE BRAIN

Concretizing abstract concepts with two objects activates bilateral movement in the brain, which neuroscience asserts is essential for healing and transformation, especially where trauma is an issue. **Bilateral stimulation: Sensory triggers that alternate in a left–right sequence.** Asking clients to choose objects that concretize two abstract concepts (e.g., "What I want" and "What I don't want") activates their visual and tactile senses, and possibly other senses as well, including the sixth sense: their response to stress, which is mediated by the vagus nerve. (A description of polyvagal theory is in Chapter 5.)

How can working with two objects activate bilateral stimulation and help clients? When you invite clients to engage in the novel activity of choosing two objects to represent polar aspects of their sexual stories, the immediate response is attention, which may range from curiosity to resistance, as demonstrated in the opening of this chapter. In neuroscience terms, clients shift from limbic responses to their negative stories (anger, fear, fight/flight) to the prefrontal cortex, where they can also respond to their positive stories, and move toward solutions. This has the immediate effect of interrupting clients' negative stories, which are often linear, hooked to the past, and so often repeated that they may be drained of juice once you deconstruct them.

By effecting an automatic shift from limbic to cortical, bilateral stimulation induces a relaxation response, increases flexibility, and promotes clients' ability to see a larger picture—as represented by the 4-D Wheel. Clients' perceived problems minimize. Instead of occupying the whole picture, they occupy only part of it. What you will notice is that a client's singular focus on a problem is diverted, so they can move from stuck-in-negative to an ability to explore any dimension on the Wheel by moving back and forth between problems and solutions. Thus, a position of permanent stuckness shifts to a position of choice. Clients will affirm that they're "sick and tired of feeling sick and tired."

What does bilateral stimulation do for therapists? When bilateral stimulation manifests through working with two concrete objects, it clearly displays both sides of a clients' issues, and allows therapists to see more closely what the client sees. Further, it offers common imagery and language for describing those issues with the client.

LEARNING FROM OUR OBJECTS: AN EXAMPLE OF SHIFTING FROM THE MIND INTO BODY AWARENESS

By engaging in the exercise of choosing an object that holds the energy of their experience, clients may learn something about themselves that they have never fully understood or validated before. A colleague reported the following example: A "low-desire" client brought in a stress ball, the kind you squeeze in your hand. This was to represent the tension she felt when her partner approached her sexually. Until she found that object, she had never noticed how tense her body was in those sexual moments. Instead, her consciousness had flown upstairs into her head, where she was totally focused on "there's something wrong with me." This new awareness allowed her to intervene in her automatic aversion response to sex. In place of focusing on the negative story she was telling herself, she could focus on sending relaxation breath into her belly and hip where she was holding tension. This was a first step in her exploring desire and sexual intimacy with her partner.

"OUR OBJECTS ARE OUR TEACHERS": WHAT DOES THIS MEAN?

My spiritual training teaches that everything has life. Rocks and trees, even chairs and clothing, all these carry energy and information. In working with core dynamics and skills of the Wheel, I've learned that clients' objects can take on distinct lives of their own. Even those ballpoint pens and dollar bills dug from a pocket at the last minute may reveal surprising insights. And as Sophie's story attests below, even objects we don't consciously bring to the Wheel can play significant roles in awakening awareness.

Because these objects have solid form, they differ from metaphors or symbols. In 4-D Wheel terms, this means the information they convey inhabits the physical dimension as well as the mental, emotional, and spiritual dimensions. They are visible. They occupy space. They have a life and presence of their own. Clients report that choosing their objects, and deciding what they mean and how to introduce them can be a power surge toward their knowing clearly what they want, and how to ask for it. Further, it means that clients can move their objects in any ways they want, to explore them in all dimensions of the Wheel. When they take their objects home, some clients place them on their personal altars, others shred, burn, or bury them. The point is that clients are in charge of these objects, and can continue to work with them as if they are wise guides. Even "shadow" objects can be wise guides, reminders of the learning opportunities implicit in dark times, and of the truth that life is always a journey.

Objects that represent shadow and light may begin to merge over time—offering the tangible wisdom that everything has opposites. When we thoroughly explore these opposites, we find they are really two extremes of the same thing. This is the crux of the Hermetic principle of polarity on which Carl Jung based much of his work: the duality of all things, as expressed in ancient Egyptian and Greek philosophy.

SOPHIE'S LOST SUITCASE

Sometimes objects become our teachers even when we don't choose them. An eloquent example arose during one of our week-long retreats at Esalen Institute in California. Sophie arrived during a howling coastal storm—without her suitcase, which was lost in aerospace. She was coming off a two-year period of horrendous loss, including a double mastectomy and her mother's death. The lost suitcase became a tangible focus for all her losses. Yet by the end of the second day, her response to this lost object began to shift. She discovered that at Esalen's "Free Box" (aka "Lost and Found") she could acquire clothing items that were more fashionable than those in her lost suitcase—designer tights, a silk shirt, even a sweater with glitter in it. She amassed a substantial pile of these, and called them her "positive objects." A highlight of our mornings became the moment when Sophie modeled her latest find. The lost suitcase became an honorary member of our group. It began to serve as a focus for all our losses—and a vehicle for some of our many transitions of that week, especially learning how to let go. As part of our closing ceremony, we sent out an invocation for its magical return to Sophie.

We were not surprised when a month later, Sophie sent an e-mail to let us know that the suitcase was on its way home. She wrote: "The lost suitcase has served me well as a metaphor for the real life work I'm about. I have mentally unpacked it a hundred times, cherishing the trivial memory of favorite leggings and white summer top, suddenly remembering another thing lost, restraining myself from replacing items, holding out hope of retrieving them . . . I've worked equally hard on summoning it back and on sending it out into the universe, untethered from me along with everything else from my past. Thanks to everyone for your loving support and every thought you put into it, into me. I remember exactly the moment when we all focused on bringing it back!"

ENCOURAGING CLIENTS TO SPEAK AS THEIR OBJECTS: FINE-TUNING YOUR WORK WITH CONCRETIZING

Recently I conducted a session with a couple who desperately wanted to trust each other. But they were so caught up in their own stories of early betrayal that they were unable to absorb the commitment and love they each felt for the other. To wake them up, interrupt their old stories, and help them toward an updated, intimate conversation, I asked them to pick up the "trust" objects they had brought to our session, and to give them voice—literally speak as those objects in each dimension of the Wheel.

One had brought a lucid crystal. The other had brought an intricately whorled nautilus shell. Neither Crystal nor Nautilus had any experience with betrayal, so they had no language with which to speak from a place of distrust. But Crystal could speak of strength and clarity, and Nautilus knew about depth and beauty and complexity and the flowing ocean. When the couple spoke as these objects, they could hear each other, and respond.

> **⦙⦙⦙** **Choice Point—Do I encourage this couple to explore their negative objects as well?** With some couples this might be important. But this couple is already expert at negative. Besides, both are, by admission, stuck in their heads—and since they are so strongly and creatively relating as Crystal and Nautilus . . . **I decide to stay with only their positive objects, and give them an opportunity to practice the language of trust and complexity and flowing exchange—so new for both of them.**

By the end of the session the couple laughed (giggled actually) and said they were thoroughly "confused." Their old arguments about trust just didn't make sense anymore. They left, each holding their objects and knowing they'd found new voices; they could call on Crystal and Nautilus whenever they needed to revisit the issue of trust. Though they soon remembered the old arguments, bilateral stimulation had kicked in and registered, and was supported by objects with resonant voices. They now had an alternative conversation to use—which continued to inform their therapy, and their life.

A client couple of mine who could benefit from speaking in the voices of their positive objects

_____

_____

A particular issue I would suggest this couple explore via their objects _____

_____

I might initiate such a session with them by _____

_____

Another client couple of mine who could benefit from speaking in the voices of their positive objects _____

_____

A particular issue I would suggest this couple explore via their objects _____

_____

I might initiate such a session with them by _____

OBJECTS THAT SPELL DANGER AND OBJECTS THAT SPELL HOPE: HOW BRINGING OBJECTS TO THE WHEEL CREATES NEW CONNECTIONS

In groups, clients have the opportunity to move their objects into every dimension of the Wheel—and to explore them in relationship to the objects others bring. As group members introduce themselves with two objects and place their objects in the Wheel, the effect is evocative, dynamic, humming with the energy of the stories and the synchronicity of connections being made. The Wheel expands to hold it all, and continuously re-patterns itself as people move their objects from one dimension to another to explore their stories, and also their relationship to stories of others in the Wheel.

Sometimes uncanny connections are made, just by the juxtaposition of objects. Like begins to gravitate to like, regardless of the story each is embodying. A red satin dragon (rage at an abusive spouse) gravitates toward the red satin bra of someone else's "bad-girl" past. In this instance, the "Aha!" is that the enraged dragon is actually panting for hot sex, and that the sexy red bra represents teenage anger as much as it does teenage rebellion and risk. And so it goes—the prayer book ends up next to the "pleasure-pack" condoms (both representing a moribund "till-death-do-us-part" commitment). The dismembered doll migrates to the cusp of Physical and Emotional, next to the loved teddy bear (both representing a need for comfort). All of these objects expand our stories and fire our neurons, even beyond the bilateral stimulation of choosing two objects. And they spur conversations as complex and layered as the warp and weft of desire and intimacy.

To end the group, all participants reclaim their objects and take them home to act as teachers, to continue the unfolding of the story. The Wheel is empty, as it was when the group began, yet the holographic after-image remains. The feeling is like witnessing a Tibetan sand painting when it is erased. The actual picture is gone, but the reverberations last long beyond.

> 🔆 **Hot Tip—If you find clients resistant to bringing in objects,** try some of the strategies for eliciting a "Yes!" response outlined in Chapter 3. Also, note that working with objects is not the only way to particularize abstract concepts, and doesn't necessarily fit all clients (or all therapists).

A PRACTITIONER SPEAKS: CONCRETIZING THE LAW OF "JANTE"

I love the stories my Swedish colleague Tina Nevin tells of her journeys with objects. She is a nurse-midwife and sexuality counselor who helps people with cancer reclaim their sexuality. She has worked with the Wheel since 2010. She presently co-leads training groups with me in Mexico and elsewhere. (Meet her again in Chapter 6.)

Of her first journey with her own objects, Tina writes: "I brought a Native-made dreamcatcher for the dreams I held inside and my inner spirituality that I wanted to nourish—especially around intimacy with my partner. And I brought a rough black rock from the Swedish forest outside my house to symbolize the messages in my culture that say I should not be so high and mighty as to think I have anything to offer anyone else. These are messages that were fed to me by my parents and by my school, and there is actually a name for them. In Sweden, it is the Law of Jante (pronounced 'Yanta'). If you look online you'll find a list of negatives that Scandinavian society heaps on anyone who attempts to succeed—but I think many of them are common to all cultures.

"The messages go like this: *Don't think you are anyone special. Don't think you are any better that anyone else. Who do you think you are, trying to be a sexuality counselor? You are a fake, and remember that.* Sometimes I feel these messages have burrowed into my skin like some black microbe that infects every breath I take.

"It has taken many times of walking around the Wheel with others as my guides and witnesses. It has taken many walks around my own Wheel that I have in my home. My black rock always ends up in the Mental. My dreamcatcher can live in any of the dimensions of the Wheel—but the Law of Jante is stuck in the linear, non-moving part of society where one part wants to have power over others.

"When dealing with Jante—I step into the Physical, where I can move my arms and my whole body in expansive gestures that say, 'That is YOUR problem and I do not own it.' Doing the gesture over and over makes me feel as if I'm flying—so I can leave that black rock behind on the ground. Even so, that rock continues to have plenty to teach me, so I keep it with me—not in my house, but outside, near the forest, where I have made a Wheel that is open to the sun and wind and rain.

"Today I have a good relationship with Jante. There will always be days when I feel the Law of Jante is still controlling me, but those days come more and more seldom."

What are negative "laws" in your culture that color your experience of desire and intimacy?

_____

_____

_____

How might you concretize these cultural "laws" with an object that represents them?_____

_____

_____

_____

Describe what an opposite object might be—to represent a "law" of acceptance and praise _____

_____

_____

_____

What are negative "laws" that you find color *your clients*' experience of desire and intimacy?

_____

_____

_____

How might you suggest that *your clients* concretize these" laws" with representative objects?

_____

_____

_____

How might you suggest that *your clients* concretize what an opposite object might be—to stand for a "law" of acceptance and praise? _____

_____

_____

WALKING THE WHEEL WITH YOUR OBJECTS: CONCRETIZING YOUR OWN ISSUES OF DESIRE AND INTIMACY—THE LIGHT AND THE SHADOW

Find two objects—one to represent a part of your sexual story you want to keep, nurture, and expand; the other to represent a part of your sexual story you want to release and move beyond. Use the template of the Wheel below to explore these objects in each dimension: physical, emotional, mental, spiritual. In the blank spaces below, note what your objects are, and what each object has to teach you about yourself in each dimension of the Wheel.

> 💡 **Hot Tip**—Be sure to work in-depth with your own objects before suggesting that clients work with their objects.

Object to Keep

Object to Release

_____
_____
_____
_____
_____
_____

Object to Keep

_____
_____
_____
_____
_____
_____
_____

Object to Keep

_____
_____
_____
_____
_____
_____
_____

SPIRITUAL

EMOTIONAL   **MENTAL**

PHYSICAL

Object to Release

_____
_____
_____
_____
_____
_____

Object to Release

_____
_____
_____
_____
_____
_____
_____

Object to Keep

Object to Release

_____
_____
_____
_____
_____
_____

_____
_____
_____
_____
_____
_____

USING OBJECTS WITH YOUR CLIENTS

(Answer all the questions that apply to you)

Reasons to introduce the idea of objects to my clients include _____

_____

Ways I plan to introduce the idea of objects to my clients _____

_____

Objects clients have brought include _____

_____

Experiences my clients have had when working with objects _____

_____

Experiences I have had when my clients brought in objects _____

_____

Ways I see that concretizing works differently from talk therapy _____

_____

SELF-EVALUATION:
WORKING WITH CONCRETE OBJECTS IN SESSIONS WITH CLIENTS

Special gifts I bring to this practice _____

_____

Ways I prevent myself from being my most effective _____

_____

What I need to learn in order to optimize my gifts _____

_____

An action step I will take _____

_____

An affirmation I offer myself _____

FOOD FOR THOUGHT: DR. RUTH ON THE SIGNIFICANCE OF OBJECTS

"When I was 10, I escaped Nazi Germany on a Kindertransport—a train that carried Jewish children to safety. I had to leave almost all my dolls and toys in Frankfurt, and I ended up in an orphanage in Switzerland. There was only one doll I could take with me, and on the train I gave it to a younger child who was crying. She needed the doll more than I did. Now I collect dollhouses . . . I collect them because I have control over them, which I did not have in my life. People think they're for my granddaughters, but they're not. They're for me. I did not get to grow up with a family, so the houses all have families of dolls and tiny toys and Teddy bears for the children . . . I don't have so much time to play with the dollhouses now, but when I'm sad, I can stand in front of one and move some of the dolls, and it gives me comfort . . . and my friend made some of my books in miniature for the dollhouse. I have *Sex for Dummies*. I have *Heavenly Sex* . . . It's very cute."

—Reprinted from Dr. Ruth Westheimer as interviewed in *AARP Magazine*, July, 2015

REFERENCES AND SUGGESTED READING FOR
CONCRETIZING ABSTRACT CONCEPTS

Blake, W. (1950). Auguries of innocence. In *Poets of the English language*. New York: Viking Press.

Omaha, J. (2004). *Psychotherapeutic interventions for emotion regulation: EMDR and bilateral stimulation for affect management*. New York: Norton.

Stoddard, J.A., Afari, N., and Hayes, S.C. (2014). *The big book of ACT metaphors: A practitioner's guide to experiential exercises and metaphors in acceptance and commitment therapy*. Oakland, CA: New Harbinger.

5

"Re-Membering"

Helping Clients Move from "No!" to "Yes!"

"Without a left side, there is no right side.
Without mud, there is no lotus."
—*Thich Nhat Hahn*

OPENING QUIZ:
YOUR ATTITUDES ABOUT EXPLORING POLARITIES IN DESIRE AND INTIMACY

This quiz is not a test! It is to help you recognize your own opinions and consider new ones. There are no right or wrong answers—interpret them as you wish, and write other questions on this page as they occur to you.

Circle the number that most closely reflects your views on the questions below:

1 always true; 2 sometimes true; 3 seldom true; 4 never true

Clients often have conflicting issues regarding desire and intimacy	1	2	3	4
Clients' ability to say "Yes" to pleasure may depend on their ability to say "No" to pain	1	2	3	4
Some clients' issues are beyond words and can best be expressed somatically	1	2	3	4
Cognitive behavioral therapy (CBT) is the most effective way to address sexual dysfunction	1	2	3	4
Men aren't as likely to have problems with low sexual desire as women are	1	2	3	4
Testosterone is the only definitive way to treat low libido in women	1	2	3	4
Women want love, men want sex	1	2	3	4
Gay and lesbian clients have totally different issues from heterosexual clients	1	2	3	4
Some clients seem permanently rooted in negative sexual habits	1	2	3	4
I have a difficult time slowing clients down enough so they can be in the moment	1	2	3	4
I'd like to expand the way I approach issues of desire and intimacy with clients	1	2	3	4
Other issues _____	1	2	3	4
Other issues _____	1	2	3	4
Other issues _____	1	2	3	4

There are many effective ways to address polarities during sessions about desire and intimacy. Which ways do you use? (Check all that apply)

___ Acknowledging that it's normal to have conflicting feelings about desire and intimacy

___ Gestalt chair work to help clients recognize and own their conflicting feelings

___ Asking clients to journal about their polarities

___ Inner child work to help clients differentiate past from present

___ Internal family systems (IFS) to help clients identify their various inner parts

___ Eye movement desensitization and reprocessing (EMDR) to help clients release trauma

___ Dialectic behavior therapy (DBT) to explore polarities

___ The "Re-Membering" activity in each dimension of the Wheel

___ Other ways _____

___ Other ways _____

___ Other ways _____

> "As we go further into the Wheel . . . sometimes we find ourselves in the land of paradoxes—where that which some clients may crave is also what they most despise; and where that which makes them weak and defensive also has the potential to make them strong and open. The lesson for us as therapists is to help clients open up new insights and solutions through collaborative inquiry rather than through judgments and diagnoses."
> —*Expanding the Practice of Sex Therapy*, pp. 29–30

This workbook is designed as a companion for *Expanding the Practice of Sex Therapy*. Chapter 5 is based on *Expanding* Chapters 3–8, which detail the 4-D Wheel of Sexual Experience.

"RE-MEMBERING": EXPLORING POLARITIES TO CREATE AWARENESS, FLEXIBILITY, AND CONNECTION

Sexual experience is complex—filled with inconsistencies, conflicts, contradictions, paradoxes, and more. Clients may express these as actual dichotomies: male vs. female (Mars–Venus attitudes), sexual vs. spiritual, heart vs. mind, past vs. present, straight vs. gay, young vs. old, and many more, including the sense of "Yes!" (power) vs. "No!" (control), as outlined in Chapter 3.

The importance of addressing polarities struck me forcefully in the mid-1970s, when I began conducting women's groups to talk about sex, for which we had surprisingly little language then. First, I offered "Let's Discuss Pleasure" groups, and women spontaneously began recounting stories of sexual distress and trauma. Then I offered trauma groups, and women wanted to talk about pleasure, orgasm, and ecstasy. I finally understood that when offering a forum for women's sexual stories (indeed, anyone's sexual stories), it is essential to allow a container for the whole spectrum—polarities, paradoxes, and all.

Fast-forwarding to now, I've explored many ways of helping clients become aware of their paradoxes and polarities in desire and intimacy. In this chapter, I introduce "Re-Membering," a basic activity that incorporates the Wheel template and the core dynamics and skills outlined in the previous chapters. Re-Membering can be adapted to fit many different clients and situations. It can be adapted for couples and groups as well as individuals. It is especially useful for clients with trauma histories, and for clients who find it challenging to stay with (or even remember) their positive experiences.

EXPLORING TWO FACES OF DESIRE AND INTIMACY

Re-Membering is an embodied, mostly non-verbal way of helping your clients experience both the light and shadow aspects of desire and intimacy. It enlists their body intelligence to help them explore moving from **Yes** to **No**, then back to **Yes** again. It invites them to notice in minute detail how they make transitions from a place of expansion and empowerment to a place of constriction and disempowerment—and how they can (literally) step back into expansion and empowerment.

You can use Re-Membering as a movement exercise or as a meditation. You can accompany it with music or rhythmic drumming—to intensify the transitions between Yes and No. Or you can keep it entirely simple. If you are an educator, you can use this activity with your students, adapting it to your classroom. You can also use it as a concept alone, to open students to a new idea. Or you can use it as a visualization exercise for students while they are in your classroom—inviting them to breathe and imagine moving between their light and dark states of desire, intimacy, or any other issue in their lives.

You can offer this activity in a variety of contexts, and mix and match the suggestions below:

- To invite clients and students to explore the light and shadow in each dimension of the Wheel—physical, emotional, mental, spiritual.
- To invite clients and students to explore objects (or events, or memories) that represent a part of their story they want to keep, and a part they want to move on from.

The basic directions are on the next page.

Re-Membering: Exploring Your Polarities of Desire and Intimacy

This activity can be adapted in numerous ways—for individuals, couples, and groups
You can use Re-Membering to explore each dimension of the Wheel
You can use Re-Membering without objects: "Remember a time when . . ."

Always begin with a brief experience of grounding or centering (see Chapter 1)

"**Imagine an object that represents a part of your sexual story you want to keep, nurture, and expand** . . . for instance, other people have chosen objects like a ripe mango to represent juicy desire, or an open rose to represent love and beauty, but you can choose anything that's right for you. Right now, call forth an object that represents *your* story and **imagine holding that object in your LEFT hand**. Notice how you feel as you hold it. Let yourself be still and breathe. Notice what it's like to be in the presence of light and fluidity and pleasure, in a place of **YES**.

"**Now let your body begin to move** as if you could dance with that object, or dance as if you *are* that object. Notice what's happening in your body—breath, posture, muscles, facial expression, and more. Notice your thoughts and memories. Notice your feelings. Allow yourself to BE in that place of **YES**!

"**Now I'm going to ask you to shift your consciousness. Imagine an object that represents a part of your sexual story you want to let go of, or maybe never have anything to do with again** . . . for instance, others have chosen objects like a black rock or broken mirror, to represent misunderstanding and abuse, but you can choose anything that's accurate for you. Right now, call forth an object that represents *your* story of what you want to let go of, and **imagine holding that object in your RIGHT hand** . . . and notice how you feel as you hold it. Be still and breathe—you don't have to stay there. But just for a moment, notice what it's like to be in the presence of shadow, in a place of **NO**.

"**Let your body begin to move** as if you could move with that object, or move as if you are that object. Notice what's happening in your body—breath, posture, muscles, facial expression, and more. Notice your thoughts and memories, your feelings. Allow yourself to BE in that place of NO—and notice especially and minutely **what you had to do to move from YES to NO**—notice your thoughts and feelings, your breathing, how your body moves.

"**Now bring your consciousness back to your LEFT hand**, where you're holding the object that represents light and movement and **YES**. Notice what it's like to be in that place again. **Let your body move—and notice especially and minutely what you had to do to move from NO to YES**—notice your thoughts and feelings, your breathing, how your body moves.

"Share your observations with a partner, or write them down while they are still fresh in your memory and body memory. Notice what emerges for you. Allow yourself to explore your experience further—on the Wheel and/or in your life.

"As you move through the rest of your day, be aware of what specific powers you have to move from Yes to No and from No to Yes—and be acutely aware of what choices you make."

THE NEUROSCIENCE OF RE-MEMBERING

Polyvagal Theory

Recent evidence from neuroscience indicates two autonomic responses to stress, which transmit through separate branches of the vagus nerve (hence the term "polyvagal"). The most evolved of these stress responses includes behaviors such as communication, soothing, and self-soothing. When these responses fail, we automatically switch to our most primitive responses: aggression, also immobilization, even to feigning death. We can chart polyvagal theory as below:

Polyvagal Responses to Stress

Receptive ("Yes!")	Reactive ("No!")
Social engagement	Fight/flight

Through the eyes of a sex therapist, it's easy to see how polyvagal theory applies to our clients' stress responses regarding desire and intimacy—and to understand how Re-Membering can help clients literally move into a more receptive state of engagement with themselves and their partners. Take, for instance, a desire-discrepant couple whose passionate attraction of new love has changed over the years to anger, turn-offs, faking orgasm, and more. As newly-weds, their early stress responses to each other included some combination of soothing, self-soothing, and loving communication. But over the years, stress began to trigger their most primitive responses: aggression, alternating with shutting down their feelings to the point of numbness. The therapeutic issue is not that our clients have responded with "No!" Rather, it is how to help them discover (and rediscover) the choice to respond with "Yes!" This is where Re-Membering can provide breakthrough information. For a central-nervous-system view of our dual responses to sex, see Emily Nagoski's analogy of our inbuilt accelerator (sympathetic nervous system) and brake (parasympathetic nervous system).

Bilateral Stimulation

In addition to expanded awareness regarding their polyvagal responses, clients who practice Re-Membering receive repeated bilateral stimulation to their brains (see Chapter 4 for a short description of bilateral stimulation). Clients have reported: "The Re-Membering activity is like embodied EMDR!" While there are substantial differences between Re-Membering and EMDR, some of the intentions and effects are similar: that is, clients who practice these can develop fluid ways of moving beyond trauma by swiftly alternating visits to remembered trauma with visits to a sense of power and pleasure within themselves. Repeating this bilateral movement initiates mental focus, physical and emotional flexibility, and the ability to see the large picture. In other words, it involves all the dimensions of the Wheel: physical, emotional, mental, and spiritual.

Take a moment to jot down stress responses clients have reported—do these responses lead to positive social engagement or to fight/flight?_____

_____

How might a knowledge of polyvagal theory help those clients?_____

_____

_____

How do concretizing and movement generate bilateral stimulation for clients?_____

_____

_____

In your practice, what other methods do you use to generate bilateral stimulation?_____

_____

_____

RE-MEMBERING—A CASE EXAMPLE:
GUIDING AN INDIVIDUAL IN THE 4-D WHEEL (WITH OBJECTS)

LORENA: "WALKING THROUGH THE VALLEY OF THE SHADOW OF LIFE"

With an individual client, the guided part of this activity should take under 10 minutes. The discussion that follows could last for the rest of the session and well beyond.

The following example centers on Lorena, who is 56, and unpartnered. Following a group during which she'd experienced moving adventures on the Wheel, she asked if she could have a session with me to practice Re-Membering. I took her request as an inbuilt "Yes!" response from her. I know she's worked deeply with her objects to explore traumatic childhood scenes that occurred in the basement of her home, with her father, a judge who was publicly above reproach. Starting when Lorena was about three, he'd take her to his basement office and play old porn movies while holding her in his lap and masturbating. "He took away my sexual desire," says Lorena, who becomes powerless and almost mute when she feels desire now, as an adult—a condition she calls finding herself in the "valley of the shadow of life."

I re-introduce Re-Membering to her as a way to help her get herself out of the basement and find ways to power and desire. We structure the activity so that she will use her objects: a chunk of cement to represent the basement stairs of her childhood, and a photo of the ocean to represent her "sea of possibility."

Introductory Directions for Lorena

"This is a non-verbal movement activity for you. I'll guide you each step of the way. As in all Wheel activities, you are in charge. You can step out at any time. The purpose is to help you discover what you do to get yourself into that basement, where you feel no desire. And to help you discover what you do to bring yourself back, as you always do—to be the vibrant woman and teacher and artist that you are. This activity will help you be aware of how much power and control you actually have over these two aspects of your life—and of your possibilities to wake up and enjoy intimacy and desire.

"I'm going to ask you to hold your ocean photo in your left hand and your chunk of cement in your right hand. You're going to take these with you into each dimension of the Wheel. You'll begin by embodying your ocean photo: literally stepping into it as if you could step into your most powerful flowing self. Next, you'll focus on your chunk of cement and descend into that basement of your childhood. Then you'll step back into your powerful self again by moving in tune with your ocean photo. By alternating these movements, your body will give you information about how you can move fluidly back and forth between these two states.

"Where do you want to begin: physical, emotional, mental, spiritual?"

Lorena chooses to begin in the mental dimension.

(Here, I adapt the basic directions from p. 64, and repeat them for each of the four dimensions.)

What I Notice

When Lorena is embodying her sea of possibilities in each quadrant of the Wheel, I notice that she looks like Venus Rising. She glows with Aphrodite energy—serene and fluid. She seems to be queen of all she surveys. I almost have an urge to bow down before her.

At the direction to focus on the hand that holds the basement cement, Lorena shrinks into a crouched ball, her arms shielding her head as if she's staving off a nuclear bomb. Her energy all but disappears. She seems to suck it deep inside herself where nobody can find it.

When asked to bring her attention back to her power object, she rises serenely again into her Venus stance. She repeats these postures almost identically in each dimension, in this order: mental, spiritual, emotional, and physical.

What Lorena Notices

L: When I focused on the ocean, I felt like I was stepping into an endless wave or fountain. In the Mental, the fountain was fire—but it didn't burn. In Spiritual, it felt like vast space. In Emotional, it was water and I could feel tears coming—not like crying, but tears in my heart—that made my heart open, like watering a flower. In Physical, I could feel my feet. They felt secure and solid and it felt as if I was standing in the shoes of the Goddess. I could actually see the shoes—red and sparkly.

With that chunk of cement—it was the same, only opposite. It was like "Clunk! Here it comes again. Cover your head till it's over." I felt dead. Like in those old black-and-white movies. Bang! You're dead!

> **⚡ Choice Point—I focus on her transitions rather than her story.** I ask Lorena what she noticed about what she actually did to move herself back and forth between these two states. What did she have to change to get from Goddess to Dead Kid, then back to Goddess again? (I basically follow the dimensions of the Wheel: mental, spiritual, emotional, physical.) Did she change her breathing? Were there images in her mind as the Goddess or as the cement? What was she feeling emotionally? What new movies was she stepping into?

L: When I was the Goddess, I was so conscious of stepping into my creative self—I feel like that when I'm starting a painting—as if the moon and stars are speaking to me—I'm wide open and nothing can stop me . . . But when I was cement, I felt nothing. I saw nothing. No images. I remembered nothing. Except in Physical. I remembered how my body felt—all covered up as best I could in my father's lap waiting for it to be over. (*She takes a deep breath. The knuckles go white on her right hand, which is still clutching the cement*). He never fucked me. But he sure messed up my sex life.

With her last statement, I see that Lorena has a major "Aha!"—connecting mind and body. In neuro-language, she has differentiated her story, and now she's beginning to integrate by creating new connections in her brain.

G: Is there anything more you want to do right now?

L: (*Still clutching the cement*) Yes, I'd like to throw this right through your window all the way to kingdom come—and I would if it wasn't going to wreck your office.

G: You want to get rid of it. (*I affirm her and mirror her power back to her.*) You can find many ways to dispose of that chunk of cement (*by naming it that, I seek to diminish its power*). Before you do, does it have anything more to teach you? (*As her collaborative investigator, I raise this question for her to consider.*)

L: Oh! Of course. It holds the memory of what actually happened. (*Another "Aha!" which comes directly from her, not suggested by me.*)

G: Right (*I affirm her discovery*)—those are the memories that are locked in your body right now—that shut you down when you get an inkling of any sexual feeling. (*I offer a new frame for her discovery, with a new image that contains a focus for possible change. I invite her to stand in the physical dimension of the Wheel.*) So your cement is still your teacher? At least for a while?

L: Yup. OK, I'll take it home with me and see what it has to tell me about my body.

What Lorena Does as a Result of the Session

First of all, Lorena understands that this is not a magic cure; that she has explorations ahead to find the threads (and neuronal synapses) of her extinguished desire. Right now, she decides to get to know her (inner) little girl better so she doesn't feel so waiflike and abandoned. I suggest she take little Lorena on a series of short trips—out for ice cream, down to the river to watch boats, the kinds of things her parents might have done if they hadn't been locked in a marital cold war. This appeals to her, especially since she had made the choice in her teens never to have children of her own. I also suggest she write a letter to her father, not to send to him, but to help her organize and express her feelings. (This would be based on the "Letter to a Sexual Abuser" in *Expanding the Practice of Sex Therapy*, pp. 50–52.)

Questions Still to Explore

- Where was her mother all this time? My guess is that she was sunk in her own version of muteness and despair, a limbic "flight" response to stress, the process of which she passed directly on to Lorena. Finding new (cortical) responses to stress will become a further layer of Lorena's healing.
- What does Lorena want to do to reconcile her feelings with any of her family members—including her father, who is now in his 80s and extremely frail? She needs to make some hard decisions, and my guess is that these decisions will involve every dimension of the Wheel.
- What steps does Lorena want to make toward entering into a sexual/intimate relationship of her own? My hope is that truly intimate relationships may become part of Lorena's story as she opens herself to updating her responses to sexual desire.

REFLECTING ON RE-MEMBERING (LORENA'S STORY)

How do you see that Re-Membering was effective with Lorena? _____
_____

How might it have been more effective? _____
_____

What further questions would you ask Lorena? _____
_____

Do you have clients with issues similar to Lorena's? (If yes, please describe) _____
_____

What can you take from Lorena's story that might help you address those issues with them?
_____

RE-MEMBERING—A CASE EXAMPLE:
GUIDING A COUPLE IN THE 4-D WHEEL (WITHOUT OBJECTS)

WILL AND JOSH: "TAKING TALK OFF THE TABLE"

With a couple, the guided part of this activity should take 10–12 minutes.
The discussion that follows could last well beyond the session.

The following example involves Will and Josh, who are exploring how they can regain the emotional passion that has disappeared over the course of the 13 years they've been together in a committed relationship and, recently, marriage. Will is a big-hearted, entertainingly talkative educator; Josh is more reserved, a math professor who is awkward and silent when it comes to expressing deep feelings. I suggest they engage in Re-Membering to help them gather information about their experience of passion directly from their bodies, without talking, and without the usual blame or self-blame.

We structure the activity so that they "Re-Member" in every part of the Wheel, without using objects—because they are not familiar with using objects, and I want to make this activity as comfortable as possible for them. I explain the activity and ask them to choose where they want to begin. They choose the physical dimension. (When a couple can't decide, I typically use the physical dimension as a default, because this is a body-centered activity.)

Introductory Directions for Josh and Will

G: This is a non-verbal activity. You'll begin by standing and facing each other. And please close your eyes for right now. (*I am hoping that eyes-closed will help take performance pressure off Josh. I ask them to breathe and ground themselves—as per instructions for breathing and grounding on p. 26. Then I add the directions that follow and ask them to explore each of their movements for 30 seconds, more or less. Adapt these directions to fit your clients.*)

In the Physical Dimension

G: In this place where your body speaks so eloquently, I want you each to remember an experience of personal power, of desire, of intimacy, of passion. Let your body begin to move . . . and notice what's happening—breath, posture, muscles, facial expression, and more. Notice your thoughts, memories, feelings. Allow your body to express actually BEING in that place of the passion you desire:

- Re-Member what it's like to be in a place of "YES!" (*Explore this place for 30 seconds.*)
- Now shift your consciousness to an experience of disconnection and powerlessness. Let your body begin to move . . . Notice what's happening—breath, posture, muscles, face . . . your thoughts memories, feelings. Allow your body to express actually BEING in that place of disconnection and powerlessness. Re-Member what it's like to be in a place of NO! . . . And **notice especially and minutely what you had to do to move from YES to NO.** (*Explore this place for 30 seconds.*)
- Now bring your consciousness back to power and desire and passion. Let your body move, into this place of YES again. (*Explore this place again for 30 seconds.*) Know in your body what it's like to be in this place—and **notice especially and minutely what you had to do to move from NO to YES.**
- When you're ready, open your eyes and look at each other—briefly, just notice, before moving on to the emotional dimension.

In the Emotional Dimension

G: In this place of the heart, Re-Member an experience . . . (*Repeat the Yes–No–Yes instructions on the previous page, using Emotional in place of Physical. Allow about 1½ minutes; 30 seconds for each shift from Yes to No to Yes.*)

In the Mental Dimension

G: In this place of illumination, Re-Member an experience . . . (*Repeat the Yes–No–Yes instructions on the previous page using Mental in place of Physical. Allow about 1½ minutes; 30 seconds for each shift from Yes to No to Yes.*)

In the Spiritual Dimension

G: In this place of connection and meaning, Re-Member an experience . . . (*Repeat the Yes–No–Yes instructions on the previous page, using Spiritual in place of Physical. Allow about 1½ minutes; 30 seconds for each shift from Yes to No to Yes.*)

Ask each partner to share their experiences of the activity (use your judgment about how much time to allow):

- Take a few minutes to share with each other what you noticed about yourself as you Re-Membered your experiences in each of the dimensions.
- Now, each of you share what you noticed about your partner as you Re-Membered your experiences in each of the dimensions.

Invite further processing—still using the Wheel:

With Will and Josh, I ask: "Is there anywhere else on the Wheel from which you wish to speak right now? Just step into that place and speak from there—directly to each other."

Will begins (he begins all of their conversations): Each time I really opened up, it was in the Emotional—because my heart opened and I could hear your words when we first met: "You are the love of my life." I took these words all around the Wheel with me.

Josh: Well, I still mean those words. (*He moves to the Mental.*) So each time I stepped into no-power, I felt the school bully and the only way I could stand up to him was to be smarter than he was and not cry.

G: Josh. Are you saying that being in an intimate relationship with Will is like being with the school bully?

J: It's scary. In a different way of course. Suppose I fail?

▥ Choice Point—Josh is finally speaking! Do I encourage him to express his powerlessness right now? This could offer valuable information about why he has such difficulty relating emotionally to Will. **I decide instead to go with the emotions that are palpable in the room, and keep the energy focused within the couple . . . and to encourage Josh to speak in another way.**

I look at Will and ask: "Did you know you mean so much to Josh?" (*Josh begins to choke up.*) "Tell him, Josh." (*I lead Josh into the emotional dimension, to stand beside Will. Josh is speechless and gawky. Will starts to speak.*)

> ▥ **Choice Point**—Do I let Will speak? Or do I intervene so Josh can speak? This would model a process that will be different for this couple. I decide to intervene.

G: Will, I know you want to rescue Josh from embarrassment and speechlessness here. This is a pattern you've both established over your 13 years together. But right now, I ask you to let Josh speak for himself. Even if it's difficult for him. Even if it's difficult for *you*.

Josh, if you're having a problem finding words, you can express in your body what you're feeling—just as you did in the Re-Membering activity. You can move to any dimension in the Wheel.

And Will, if you're feeling silenced by my asking you not to speak, you're welcome to move to any dimension that reflects those feelings. OK?

At this point, Josh takes Will's hand and they both begin to move together in a dance, which becomes hip-grinding and entirely sensual. We all laugh—and agree that they need to practice their moves at home.

We meet for several more sessions, and both Will and Josh agree that doing the Re-Membering experience helped them move to a more connected place in their relationship—because it didn't depend on talking. They also say that they're using Re-Membering on their own as a way to get back on track with each other. In Will's words, "It makes great foreplay."

REFLECTING ON RE-MEMBERING (JOSH AND WILL'S STORY)

How do you see that Re-Membering was effective with Josh and Will? _____

_____

How might it have been more effective? _____

_____

What further questions would you ask Josh and Will?_____

_____

Do you have clients with issues similar to Josh's and Will's? (If yes, please describe) _____

_____

What can you take from Josh and Will's story that might help you address those issues with them?

_____

> 💡 **Hot Tip**—In Re-Membering sessions, clients do their own work. Our job is to create and hold space, notice, reflect, and ask questions that encourage further awareness.

RE-MEMBERING: ADAPTING THE EXERCISE FOR GROUPS

I often use Re-Membering in trainings, retreats, and even lectures. Other practitioners use it in groups for clients who are transitioning, or confronting questions about their gender identity, sexual orientation, pornography use, affairs, low desire, and more. Introducing Re-Membering adds movement, provides information about differentiation, and offers experiences for group members who may not be comfortable speaking up. You can use it effectively with or without objects.

RE-MEMBERING FOR A 4-D WHEEL GROUP OF 50 OR FEWER MEMBERS: EXPLORING ALL FOUR DIMENSIONS OF THE WHEEL

Ask group members to choose partners for this activity. If numbers are uneven, ask one of the pairs to open up to become three. (If it feels appropriate, you can use this moment to interject a comment about "poly" relationships.) Adapt your ongoing directions for the group of three, and allow a bit of extra time for them to complete the exercise.

Basic Directions to the Group

Begin this activity in the dimension in which you are standing around the Wheel. You'll get to experience all the dimensions. Notice where you're positioned: in Physical, Emotional, Mental, or Spiritual. (If the group is large you can spread out to make the space work.) If you can't find a place exactly in a given dimension, imagine that you're positioned where you want to be.

This is a non-verbal activity—to let your body speak . . . Proceed with directions provided for the couples Re-Membering on pp. 69–70. Allow 30–60 seconds for each transition.

If this group has been working with objects in the Wheel . . . You can have them physically hold their objects as they Re-Member.

I ask them to hold their positive object in their left hands (traditionally the receiving hand) and their negative object in their right hand (traditionally the giving hand or, in this case, the letting-go hand).

Adjust the directions by including how they will use their objects:

- "Begin by focusing your attention on your left hand and the object you want to keep. Allow your body to move as if you could dance with that object, or move as that object might move."
- "Now focus your attention on your right hand, and the object you want to release. Allow your body to move as if you could dance with that object or move as that object might move."
- "Now focus your attention again on your left hand, and the object you want to keep. Allow your body to move as if you could dance with that object or move as that object might move."

As in the couples version of Re-Membering, ask the group members to share with their partners their experience of themselves, and their experience of their partner. Then invite sharing among the whole group. Allow plenty of time, as there will likely be questions and "Aha's" to share.

To end the activity, ask them to walk mindfully around the Wheel and place their objects where they belong now that they've "Re-Membered." Allow this walk around the Wheel to take whatever time it needs, as participants may find themselves in a different place after this activity and may be deeply reevaluating their objects—and the issues they brought to the group.

ADAPTING RE-MEMBERING FOR A GROUP OF 50 OR MORE: EXPLORING ONLY ONE DIMENSION OF THE WHEEL

The activity should take about 10 minutes—about 4 minutes to do one sequence of the Re-Membering activity, and another 6 minutes for partners to share (allow about 2–3 minutes for each partner). You can then take as long as you have time for to complete the conversation the activity generates.

Ask group members to choose partners for this activity.

Keep it Simple

- Use one sequence of Re-Membering (Yes to No to Yes).
- You can do the activity with or without objects, and without exploring each dimension of the Wheel.

Basic Directions without Objects

Adapt from directions for Will and Josh, on pp. 69–70.

Basic Directions with Objects

Adapt from basic directions p. 64.

When I have offered Re-Membering to groups of about 50 therapists and educators, the most moving part has been the general sharing following the activity, as participants build on each other's experiences. There is always a gratifying mix of personal sharing, along with discussion of how participants might use the activity with their clients and students.

A retreat or training group that could benefit from exploring polarities of desire and intimacy

_____

_____

A particular issue I would suggest this group explore _____

_____

💡 **Hot Tip—Before introducing this activity to clients and students,** use it to explore your own polarities and paradoxes about sexuality or any other issue in your life.

ADAPTING RE-MEMBERING FOR A GROUP OF 250 OR MORE

The one-sequence version of the Re-Membering activity can be effective even in a lecture hall. I've used it in two different ways—as a mindfulness exercise and as a partner exercise to energize the room.

Re-Membering as a Mindfulness Exercise: Basic Directions for a Large Group

Approximate time: 3–5 minutes, depending on the amount of feedback you invite

"Sitting where you are in this hall, imagine yourself in your own place of expanded energy and personal power. Breathe into this energy and power and allow it to nourish you: desire, intimacy, light, color . . . Send this positive energy all the way up to your crown chakra, at the top of your head—and all the way down to your feet—and down into the very center of the earth. Notice your breathing. Notice what's going on in your mind and in your heart. Notice what this energy means in your life.

"Now let yourself move from this place of power into the shadow part of your energy—just for a few seconds—you don't have to stay there. Allow yourself to step into the shadow aspect of your sexual story, and Re-Member what that's like. Notice clearly what you had to do to move yourself into this place of shadow from your place of light and power. Notice how you had to change your breathing, your posture. Notice what you changed about what you were thinking and feeling. Just notice.

"And now, bring yourself back into that place of power . . . you know the way. Notice what you have to do to get from darkness into light—your breath, your posture, your thinking, feeling . . . and come back into this room knowing that you can move into this place of personal power whenever you want; all you have to do is breathe."

At this point, invite participants to share how they moved from Yes to No, and most importantly from No back to Yes again.

Re-Membering as a Partner Activity: Basic Directions for a Large Group

Approximate Time: 12+ minutes (2 minutes to get people into partners, 2 minutes to describe the Re-Membering activity, 2 minutes to lead them through all three phases of the activity, 2 minutes for them to share, 3+ minutes to process the activity). Adjust the actual timing to meet your own schedule.

Basic Directions

"Find a partner in the room to share this activity with you—if you need to be in a group of three, that's fine—open up your relationship." (Proceed as the directions above.)

When the Re-Membering sequence is over: "Share with your partner(s) what you noticed that you had to do in order to move from Yes to No, and most importantly from No back to Yes again."

A large group or lecture presentation that could benefit from the Re-Membering activity_____

_____

A particular issue I would suggest for this audience _____

_____

RE-MEMBERING YOURSELF:
WALKING THE WHEEL WITH YOUR LIGHT AND SHADOW DIMENSIONS

Practice Re-Membering your own issues of desire and intimacy by stepping into each dimension: physical, emotional, mental, spiritual—first light, then shadow, then back to light. Note in the blank spaces below what you learn about yourself in each dimension and what you need to do to move from one polarity to the other—notice movements, breath, thoughts, emotions, and more.

Light

Shadow

_____   _____
_____   _____
_____   _____
_____   _____
_____   _____
_____   _____

Light   Light

_____   _____
_____   _____
_____   _____
_____   _____
_____   _____

Shadow   Shadow

_____   SPIRITUAL   _____
_____   _____
_____   EMOTIONAL   MENTAL   _____
_____   _____
_____   PHYSICAL   _____
_____   _____

Light   Shadow

_____   _____
_____   _____
_____   _____
_____   _____
_____   _____
_____   _____

© 2017, Exploring Desire and Intimacy: A Workbook for Creative Clinicians, Gina Ogden, Routledge

75

INTRODUCING RE-MEMBERING TO YOUR CLIENTS

Describe how you would introduce Re-Membering to individual clients_____

_____

_____

Describe how you would introduce Re-Membering to couples _____

_____

_____

Describe how you would introduce Re-Membering to a group _____

_____

SELF-EVALUATION:
WORKING WITH RE-MEMBERING AS A ROUTE TO SEXUAL DESIRE AND INTIMACY

Special gifts I bring to this practice _____

_____

Ways I might prevent myself from being my most effective _____

_____

What I need to learn in order to optimize my gifts _____

_____

An action step I will take _____

_____

An affirmation I offer myself _____

FOOD FOR THOUGHT

Don't Try Techniques on Your Clients Without Trying Them on Yourself First
A mother came to Gandhi and asked him, "Dear Gandhi, can you please tell my son not to eat sugar anymore?" Gandhi paused for a moment and said, "Come back in two weeks." Two weeks later the mother came back, and Gandhi looked at her son and said to him, "Don't eat any more sugar!" The woman then asked Gandhi, "But why did you not tell him this two weeks ago? I would not have had to make the long journey to you twice!" Gandhi smiled, and said, "I understand, but two weeks ago I was eating sugar."
—Thanks to Ruth Fishel for this story, probably apocryphal, but still very useful

---

REFERENCES AND SUGGESTED READING FOR EXPLORING POLARITIES

Fishel, R. (1998). *Time for joy*. Deerfield Beach, FL: Health Communications.

Linehan, M.M. (2014). *DBT skills training manual*. New York: Guilford.

Nagoski, E. (2015). *Come as you are: The surprising new science that will transform your sex life*. New York: Simon & Schuster.

Nhat Hanh, T. (2004). *No mud, no lotus: The art of transforming suffering*. Berkeley, CA: Parallax Press.

Ogden, G. (2008). *The return of desire: A guide to rediscovering your sexual passion*. Boston: Trumpeter.

Omaha, J. (2004). *Psychotherapeutic interventions for emotion regulation: EMDR and bilateral stimulation for affect management*. New York: Norton.

Porges, S.W. (2011). *The polyvagal theory: Neurophysiological foundations of emotions, attachment, communication, and self-regulation*. New York: Norton.

Schwartz, R.C. (1997). *Internal family systems therapy*. New York: Guilford.

Three Initiates. (2008). *The Kybalion: A study of the hermetic philosophy of ancient Egypt and Greece* (1st Jeremy P. Tarcher/Penguin ed.). New York: Jeremy P. Tarcher/Penguin.

6

Core Knowledge Areas and More

What We Need to Know about Desire and Intimacy

Q: How many therapists does it take to change a lightbulb?
A: Only one. But the lightbulb has to really want to change.

—*Anon.*

OPENING QUIZ:
YOUR ATTITUDES ABOUT HOW YOU EXPLORE DESIRE AND INTIMACY

This quiz is not a test! It is to help you recognize your own opinions and consider new ones. There are no right or wrong answers—interpret them as you wish, and write other questions on this page as they occur to you.

Circle the number that most closely reflects your views on the questions below:

1 always true; 2 sometimes true; 3 seldom true; 4 never true

Listening closely to clients gives me all the information I need about desire and intimacy....	1	2	3	4
Reading books by experts is a major way to stay current with trends.............................	1	2	3	4
I feel I don't know enough about desire and intimacy to be able to help clients...........	1	2	3	4
Watching porn videos and Internet porn keeps professionals aware of what men want.....	1	2	3	4
I'm unclear about my own desire and intimacy—so I don't raise the issue with clients...	1	2	3	4
Attending sexuality conferences is a way to meet top thinkers in the field....................	1	2	3	4
Romance novels are full of insights about desire and intimacy.......................................	1	2	3	4
Scholarly journal articles are the only reliable source of information about sex	1	2	3	4
Neuroscience offers updated information about our sexual reward systems....................	1	2	3	4
Pharmaceutical ads offer a special perspective on sexual dysfunction	1	2	3	4
I'd like to expand the way I approach issues of desire and intimacy with clients	1	2	3	4
Other issues _____	1	2	3	4
Other issues _____	1	2	3	4
Other issues _____	1	2	3	4

There are many effective ways of learning facts about desire and intimacy—which ways do you use? (Check all that apply)

___ I take courses every year to earn continuing education credits
___ I learn facts about sexual behavior from sex surveys
___ I've taken numerous sex-education courses during my training
___ I constantly read books about sex and sex therapy
___ I belong to several sexuality organizations and avidly read their listserves
___ I keep up with trends by binge-watching films and TV
___ Other ways _____
___ Other ways _____
___ Other ways _____

"The kinds of issues that arise in therapy may involve skills-training for therapists in a number of related areas that help clients open their hearts to their partners—and to themselves. The skills may include coaching clients to access and express their feelings—through words, eye contact, heart contact, and that indefinable something called 'presence.'"
—*Expanding the Practice of Sex Therapy*, p. 47

This workbook is designed as a companion for *Expanding the Practice of Sex Therapy*. Chapter 6 is based on *Expanding* Chapters 3–8, which detail the 4-D Wheel of Sexual Experience.

HOW MUCH DO WE *REALLY* NEED TO KNOW TO HELP OUR CLIENTS WITH DESIRE AND INTIMACY?

What information and skills do we need in order to offer optimal help to our clients? And how do these areas of expertise relate to the 4-D Wheel approach? This chapter addresses these questions, and more. It outlines the 17 Core Knowledge Areas that are required for our certification as sexuality professionals, and also outlines how the sensitivities we develop by using the Wheel can open us to subtle and nuanced information that may not be possible to measure, at least by current scientific methods. Material in this chapter is offered with the caveat that no practitioner can ever know everything there is to know about desire and intimacy. These subjects are too vast, too complex, too subjective, and too interwoven with other facets of human existence: physical, emotional, mental, and spiritual.

The "Sex Spider" below conveys this idea, though it shows only the tip of the iceberg.
On the empty legs of the Spider write other issues that inform your work.
Add more legs and issues if you want.

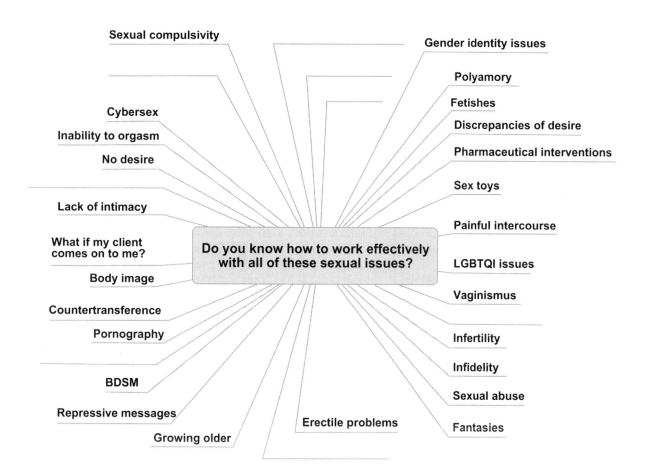

The 17 Core Knowledge Areas for Sexuality Professionals

as identified by The American Association of Sexuality Educators, Counselors, and Therapists (AASECT) the international certifying organization for sexuality professionals

"All candidates for certification must have knowledge of the following as they relate to sexual health and pleasure."

Check the Knowledge Areas below *in which you feel confident* as a therapist and/or sex therapist:

___ Ethics and ethical behavior

___ Developmental sexuality from a bio-psycho-social perspective across the life course

___ Sociocultural, familial factors (e.g., ethnicity, culture, religion, spirituality, socioeconomic status, family values), in relation to sexual values and behaviors

___ Issues related to sexual orientation and/or gender identity: heterosexuality; issues and themes impacting lesbian, gay, bisexual, pansexual, asexual people; gender identity and expression

___ Intimacy skills (e.g., social, emotional, sexual), intimate relationships, interpersonal relationships and family dynamics

___ Diversities in sexual expression and lifestyles, including, but not limited to polyamory, swinging, BDSM, Tantra

___ Sexual and reproductive anatomy/physiology

___ Health/medical factors that may influence sexuality including, but not limited to illness, disability, drugs, mental health, conception, pregnancy, childbirth, pregnancy termination, contraception, fertility, HIV/AIDS, sexually transmitted infection, other infections, sexual trauma, injury, and safer-sex practices

___ Range of sexual functioning and behavior, from optimal to problematic, including, but not limited to, common issues such as: desire discrepancy, lack of desire, difficulty achieving or maintaining arousal, sexual pain and penetration problems, difficulty with orgasm

___ Sexual exploitation, including sexual abuse, sexual harassment, and sexual assault

___ Cyber sexuality and social media

___ Substance use/abuse and sexuality

___ Pleasure-enhancement skills

___ Learning theory and its application

___ Professional communication and personal reflection skills

___ History of the disciplines of sex research, theory, education, counseling, and therapy

___ Principles of sexuality research and research methods

Bringing the 17 Core Knowledge Areas into the 4-D Wheel

Below, the Core Knowledge Areas from the previous page are organized via the 4-D Wheel, so that you can more readily observe how they relate to your clients' issues—and also see the large picture of what educational requirements are believed necessary for certification as a sexuality professional. Note that these requirements are pretty evenly divided among physical, emotional, and mental dimensions, and that there is less explicit inclusion of spiritual connections or meanings. Note also, that many of the Core Knowledge Areas overlap, all of them interact, and several of them ultimately belong in more than one dimension of the Wheel—so feel free to make those judgments for yourself.

Check the Knowledge Areas below *in which you need more skills* as a therapist and/or sex therapist:

Core Knowledge Areas that focus especially on the physical dimension of the Wheel—for clients who need help with specific performance issues, understanding how their bodies function, sexual health, safe sex, how alcohol and drugs interact with desire, arousal, lubrication, erection, orgasm, and more.

___ Sexual and reproductive anatomy/physiology
___ Range of sexuality functioning and behavior
___ Substance use/abuse and sexuality
___ Health and medical factors that may influence sexuality—including, but not limited to, illness, disability, drugs, mental health, conception, pregnancy, childbirth, pregnancy termination, contraception, fertility, HIV/AIDS, sexually transmitted infection, other infections, sexual trauma, injury, and safer-sex practices

Core Knowledge Areas that focus especially on the emotional dimension of the Wheel—for clients whose issues include intimacy, pleasure, trauma, communication, and couple and family dynamics.

___ Intimacy skills (social, emotional, sexual), intimate relationships, interpersonal relationships and family dynamics
___ Sociocultural and familial factors
___ Communication and personal reflection skills
___ Pleasure-enhancement skills
___ Sexual exploitation

Core Knowledge Areas that focus especially on the mental dimension of the Wheel—for clients whose issues include questions about diversity and developmental issues, and for professionals who need basic knowledge of sex research and ethics.

___ Ethics and ethical behavior
___ Developmental sexuality from a bio-psycho-social perspective across the life course
___ Sexual orientation and/or gender Identity: heterosexuality; lesbian, gay, bisexual, pansexual, asexual people; gender identity and expression
___ Diversities in sexual expression and lifestyles, including, but not limited to, polyamory, swinging, BDSM
___ Cyber sexuality and social media
___ Principles of sexuality research and research skills
___ History of sex research
___ Learning theory and its application

Core Knowledge Areas that focus especially on the spiritual dimension of the Wheel—for clients whose issues include connection and meaning.

___ Religion
___ Spirituality
___ Tantra

CORE KNOWLEDGE AREAS ORGANIZED VIA DIMENSIONS OF THE 4-D WHEEL

FILLING IN THE BLANKS

Awareness of the required Core Knowledge Areas is important because it outlines a range of issues that sexuality professionals may be called on to address with their clients. Organizing this list via the dimensions of the Wheel can offer a picture of how these issues might interact, and how you might focus these areas for your clients during specific choice points in the course of your sessions. Review the items you checked on the previous two pages, and note in the box below the top three areas where you feel you need more education and practice. Beside these areas, note in which dimensions of the Wheel they belong. Then note your action steps: how you plan to fill in your blanks.

NEXT STEPS IN YOUR EDUCATION AND PRACTICE

**Top three Core Knowledge Areas
I need to focus on**

_____

_____

_____

Action steps I will take

_____

_____

_____

**Dimensions in which I need
to focus my learning**

_____

_____

_____

Action steps I will take

_____

_____

_____

**BEYOND "JUST THE FACTS":
MORE CORE KNOWLEDGE AREAS FOR HELPING YOUR CLIENTS—
EXCERPTS FROM *FIVE SECRETS OF GREAT SEX THERAPY***

The 17 Core Knowledge Areas required for sex-therapy certification are relatively comprehensive in terms of the subject matter they cover. But they leave out many of the process issues and skills that so often determine how we actually are with clients, and what clients take away from our sessions. These continually emerge in what my supervisees call "Wheel Work," so I want to share them with you here—with space for you to add your own observations about your approach to clients, whether or not you are working within the approved Core Knowledge Areas.

💡 **Hot Tip—Acknowledging and validating your clients' questions may be as important as your trying to solve their sexual problems,** even when some of their problems seem to cry out for help. If you're a born rescuer, you may need to train yourself to say simply: "Tell me more about that . . ." Or: "How does that relate to other aspects of your sexual story?" Once you engage your clients in stepping into significant pieces of their own stories, they may discover their own solutions—and over time, you will find you don't have to be the ultimate authority.

That said, if a client conversation about desire and intimacy raises issues that are clearly beyond your expertise, by all means refer your client for some sessions with a certified sex therapist—or consider training and supervision for yourself. Either way, find information at: www.AASECT.org.

SECRET # 1: LISTEN CLOSELY TO YOUR CLIENTS

The details of our clients' lives are keys to their sexual mysteries. To evoke them takes more than just a routine sex history of the kind that asks "When did you first have intercourse?" etc. It takes openly inviting our clients to share nuances of their own unique erotic experience: their sensations, preferences, fears, longings, memories, wishes, dreams, and other connections of body, mind, heart, and spirit. Let yourself listen with curiosity and wonder. Witnessing and accepting your clients' experience can be a potent therapeutic strategy.

How I listen to my clients—physically, emotionally, mentally, spiritually _____
_____

How I distinguish between just hearing my clients' words, and deeply hearing their issues _____
_____

The 4-D Wheel approach helps me deeply hear my clients' issues by _____
_____

Other approaches that help me deeply hear my clients' issues include _____
_____

SECRET # 2: THERE'S MORE TO SEX THERAPY THAN PERFORMANCE

Great sex therapy often involves more than diagnosis and treatment of sexual dysfunction. Sexual experience is complex. Focusing only on the performance aspects of sex leaves out much of what is crucially important for men, women, and the rest of us, especially as we all grow older: self-esteem, pleasure, and the immeasurable joys of erotic connection. Think beyond symptoms of dysfunction and the sexual goals of intercourse or orgasm. As you ask new questions, so will your clients. What is out there for them to discover is a rich new sexual landscape of sensation, feelings, meanings, and connections.

I look beyond my clients' physical symptoms by _____
_____

I help some of my clients expand their goals beyond performance by _____
_____

The 4-D Wheel approach helps me open up new areas for clients to explore by _____
_____

Other approaches that help me open up new areas for clients to explore include _____
_____

SECRET # 3: YOU DON'T HAVE TO HAVE ALL THE ANSWERS (REALLY!)

No therapist can possibly know everything there is to know about sex and intimacy. Sometimes the most empowering intervention we can offer is to support our clients in exploring their sexual dilemmas for themselves. Solving all our clients' problems is not our job. Predicting outcomes for our clients' lives is not our job. Our job is to inspire self-esteem and create a safe, confidential space in which clients can begin to rewrite the negative scripts that keep them locked in unwanted sexual dynamics.

I encourage my clients to develop self-esteem by _____
_____

I help my clients develop problem-solving skills by _____
_____

The 4-D Wheel approach helps me create and hold safe space for my clients by _____
_____

Other approaches that help me create and hold safe space for clients include _____
_____

SECRET # 4: WORKING HARDER THAN YOUR CLIENTS IS SELDOM HELPFUL

It's your client's life, not yours. If you find yourself working harder than a client, this is a recipe for burnout—plus a mixed message about responsibility. Great sex therapy involves trust that your clients are capable of acting in their own behalf (and teaching them how to if they come to you not knowing). Work collaboratively with them rather than trying to fix them. Engage them in becoming aware of the sexual complexities of their lives—past, present, and future. Above all, encourage every independent step your clients take toward sexual healing and pleasure.

I keep myself from trying to fix my clients by _____

_____

I encourage my clients to take their own steps to sexual healing by _____

_____

The 4-D Wheel approach helps me work collaboratively with my clients by _____

_____

Other approaches that help me work collaboratively with clients include _____

_____

SECRET # 5: CHECK YOUR OWN ISSUES AT THE DOOR

Great sex therapy focuses on our clients, not ourselves—even when our clients' issues bring us face-to-face with our own. Professional ethics dictate that the therapy room is a place to model compassionate connection and clear, empathic boundaries along with confidentiality and safety. Summon whatever it takes to resolve your own issues about love, sex, and relationships so you don't get caught up in clients' stories and projections, or act on ego needs to enter into romantic or sexual relationships with your clients.

My clients' issues that are likely to trigger my own unresolved issues include _____

_____

Methods I use to be aware of my countertransference issues with my clients include _____

_____

The 4-D Wheel approach helps me deal with my own issues by _____

_____

Other approaches that help me deal with my own issues include _____

_____

YOUR OWN SECRET(S) OF GREAT SEX THERAPY

What I bring into my practice of sex therapy that is uniquely beneficial to my clients:

_____
_____
_____

What qualities of mine enable me to bring my own "secret(s)" into my practice of sex therapy:

_____
_____
_____

I perceive my sex therapy "secret(s)" to be most beneficial to my clients in the following dimensions of the Wheel:

Physical (describe how) _____
_____
_____

Emotional (describe how) _____
_____
_____

Mental (describe how) _____
_____
_____

Spiritual (describe how) _____
_____
_____

🔆 **Hot Tip—"Promoting positive change for our clients involves more than being proficient at the models and techniques we use.** It also involves the energies we embody ourselves, as therapists. Call it mirror neurons, vibrational resonance, or Freudian transference, our presence may actually spark the change our clients seek—as long as we take the ego out of that statement. When we can step beyond goals and outcomes to encourage (and sometimes surprise) our clients to step into their own experiences of acceptance, trust, compassion, appreciation, and on and on, we are helping them find their own paths to sexual potential."
—_Extraordinary Sex Therapy_, p. 5

SPARKING, EXPANDING, AWAKENING:
SEVEN WISDOM AREAS TO HELP YOU HELP YOUR CLIENTS—
BODY, MIND, HEART, AND SPIRIT

There are numerous wisdom areas that reach beyond the core knowledge areas required for certification as a sexuality professional. These are not necessarily taught in classrooms. Some come to us innately and some accrete through clinical experience. Below, find seven of these wisdom areas that are crucial to a practice of sex therapy that is both engaging and transformative for clients. You may recognize these as part of what you routinely bring into your interactions with clients. Here is an opportunity for you to acknowledge and name them.

1) Complex Thinking Sparks Erotic Creativity

The nature of both sexual experience and sex therapy can be paradoxical. To fully understand these involves a conceptual framework that acknowledges and celebrates the erotic, and helps clients travel the often surprising distances between intimacy and passion. If you instinctively see many facets of the issues your clients bring to therapy, you are a complex thinker. I call this "thinking in the round," which is both a prerequisite for and a byproduct of using the 4-D-Wheel approach.

An example of my "thinking in the round" as a therapist is _____
_____

I help myself "think in the round" during therapy sessions by _____
_____

I promote complex thinking in my clients by _____
_____

2) Curiosity Promotes Sexual Healing

Sometimes the most therapeutic service we can offer clients is to listen—deeply, completely, intelligently. This is especially true in sex therapy, where clients' stories may reflect desires and behaviors that are stigmatized so that they carry with them a heavy load of thoughts, feelings, sensations, and meanings—and sometimes diagnoses. One colleague speaks of clients who inhabit "the geography of desperation." I find it helpful to approach each client's story as if it's a sacred portal into a geography that is new to me. My intention is to learn enough nuances of that client's experience so that we can travel into that landscape together with common language and purpose.

An example of my curiosity as a therapist is _____
_____

I activate my curiosity during a therapy session by _____
_____

I encourage curiosity in my clients by _____
_____

3) New Information Awakens Sexual Awareness and Desire

It is often said that the greatest predictor of great sex is novelty. It has been my experience that introducing new information into a session can be a predictor of great sex therapy—as innovative models can spark transformative experiences in clients' lives. The 4-D Wheel opens multiple perspectives that can unlock impasses for clients. As clients explore each dimension, they have opportunities to discover new information that may range from the depths of their own emotions to how neuroscience offers insights into post-traumatic indices of low sexual desire. For some clients, awakening means moving beyond cultural messages; for others it's about differentiating from their partners. Still others use information as a kind of aphrodisiac to redefine sexual and emotional caretaking, build curiosity about their own sensuality, and activate new neuronal paths for pleasure. It doesn't stop.

An example of my generating new information for clients is _____
_____

I offer new information during therapy sessions by _____
_____

I encourage clients to seek new information by _____
_____

4) Intelligent Touch Wakes Up Our Bodies

Of all the senses, touch is as essential to life as it is to sexual development. Yet therapists and other sexuality professionals often avoid teaching touch to help desire and intimacy issues because they're not trained to use touch in a therapeutic way or even to recognize its benefits. Moreover, in our litigious society, any touching of clients during a therapy session may carry with it the risk of misconduct, even malpractice. In traditional sex therapy, touching may be assigned as "sensate focus" homework. But even this is not always adequately explained; too often, it's left for clients to fumble through at home, on their own. Clients may "forget" to do their homework, or say "It doesn't work." Relating touch to all the dimensions of the Wheel can help open the conversation about how to give—and receive—intelligent touch.

I assess when and how to open the conversation about touch by _____
_____

I encourage clients to develop sensitivities to intelligent touch by _____
_____

5) Active Education Creates Active Change

Sometimes practical solutions are what a client needs most. Are you a down-to-earth, just-do-it practitioner with the sensitivities of a coach rather than a therapist, whose training focuses on personal and relational problems? The behavioral, solution-focused elements that coaching techniques offer to help clients experience desire and intimacy include educating and supporting them in their quest for self-esteem and pleasure—body, mind, heart, and spirit. Does one of your clients need help shopping for sex toys or other paraphernalia? Is it appropriate for you to take on this role? If not, it may be the right time to actively prepare your client to take this special journey solo, or else to refer to another sexuality professional whose job includes accompanying clients on shopping sprees.

I offer practical solutions during the course of therapy by _____
_____

I encourage my clients to seek their own practical solutions by _____
_____

6) Inclusive Language Expands Sexual Diversity

Language (both verbal and non-verbal) transmits sexual information and is a potent vehicle through which we can encourage clients to expand their norms—or in worst-case scenarios actually constrict them. When the issue includes sexual desire and intimacy for clients who identify as gay, lesbian, bi, trans, poly, queer, and more, our binary ("his/her") language reflects inbuilt prejudices against sexual diversity. In the sexuality field today, there is movement to develop queer-friendly consciousness and syntax that is plural enough to welcome all genders, orientations, and varieties of relationship, no matter how creative or unusual these may seem to dyed-in-the-wool monogamous heterosexuals.

> 🔆 **Hot Tip—Ask your clients what pronoun they prefer when you refer to them** (e.g., "he," "she," "they"—or something else). Being clear with your clients helps you avoid unintended discrimination or microaggressions, builds trust with your clients, and models your ability to ask for specific guidance into the mysteries of your clients' sexual culture and language.

I help myself become aware of diversity during therapy sessions by _____
_____

I help clients affirm and express their own diversity by _____
_____

7) Non-Ordinary Paths Open New Vistas for Desire and Intimacy

There are many paths to sexual healing, and some of them lead through opening the proverbial "doors of perception" into non-ordinary realms. If you are ready to listen, some clients will tell you of sexual, sensual, erotic experiences way beyond orgasm, in which they've felt transported to new landscapes where both sensory and cognitive awareness are magnified, where they feel connected with subtle energies—nature, the spirit world, and whatever they name as God. These are experiences often expressed as the very center of the Wheel, where all the dimensions meet: physical, emotional, mental, and spiritual. (The "ISIS" survey recounts thousands of such experiences; you can read about them in *The Heart & Soul of Sex*.)

In the therapy office, non-ordinary experiences occur as spontaneous shifts or transitions when clients have flashes of insight that come suddenly, and seemingly from nowhere. Or when they "dissociate" while exploring the depths of old sexual traumas. These are potent events, neurologically as well as emotionally. And they are often momentary; you can miss them if you are not attuned. As you learn to recognize them and hold space for them, you can help clients walk through them, as significant gateways to transformation. With some clients, you can set the stage for non-ordinary shifts by initiating yoga breathing, guided meditations, rhythmic movements and even aspects of shamanic ritual, such as clearing energy and lighting candles, as described in Chapter 2.

I help myself be conscious of non-ordinary information during a therapy session by _____
_____

I affirm clients' exploring non-ordinary realms by _____
_____

YOUR CORE KNOWLEDGE AREAS AND WISDOM AREAS

From your own observations throughout this chapter, note on the Wheel below what issues you need to expand for yourself in each dimension of the Wheel, and what action steps you will take.

I need to expand

Action steps

_____   _____
_____   _____
_____   _____
_____   _____
_____   _____

I need to expand   _____   _____   I need to expand
                     _____   _____

_____   _____
_____   _____
_____   _____
_____   _____
_____   _____

Action steps

SPIRITUAL

EMOTIONAL   **MENTAL**

PHYSICAL

Action steps

_____   _____
_____   _____
_____   _____
_____   _____
_____   _____

I need to expand

Action steps

_____   _____
_____   _____
_____   _____
_____   _____
_____   _____

SELF-EVALUATION:
WORKING WITH CORE KNOWLEDGE AREAS AND WISDOM AREAS
TO HELP CLIENTS WITH SEXUAL DESIRE AND INTIMACY

Special gifts I bring to this practice _____

_____

Ways I prevent myself from being my most effective _____

_____

What I need to learn in order to optimize my gifts _____

_____

An action step I will take _____

_____

An affirmation I offer myself _____

FOOD FOR THOUGHT

It doesn't matter how smart you are or how much you know about sex. What matters is what clients take away from your sessions to help them transform their lives.

REFERENCES AND SUGGESTED READING FOR EXPLORING
CORE KNOWLEDGE AND SKILLS AREAS

Annon, J.S. (1976, April 1). The PLISSIT model: A proposed conceptual scheme for the behavioral treatment of sexual problems. *Journal of Sex Education and Therapy*, 2(1): 1–15.

Barker, M. (2012). *Rewriting the rules: An integrative guide to love, sex and relationships.* New York: Routledge.

Binik, Y.M., and Hall, S.K. (Eds.) (2014). *Principles and practice of sex therapy* (5th ed.). Binghamton, NY: Guilford.

Cohn, R. (2011). *Coming home to passion: Restoring loving sexuality in couples with histories of childhood trauma and neglect.* Santa Barbara, CA: Praeger.

Eisler, R. (1995). *Sacred pleasure: Sex, myth, and the politics of the body.* New York: HarperCollins.

Heiman, J., and LoPiccolo, J. (1987). *Becoming orgasmic: A sexual and personal growth program for women* (rev. ed.). New York: Fireside.

Joannides, P. (2015). *The guide to getting it on* (8th ed.). Waldport, OR: Goofyfoot Press.

Kaplan, H.S. (1988). *The illustrated manual of sex therapy* (2nd ed.). New York: Routledge.

Kleinplatz, P.J. (Ed.) (2012). *New directions in sex therapy: Innovations and alternatives.* New York: Routledge.

Montague, A. (1971). *Touching: The human significance of the skin.* New York: Columbia University Press.

Morin, J. (1995). *The erotic mind: Unlocking the inner sources of sexual passion and fulfillment.* New York: Harper Collins.

Ogden, G. (2006). *The heart and soul of sex: Keys to the sexual mysteries.* Boston: Trumpeter.

Ogden, G. (2011). *Five secrets of great sex therapy.* Self-published e-book.

Ogden, G. (Ed.) (2015). *Extraordinary sex therapy: Creative approaches for clinicians.* New York: Routledge.

Shapiro, F. (1997). *EMDR: The breakthrough therapy for overcoming anxiety, stress, and trauma.* New York: Basic Books.

Shapiro, F. (2012). *EMDR: Getting past your past: Take control of your life with self-help techniques from EMDR therapy.* Emmaus, PA: Rodale.

Tiefer, L., and Kaschak, E. (2001). *A new view of women's sexual problems.* Binghamton, NY: Haworth Press.

Weiner, L., and Avery-Clark, C. (2014). "Sensate focus: Clarifying the Masters and Johnson's model." *Journal of Sexual and Relationship Therapy*, 29(3): 307–319.

7

Making Your Own Wheel

Adapting It to Your Office and Your Unique Strengths

"If we wait until we're ready, we'll be waiting for the rest of our lives."
—*Lemony Snickett*

OPENING QUIZ:
YOUR ATTITUDES ABOUT CREATING YOUR OWN WHEEL

This quiz is not a test! It is to help you recognize your own opinions and consider new ones. There are no right or wrong answers—interpret them as you wish, and write other questions on this page as they occur to you.

Circle the number that most closely reflects your views on the questions below:

1 always true; 2 sometimes true; 3 seldom true; 4 never true

The idea of creating a 4-D Wheel feels really exciting	1 2 3 4
I have a lot of anxiety about creating my own Wheel	1 2 3 4
I'm not an artist so my Wheel will be direct and simple	1 2 3 4
It's not important for the Wheel to be a work of art	1 2 3 4
Using the Wheel sets special space in an office for working with clients	1 2 3 4
Just using a diagram on a piece of paper is enough	1 2 3 4
Creating a Wheel activates clients' imagination and makes my therapy more creative	1 2 3 4
Using the Wheel awakens the therapist as well as the client	1 2 3 4
Using a Wheel distracts from the serious business of therapy	1 2 3 4
Creating a Wheel is an innovative way of inviting clients to tell their sex histories	1 2 3 4
The Wheel I created brings wonderful energy into the room	1 2 3 4
Other issues _____	1 2 3 4
Other issues _____	1 2 3 4
Other issues _____	1 2 3 4

There are many ways to create a four-dimensional Wheel that offers safe space and effective ritual for clients. Which ones do you use? (Check all that apply)

___ I use four Post-Its labeled "Physical," "Emotional," "Mental," and "Spiritual"

___ I have an elaborate Wheel that I keep set up in my office all the time

___ Instead of a Wheel, I use copies of the 4-D Wheel Handout (see p. 7 or p. 175 for a copy)

___ I constantly keep the Wheel in my mind as I'm working with clients

___ I don't need an actual Wheel; it's just as effective to tell clients about it

___ I ask clients to make their own Wheels as part of their homework

___ Other ways _____

___ Other ways _____

___ Other ways _____

"[Clients] identify with the [4-D] Wheel in a new consciousness of the circles and wheels all around them—in nature, in mandalas and labyrinths, and in the multidimensional components in almost every situation in their lives. All of these call up the [therapeutic] experience and remind them that there are ways to explore their stories, and their lives, from different perspectives."
—*Expanding the Practice of Sex Therapy*, p. 153

This workbook is designed as a companion for *Expanding the Practice of Sex Therapy*. Chapter 7 is based on *Expanding* Chapters 10 and 12, which detail using the 4-D Wheel with groups, couples, and individuals.

CREATING YOUR OWN WHEEL: ADAPTING IT TO YOUR OFFICE AND YOUR CLIENTS

Creating and using your own 4-D Wheel is like having an ally in your therapy room when you work with clients. This is an ally who helps you set safe space, generate appropriate ritual, develop an intelligent container for clients' objects, and invite the kinds of movement that can help your clients expand their stories of desire and intimacy beyond performance and pathology. Clinicians who train with me affirm that walking their own Wheels with their clients sparks their therapeutic creativity along with deepening their understanding of their clients' issues.

I'm often asked why I don't offer a ready-made "4-D Wheel kit" on my website. My answer is that I believe that each Wheel uniquely reflects the therapeutic essence of each practitioner—in a way that ready-made Wheels cannot. Plus, the process of making one's own Wheel can be transformative in a variety of ways. That said, my colleague Patti Britton has long visualized a four-quadrant quilt, and she is now offering "mandala" quilts handcrafted by her designer sister (www.drpattibritton.com).

WHEELS, WHEELS, WHEELS

When you consider making your own Wheel, it's important that you create it from your own heart as well as keeping it appropriate for your clients. You can use the process as a reminder of the basic tenet of counseling and therapy: be fully in your own space as well as reaching out to your client's.

Your Wheel Can Be Imaginative and Elaborate

A landscape architect created the Wheel entirely with flowers.
An engineer conceptualized the Wheel as an owner's manual of many pages.
A dancer created her Wheel in a bowl of water to demonstrate its intrinsic fluidity.
A Jungian analyst painted the Wheel as a series of concentric galaxies connecting the Self with Infinity.
A movement therapist created a Wheel with scarves on her deck overlooking a lake.
A sexuality course at a Santa Fe college turned the Wheel into a group art-therapy project.

Or You Can Keep It Simple . . . as These Practitioners Do

"I put four Post-Its on the floor and get my clients up and walking their issues."
"I criss-cross two ribbons on my office carpet and use file cards for the quadrants."
"I draw the Wheel on a whiteboard in my office."
"I give the 4-D Wheel diagram to my clients and ask them to point to the quadrants as they talk about their issues."

"Training Wheels"

Many 4-D Wheel practitioners train their students and supervisees. Kristin Hodson asks members of her sexuality classes at the University of Utah to create Wheels and then video each other inviting clients into their Wheels. This is one of the ways she helps students think about the complexity of sexual issues and also practice developing their communication skills.

WHAT YOU WILL NEED

Aside from your imagination and your understanding of how you want to begin using the 4-D approach, you may want a variety of materials to help bring your own Wheel into being. For some practitioners, making a Wheel becomes a full-scale creative project. For others it's more of a spiritual journey—rather like searching for the kinds of objects you ask your clients to bring into 4-D Wheel sessions. You may even find that just the right materials find you. Others conceptualize their Wheels as means to creating safe and potent space in their offices—so that the outward design of the Wheel becomes secondary to its purpose.

Whatever your approach, I urge you to follow your instincts. At the end of this chapter is a space for you to make preliminary sketches of your own Wheel and to jot down the kinds of materials you might be using. Meanwhile, have a look below at some of the Wheels now in use by practitioners in this country and beyond.

WHEELS, WHEELS, WHEELS: THE VISUALS

In my professional archives are scores of Wheels that have been sent to me by colleagues and participants. You can see many of these on www.4-DNetwork.com. Below are nine Wheels to illustrate the kinds of Wheels that are being used by me and others. Note that each of these Wheels begins with a special vision and serves a specific purpose.

Gina's "Training Wheel"

A cloth napkin, four embroidered ribbons, four folded-over file cards for labels—these are what I carry as a basic 4-D Wheel to use when I train professionals. Everything fits in a small pouch, and I can set up the Wheel instantly on the floor—to invite participants out of their chairs to experience what it's like to literally step into each dimension in an embodied way. Well OK, here, I've added four stones to mark the quadrants, and placed a candle in the center. These are not necessary, but I have a hard time saying "No!" when it comes to objects that invest the Wheel with special meaning for me. The black stones are ancient *kuyas* (sacred healing stones) from Peru, the white heart stone was a gift from the beach outside the Casa de los Artistas in Mexico, where I conduct annual trainings, and the flaming pottery bowl in the center came from Reuben, the resident sage whose open-air market is up the jungle path from the Casa.

Gina's Ceremonial Wheel—Waiting for Participants

This is a Wheel ready to welcome 40 participants to a retreat. It will be introduced as "a ceremonial circle, which is a container for our sexual stories—to help us explore the sexual mysteries." Participants are invited to introduce themselves by placing two objects in the Wheel, and to "light their own fire" (each one lights a candle). By the end of introductions, we are sitting around a ring of fire that contains the energy of countless stories waiting to be told. Ceremonial items on the Wheel include feathers, stones, shells, flowers, singing bowls, and more—all to create sacred space, invite objects, movement, and ritual, and welcome benevolent spirits to our gathering to help our stories unfold.

Gina's Ceremonial Wheel—with Participants' Objects

Here is a view of the same Wheel, transformed into a living, breathing, somewhat chaotic mandala—after participants have introduced the stories that accompany their objects and lit their way into the circle. (The visible chaos is useful to help participants understand that desire and intimacy are complex, often messy, and contain immensely rich material.) We work with all these objects throughout the retreat, moving them to help us experience all four dimensions of the Wheel. Participants then take their objects home, where they can continue to use them as their teachers.

Kamara's Therapy Wheel

This Wheel is created by Kamara McAndrews, who co-leads retreats and trainings with me at Esalen Institute. (Meet her in Chapter 9.) Here, she has set a Wheel for a client couple in her office in Colorado Springs. Notice the precision with which she designates the four quadrants of the Wheel—in this instance, to offset the turmoil brought by a couple grappling with the aftermath of an affair. The physical container of the Wheel helps ground both partners, so that each can share from a place of physical, emotional, mental, and spiritual truth, and they can each position themselves to listen from the place that best allows them to hear the other.

Tina's Garden Wheel

This Wheel is in Lenhovda, Sweden, in the healing garden of Tina Nevin, who co-leads trainings with me in Mexico. When she conducts 4-D Wheel groups, she often takes participants outdoors into nature to put their feet on the earth as a way to reconnect body, mind, heart, and spirit. To me, her Wheel evokes the ancient stone labyrinths that dot the Swedish landscape, if you know where to look for them.

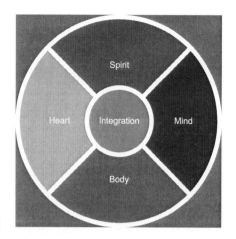

The Techie Wheel

Increasingly, I ask participants in trainings and retreats to send me pictures of the Wheels they create. This is one participant's vision—clean-cut geometry, clearly labeled, with a different color for each quadrant. I find that this Wheel appeals especially to participants who need clarity and who may be put off by the more spontaneous and chaotic aspects of the ceremonial Wheels.

The "IPEP" Wheel

This "IPEP" Wheel (for Integrative Pelvic Exam Protocol) is the creation of Debra Wickman, an Ob-Gyn physician in Phoenix, Arizona, who uses it to help women identify and discuss their pelvic pain. She introduces them to a vulva puppet she places in the center—her way of focusing them on their issues without asking them to bring objects. She labels her Wheel and explains that pelvic pain is more than just physical—it is emotional, mental, and spiritual as well. She asks women to provide a word in each dimension that describes their pain. She then asks them for a word in each dimension that describes their hoped-for outcomes. In this way, she creates a structured (and efficient) "Yes/No" dialogue, which makes her pelvic exams more comfortable, engaging, and meaningful for her patients, especially those who have experienced trauma, and despair of being understood. We are developing this approach as part of a protocol for other gynecologists, to remind them of the 4-D implications of pelvic pain, and to offer a structured practice to help them communicate more fully, and way less awkwardly, with women who need focused attention and encouragement to express their feelings and expand sexual hope.

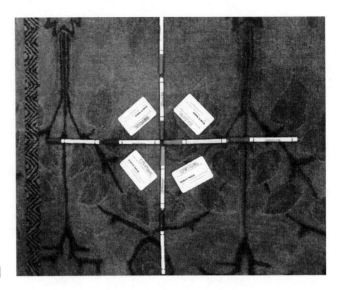

The Impromptu Wheel

When it's time to do Wheel work, use what's at hand! A 4-D practitioner was asked at a conference to demonstrate how to create a Wheel. She made this minimalist Wheel from eight hotel ballpoint pens, and used four of her business cards to label the quadrants.

"It Fits in My Office"

This is a snapshot of a Wheel being used in the therapy office of a 4-D practitioner. You can see some of the objects brought by a client: pad and pencil, and more. This Wheel is very simply four strips of tape, with a label for each quadrant. It eloquently demonstrates that your Wheel does not have to be a work of art in order to be effective with clients. It also demonstrates how useful it might be for clients to take on-the-spot photos of their objects in the Wheel, to document their therapeutic journeys over time.

CREATE YOUR OWN WHEEL BELOW

This page is for you to use—to create ideas and sketches for your own 4-D Wheel. Think about how you will use your Wheel, where you will use it, and what clients you imagine using it with. Will you be using it for therapy clients, in group retreats, or teaching sessions—or all three? Or maybe you'll create one for yourself first. Note what kind of general effect you want to create (the Wheels on the previous pages depict a range from spiritual, to techie, to expedient). Note how you want to identify the quadrants. And know that you don't have to limit yourself to just one Wheel.

TO-DO LIST FOR MAKING YOUR OWN WHEEL

Materials I will need _____

_____

_____

Friends and colleagues I will ask to practice walking the Wheel _____

_____

_____

I plan to create my Wheel by the following date (day/month/year) _____

SELF-EVALUATION: CREATING YOUR OWN WHEEL

The special gifts I bring to this practice _____

Ways I can prevent myself from being my most effective _____

What I need to learn _____

An action step I will take _____

An affirmation I give myself _____

FOOD FOR THOUGHT

"Creativity is just connecting things. When you ask creative people how they did something, they feel a little guilty because they didn't really do it, they just saw something. It seemed obvious to them after a while. That's because they were able to connect experiences they've had and synthesize new things."

—Steve Jobs

REFERENCES AND SUGGESTED READING FOR MAKING YOUR OWN WHEEL

Ogden, G. (2006). *The heart and soul of sex: Keys to the sexual mysteries*. Boston: Trumpeter.

Ogden, G. (2013). *Expanding the practice of sex therapy: An integrative model for exploring desire and intimacy*. New York: Routledge.

Snickett, L. (2001). *The ersatz elevator*. New York: HarperCollins.

Wolf, Gary. (1996, Feb 1). Steve Jobs: The next insanely great thing. *Wired*.

Part II

Practical Applications

Protocols for Challenging Clients
Using the Four-Dimensional Wheel
of Sexual Experience

Introduction
4-D Wheel Protocols for Challenging Clients

Part II offers case examples that illustrate how five seasoned practitioners incorporate Wheel work into the kinds of therapy and sex therapy they already do well. It also offers explicit questions, activities, resources, and worksheets that will help you incorporate the 4-D Wheel into your own practice—even if what you do differs from the work of these practitioners. The final chapter in Part II offers an opportunity for you to practice tracking a case or cases of your own around the Wheel.

Note that the case examples in Part II are just snapshots to show how the 4-D Wheel approach works with a particular client at a particular moment in the course of therapy. They do not represent the entire story of possible applications of the Wheel. Other practitioners have incorporated into the Wheel a wide range of methodologies and protocols they have acquired during their practices of sex therapy, counseling, and coaching, psychotherapy, couples therapy, social work, gynecology, pelvic-floor therapy, sensorimotor work, energy healing, Emotionally Focused Therapy (EFT), internal family systems (IFS), Gestalt therapy, bioenergetics, psychodrama, meditation, hypnosis, narrative therapy, imago therapy, recovery groups, and more.

What are the primary therapeutic models you use? _____
How might you incorporate them into the Wheel? _____

Note also that the first four case examples involve heterosexual individuals and couples. Please allow yourself to freely adapt the techniques, sensitivities, and questions generated by Wheel work with these clients to the full diversity of the clients in your practice.

What is the range of your clients' diversities (LGBT, single, poly, other)? _____
How might you adapt your work with the Wheel to benefit them? _____

Finally, note that these five case examples represent only a few of the diverse issues with which the 4-D Wheel approach can be both effective and efficient. Using the Wheel has proven valuable for clients who present with issues involving low desire, desire discrepancies, cultural and language differences, body image, sexual self-image, empathy, communication, gender identity, sexual orientation, kink, affairs, polyamory, anorgasmia, ejaculatory problems, attachment disorders, compulsivity, dissociation, aging, illness, disability, and transitions of all kinds—the list could go on (see the Core Knowledge Areas in Chapter 6).

What issues are important to your clients? _____
How do you see possibly using the Wheel with them? _____

8

Naomi

Discovering the Heart in Sexual Desire

"The longest journey in the world is the one
we make from the head to the heart."
—*Oscar Miro-Quesada*

LINDSAY JERNIGAN

Lindsay Jernigan, PhD, MA, is a licensed clinical psychologist who offers therapy and sex therapy for individuals and couples. She also offers workshops and therapeutic intensives for adults, and clinical supervision for therapists. Her practice is located in South Burlington, Vermont in Eastern View Mental Health: A Center for Authentic Development, an integrated healthcare center she co-founded with a team of colleagues. She writes: "Being our most authentic selves is the greatest gift and the most compassionate act we can offer in this life. I have developed a model for transformational change based on these convictions. I call it Compassionate Authenticity." www.DrLindsayJernigan.com.

USING THE 4-D WHEEL APPROACH WITH COGNITIVE BEHAVIORAL THERAPY (CBT)

I often utilize CBT in my work because I find thoughts are an efficient way to access our internal experience; the mind is a portal through which many clients feel safe and comfortable entering into an exploration of themselves. By using the Wheel in conjunction with CBT, I can help clients who are less comfortable or familiar with other layers of their experience enter into a more holistic healing process. With the Wheel, we can literally step *in* through the mind via thought analysis, and then walk the Wheel to integrate the corresponding experiences in body, heart, and spirit. Instead of consciously changing thoughts, we explore alternative states of body, heart and spirit, and then we *experience* the corresponding difference in the mind.

For example, clients frequently begin a session in the Wheel by describing racing thoughts, loud self-criticism, and distortions of helplessness and hopelessness in the mind. We then walk the Wheel to explore the whole "felt" experience that accompanies these thoughts—in the heart, body, and spirit. After working in the Wheel to tend to the needs of the body, mind, and spirit and create new flow and energy, clients very often return to the mind quadrant and report experiencing "a quiet mind" that offers self-affirming and optimistic thoughts. This happens without them having to choose or construct a new adaptive thought. Instead it happens naturally by awakening the healing voices of other parts of the self.

I am amazed every single time I use the Wheel with my clients. It has never failed to deepen the content of the clinical work. Using it moves clients rapidly into a stage of insight and healing that would have taken many months to achieve through standard therapies such as CBT and psychodynamic therapy, and generates hope and optimism as clients rediscover their own potential rather than being stuck in their negative stories about themselves. I enter into these sessions as a guide and fellow explorer. I find using the Wheel an invigorating and effortless way to help clients step outside repetitive thoughts cycles and into new states of being and am routinely awed by clients' ability to generate new felt experiences and deeper insights.

The vignette of Naomi's case in this chapter reflects the efficiency and efficacy of using the Wheel. It was particularly exciting to watch a young woman trained, herself, in standard modes of therapy, step so rapidly out of ingrained patterns of intellectualization with the help of the Wheel. I am so grateful to have the Wheel in my therapeutic toolbox, and for having had the opportunity to witness Gina in action so I know how to make use of its power and potential.

USING THE WHEEL TO EXPAND SEXUAL CONSCIOUSNESS AND THE EFFECTIVENESS OF CBT

A CASE NARRATIVE WITH ACCOMPANYING CASE SUPERVISION AND INTERACTIVE COMMENTS

Chapter 8 demonstrates how a psychologist and sex therapist incorporates cognitive behavioral therapy (CBT) into the Wheel to help Naomi, a "stuck-in-her-head" client who presents with desire and intimacy issues. Note the use of the Wheel and all of the core dynamics and skill sets. Especially note how seamlessly the core dynamics of movement and concretizing expand Naomi's therapy beyond CBT and into mindfulness, imagination, and emotions. This is an example of a 4-D Wheel application for clients who can benefit from expanding sexual consciousness to explore their story—past, present, and future.

Lindsay's case narrative is accompanied by a running commentary by me, set in shaded boxes— as a kind of clinical case supervision. Most importantly, this chapter is interactive. There are spaces that invite your observations and comments alongside the case supervision. At the end of the chapter Naomi's case is revisited, so that you can see it described via the Wheel. Note that the purpose of this chapter is not to describe CBT, but to illustrate how a practitioner uses the Wheel as a way to incorporate and expand that approach.

NAOMI, SESSION ONE: THE PRESENTING ISSUE

Lindsay's Case Narrative: In my latest Wheel example, I worked with Naomi, age 38, who wanted to overcome her automatic anxious and avoidant response to sexual contact with her husband.

> **Gina's Supervisory Comments:** The way Lindsay phrases Naomi's presenting problem and wish for change suggests that Naomi is literally stuck. My initial guess is that she's stuck in a story in her past—since she says that her "avoidance" to sex is "automatic."
>
> When responses are "automatic" this almost always means that they are habitual, ingrained over a long time. The pairing of "automatic" with "anxiety" also suggests that it would help to understand the basic neuroscience of Naomi's particular pattern, and to outline it for her at some point in the therapy. This will provide measurable markers to help Naomi accept and articulate therapeutic transformations that are taking place.
>
> I wonder what Naomi's body language is saying right now? Let's hear more of her story . . .

[Your comments:]
What do you notice at this point?_____
What would you do at this point?_____
If you were Naomi's therapist or counselor, what countertransference issues do you imagine might arise with this case?_____

L: Naomi is, herself, a therapist in private practice, and well versed in therapeutic, clinical language; she knew what she "should" think and feel in order to be healthy in her own assessment, and she had analyzed and attacked her own responses with all of her well-honed psychodynamic and cognitive-behavioral skills. That approach was actually working against her. She was repeatedly talking about herself from a purely cognitive perspective, anxiously avoiding her own bodily, emotional, and spiritual experiences in therapy, just as she was anxiously avoiding them in sexual contact with her partner.

G: Naomi says she has tried everything she knows, and has all the answers to her problems. But she admits that knowing it all isn't helping her with desire and intimacy. To continue with CBT as the only modality would be a repetition of what hasn't worked, and would undermine what Naomi wants—which is to experience more spontaneous emotions and sensations with her husband during their sexual encounters.

To help Naomi move toward her therapy goals, an approach beyond CBT is definitely recommended. My initial urge is to introduce her to the concept of the Wheel, to open her mind to the notion that sexual response is four-dimensional—physical, emotional, mental, and spiritual.

What do you notice at this point? _____
What would you do at this point? _____
What other therapeutic approaches might you consider for Naomi? _____

_____

At the end of this introductory session, Lindsay gives Naomi an assignment to bring in two objects for the next session: one object is to represent a part of her sexual story she wants to keep, the other is to represent a part of her sexual story she wants to release (see Chapter 4 for full description of this concretizing technique).

G: The assignment to bring objects to the next session undoubtedly engages Naomi at levels that are different from her usual mental/intellectual approach to her issues. First, the surprise element potentially activates Naomi's polyvagal response to stress (will she be receptive, or reactive?). Second, Naomi is asked to consider positive as well as negative aspects of her underlying issue, which is a departure from the traditional CBT approach of focusing on the problem and its solutions. Further, Naomi is asked to bring two opposing objects. Wait! She is already at war with a part of herself. These two objects set up a thematic possibility that she might ultimately acknowledge and accept seemingly opposing parts of herself—especially parts she's been "avoiding."

What do you notice at this point?_____
What would you do at this point?_____

NAOMI, SESSION TWO: WALKING THE WHEEL WITH HER OBJECTS

L: Naomi brought two objects, as instructed. The first was a square piece of paper that represented the bedroom window her high-school lover used to climb in for secret late-night sexual visits—this was the image and memory that came to mind for her when she thought of the feeling of anxious avoidance. She had craved an emotional and spiritual connection with this partner, and had been hurt again and again when he would immediately climb back out the window after their trysts. The second object Naomi brought was a puzzle piece. Specifically, this was the chest piece of a puzzle of a woman, no head attached. To her, this represented "getting out of her head," which she saw as her goal during sex, and also sex therapy.

> G: Naomi's two objects open up volumes of material to explore. The story of the old longing and hurt during the high-school trysts is emotionally moving and evocative—yet Naomi's paper is blank . . . (I wonder what Naomi might eventually write or draw on this paper—but if I were the therapist, I'd refrain from asking the question. This is a question Naomi would most powerfully come around to asking for herself.)
>
> The wished-for piece of the puzzle is intriguingly ambiguous. Naomi brings in a woman's "chest"—is this what contains the heart that's missing from Naomi's marital sex (?). Whatever it comes to represent, this puzzle piece suggests that Naomi will find much in the emotional dimension to explore. Perhaps in the physical dimension, as well.
>
> Also, the statement that this puzzle-woman is headless is a clue to how important it is that Naomi finds ways to connect the fragmented parts of herself—so she can put together the whole puzzle. I am hoping that Lindsay will guide her to explore every dimension of the Wheel—and help her find her own ways to move fluidly between them all.
>
> To sum up: both of Naomi's objects point to a theme of incompletion. It will be crucial to focus on helping Naomi fill in the blanks in her journey as she explores the Wheel.

What else do you notice at this point? _____

What else would you do at this point? _____

L: I set up a very simple Wheel on my office floor, made of ribbons and stones, and briefly described the quadrants to Naomi.

> G: Lindsay's Wheel not only sets safe space, it is another therapeutic surprise to Naomi—visual input that takes her even farther beyond her usual experience of CBT, and that expands the possible cascade of neurological information.

What do you notice at this point? _____

What would you do at this point? _____

L: Naomi was so curious that she stood up right away and we could begin our exploration. Using the Wheel allowed us to step past the barrier of Naomi's "head" literally and instantaneously, with one actual step into the Wheel.

> **G:** Getting Naomi to move out of her chair is yet another therapeutic surprise to her—beyond her usual CBT experience of sitting and talking. Changing physical posture and location activates neurological changes and enables her to access "non-cognitive" intelligence—through her vagus nerve, which mediates the emotions, and also transmits information between the brain and the genitals.

What do you notice at this point?_____

What would you do at this point?_____

L: As we explored Naomi's experiences in the dimensions of body, mind, heart, and spirit with each of her objects, she made a few important discoveries that her analytical and cognitive explorations hadn't illuminated for her. First, she was able to see the role her avoidance was playing for her.

> **G:** The 4-D Wheel offers a structure that opens up a larger picture to Naomi, and with it the possibility of new pathways to explore—including questions about her "avoidance."

What do you notice at this point?_____

What would you do at this point?_____

L: She came to see this avoidance response as a protective part of herself that she could respect, rather than as a pathological response with which she had to battle. This avoidance part of her wanted to protect her from the possibility of emotionally and spiritually disconnected sex, which she knew from her high-school experience left her feeling empty and abandoned.

> **G:** Opening up Naomi's access points to the 4-D information available in the Wheel suddenly leads her to a crucial new understanding: that "avoidance" is not her enemy. Rather, she can embrace her avoidance as a skill she has developed to keep herself from feeling hurt. In reaching this understanding, she is effectively owning a disowned part of herself, thus expanding her own capacity to feel, think, and make meaning.
>
> Let's see if this also expands her ability for physical sensation during sex with her husband—a note for future Wheel work, perhaps.

What do you notice at this point?_____

What would you do at this point?_____

L: She could honor this avoidance part of herself while also seeing that it was over-functioning in her marriage, where emotionally and spiritually connected sex was actually available. So she picked up the trysting window, represented by a blank square of paper, and moved it outside the Wheel, to a spot where it could "observe" and "be ready" if she needed it, just outside her body and her mind. She was able to trust that her body and her mind would know if they needed this part's protection.

G: Relating to her objects is helping Naomi relate to herself in new ways. A complex inner interaction begins to occur, which Naomi enacts overtly with her objects. On the one hand, she respects her abilities for avoidance as a protective skill. On the other hand, she is able (literally) to place that skill outside the circle of her "automatic" responses, where she can be aware of it, but take control over it rather than allowing it to control her.

Plus (a huge plus!), Naomi now articulates that she is able to trust her body as well as her mind—a big departure from the woman who is all head (or who is headless and all heart—or rather chest). This can open up future discussion about connection—connection with herself, with her husband, with her anxiety, past and present, and more.

In a future session, it could be important to bring Naomi back to this place of trust and offer her the Re-Membering activity in Chapter 5, to deepen her exploration. Meanwhile, let's follow Naomi's story in the Wheel and see what happens.

What do you notice at this point?_____

What would you do at this point?_____

L: Naomi also made a dramatic shift in her relationship to her own goals, represented by the puzzle piece. She had initially placed the puzzle piece in the body section of the Wheel, because she wanted to feel more present in her body and less stuck in her head during sex. But after exploring her non-cognitive experience more thoroughly with the Wheel, she recognized that her goal, more deeply, was to be present in her heart and her spirit during sex. Indeed, the puzzle piece she had (she thought) randomly selected was the piece depicting the woman's heart space.

G: Aha! Naomi finally gets it—in her mind anyway. Does she also get it in her body, heart, and spirit? (I feel my own "fix-it" impulse beginning to kick in.)

What do you notice at this point?_____

What would you do at this point?_____

L: She was struck as she looked down at the Wheel by a visual insight that cut through her usual cognitive processing style. She saw, literally by seeing where the puzzle piece sat in the Wheel, that although what she craved was emotional and spiritual connection, she was going about attaining this by putting pressure on her body to feel something.

> G: Yes! Whew! Now Naomi is in her body. She allows her eyes to work for her. She filters her insights through her sense of sight. What more does she see? Stay tuned!

What do you notice at this point?_____

What would you do at this point?_____

L: She saw that the emotional and spiritual segments of her Wheel were, literally, empty. She picked up her headless puzzle piece, and placed it on the line where heart and spirit come together, on the Wheel.

> G: Now Naomi is filling in the blanks—in a way that I hadn't imagined she'd get to so fast when she began the session in the Wheel. She is using her object to literally fill in the Wheel of her self.
>
> So far, the session has been mainly to create safe and potent space, then to track and follow Naomi as she works with her objects in the four dimensions. Now is the time to intervene and move the session toward some kind of integration—still following Naomi, but suggesting closure for the session and also for future exploration.

What do you notice at this point?_____

What would you do at this point?_____

L: When Naomi walked the Wheel with her objects in their new positions, her relationship to her own experience completely changed. She discovered a quieter mind, a sense of presence in her body ("I feel my feet on the floor!"), an open heart, and a "brave and wild spirit."

> G: This sense of groundedness, open heart, and brave wild spirit is the expected kind of "unexpected" outcome so many clients experience with the Four-Dimensional Wheel approach. Is it "magic"?

What do you notice at this point?_____

What would you do at this point?_____

In your estimation, might CBT have elicited a similar response from Naomi?_____

L: Naomi left the session eager to experience physical connection with her husband from this new, integrated place within herself—a positive basis for future work with her and her husband.

> G: Here, I find it important to stress that a form of therapeutic magic has transpired, in that Naomi has experienced a quantum shift in perception. Lest this shift look too easy, note that there has been a structure to the magic: Lindsay has carefully created and held space for Naomi to position herself and her objects in the four dimensions of the Wheel. This way, Naomi knows she can invoke the Wheel and differentiate her issues via its dimensions when her anxiety returns, which it inevitably will, though hopefully less often and with less vengeance.
>
> It is important for Naomi to take her objects home with her, with encouragement to use them as her teachers (as in Chapter 4).
>
> It is also important for Naomi to make another appointment—with some follow-up couple sessions if that is appropriate. This breakthrough session may provide many of the answers Naomi seeks, or it may be only the tip of the iceberg—that will inform countless sessions to follow.

What do you notice at this point? _____

What would you do at this point? _____

How would you close this session? _____

How do you think CBT and the 4-D Wheel enhanced each other? _____

_____

Are there any ways you see that they limited each other? _____

_____

How do you think using objects enhanced sex therapy for Naomi? _____

_____

Are there any ways you see that they limited each other? _____

_____

How do you think using movement enhanced sex therapy for Naomi? _____

_____

Are there any ways you see that they limited each other? _____

_____

What kernels of Lindsay's wisdom or skill can you incorporate into your practice?_____

_____

NAOMI'S 4-D WHEEL SESSION AT A GLANCE

On the following pages, you'll find a two-page form: "Inviting Clients Into the 4-D Wheel." On it are jotted details of the session with Naomi on the Wheel, so that you can see them at a glance as well as reading through the linear narrative. Recording these details in this way also demonstrates how you might record your own 4-D-Wheel sessions with your clients—as outlined in Chapter 13.

INVITING CLIENTS INTO THE 4-D WHEEL

Name of Client: Naomi   **Date:** xxx
CASE NARRATIVE: Describe client's issues that led you to suggest exploring the Wheel

Naomi wants to overcome automatic avoidance of sex with her husband. She's a therapist who's "stuck in her head." The Wheel and core dynamics are a way to help her expand her consciousness—quickly and non-judgmentally.

ISSUES FOR THERAPIST: Describe what occurred for you during session(s), including any countertransference

Empathy and understanding of Naomi's issues—I'm also a therapist with a tendency to retreat into mental aspects of experience ... my familiarity with her issues help me grasp her story and help her enter into deeper levels of her experience.

4-D WHEEL DYNAMICS USED: Describe what you did (and how) during your session(s) on the Wheel

Created safe space: Validated her experience; offered cognitive explanations; Created Wheel—ribbons & stones

Invited movement: In session 2, asked her to walk Wheel—all dimensions

Introduced ritual: Asked her to move objects into each dimension—getting out of her chair was a breakthrough—got her out of her head

Suggested concretizing abstract concepts with tangible objects: she brought in window (betrayal) and puzzle piece (missing head) both help her fill in her blanks about desire

Other _____

Name of Client: Naomi   **Date:** xxx
PROGRESS OF THE SESSION(S): List client's movement from quadrant to quadrant, from beginning to end of your session(s) with the Wheel, also where objects were placed, if they were used. Add another sheet if necessary.

1. Explores 2 objects in ea. dimension   11. _____
2. BODY: "Puzzle"—to feel more connected   12. _____
3. MIND: Trying to figure it all out   13. _____
4 HEART: Empty at first   14. _____
5. SPIRIT: Empty at first   15. _____
6. OUTSIDE Body/Mind—moved "window"   16. _____
7. MIND: she saw the pattern!   17. _____
8. BODY: "My feet are on the floor!"   18. _____
9. HEART: Open!   19. _____
10. SPIRIT: "Brave and Wild!"   20. _____

MOVEMENT OF CLIENT: List the major issues and transformations in each quadrant

Empty →
"Brave and Wild"

Empty →
Open

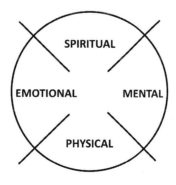

Agitation →
Quiet Mind

Pressure →
Feet on floor
Connected, excited

REFERENCES AND SUGGESTED READING FOR WOMEN, COGNITIVE BEHAVIORAL THERAPY, ATTACHMENT, AND MORE

Beck, J.S, and Beck, A.T. (2011). *Cognitive behavior therapy: Basics and beyond* (2nd ed.). Binghamton, NY: Guilford.

Binik, Y.M., and Hall, S.K. (Eds.) (2014). *Principles and practice of sex therapy* (5th ed.). Binghamton, NY: Guilford.

Boston Women's Health Book Collective. (2011). *Our bodies, ourselves* (40th anniv. rev. ed.). New York: Touchstone.

Bowlby, John (1969). *Attachment and loss*. London: Hogarth Press.

Chalker, R. (2000). *The clitoral truth: The secret world at our fingertips*. New York: Seven Stories Press.

Ensler, E. (2000). *The vagina monologues: The V-day edition*. New York: Villard.

Foley S., Kope, S., and Sugrue, D. (2012). *Sex matters for women: A complete guide to taking care of your sexual self* (rev. ed.). Binghamton, NY: Guilford Press.

Jernigan, L. (2014, February). Compassionate authenticity: A treatment model for working with women with low libido. *Sexual and Relationship Therapy*, 29 (1): 56–67.

Johnson, S.M. (2004). *The practice of emotionally focused couple therapy: Creating connections* (2nd ed.). New York: Routledge.

Johnson, S.M. (2008). *Hold me tight: Seven conversations for a lifetime of love*. Boston: Little, Brown.

Kleinplatz, P.J. (Ed.) (2012). *New directions in sex therapy: Innovations and alternatives*. New York: Routledge.

Miro-Quesada, O. and Coffin, B.G. (2014). *Lessons in courage: Peruvian shamanic wisdom for everyday life*. Faber, VA: Rainbow Ridge Publishing.

Nagoski, E. (2015). *Come as you are: The surprising new science that will transform your sex life*. New York: Simon & Schuster.

Northrup, Christiane (1995). *Women's bodies, women's wisdom: Creating physical and emotional health and healing*. New York: Bantam.

Ogden, G. (2007). *Women who love sex: Ordinary women describe their paths to pleasure, intimacy, and ecstasy* (3rd ed.). Boston: Trumpeter.

Ogden, G. (2008). *The return of desire: A guide to rediscovering your sexual passion*. Boston: Trumpeter.

Ogden, G. (2009). It's not just a headache dear: Why some women say no to connecting sex and spirit. In A. Mahoney and O. Espin (Eds.) *Sin or salvation: Implications for psychotherapy*. New York: Routledge, pp. 105–125.

Resnick, S. (2012). *The heart of desire: Keys to the pleasures of love*. New York: Wiley.

Winston, S. (2009). *Women's anatomy of arousal*. Kingston, NY: Mango Garden Press.

9

Steve

Erectile Dysfunction Meets "Two Objects"

"Sex is always about emotions.
Good sex is about free emotions;
bad sex is about blocked emotions."
—*Deepak Chopra*

KAMARA MCANDREWS

Kamara McAndrews, MA, LMFT, is a licensed marriage and family therapist, clinical sexologist, and certified sex therapist with a private practice in Colorado Springs, Colorado. She has been co-leading retreats and trainings with Gina at Esalen Institute since 2011. www.KamaraTherapy.com.

USING THE WHEEL WITH SEX-THERAPY TECHNIQUES

I discovered the 4-D Wheel at Gina's week-long workshop in Mexico in January, 2010. After an amazing personal experience there, I realized how helpful the Wheel process could be for clients who have sexual desire, anxiety, and pain disorders. I gathered items from around my house and began creating my own Wheel. Before I asked clients to try the process, I did a session for myself, pretending to be both therapist and client, then asked my mother and a friend to have a session with me. When I first asked clients to do the Wheel, I chose those who knew and trusted me and were at a place in treatment where it was refreshing to try something new.

Using the Wheel gave me permission to get clients up out of their chairs, moving, and deciphering what their dilemmas were for themselves. Right away, I noticed that they started to rely on their self-knowledge and intuition rather than asking me for explanations, answers, and suggestions. I was surprised at how smoothly catharsis would emerge as I simply inquired about a client's object as we moved from quadrant to quadrant. Solutions would begin to develop that I could never have dreamed of myself. The process enabled a depth of story and meaning beyond any theoretical approach I had learned in my 15 years as a therapist. I was so excited that I must have done 90 Wheel sessions in that first month after returning from Mexico.

I have been using the Wheel ever since in many ways, with a variety of clients. The 4-D template expands and contracts to meet my time and my clients' needs. Sometimes I use it silently, to organize my questions during intakes. I frequently show the Wheel handout to clients and ask them to use their fingers to point to where on the Wheel they are, and to express what they need in each quadrant to get to where they desire. I often pull out my square cloth, the four strips to demarcate each quadrant, and the cards that say what each quadrant represents—then ask clients to walk around the Wheel with me, so they can show me in detail what is going on for them. This is extremely helpful when my therapeutic questions (as good as they might be) leave me confused about what is at the root of my clients' issues.

As much as I love to lead five-day workshops with Gina, it's not possible to offer that for every client. So, I created a two-hour version that makes the experience on the Wheel usable for my practice and my clients' busy lives, and allows me to go more in-depth than I can with a regular one-hour therapy session. In this longer version, I set up a full Wheel [see photo of Kamara's Wheel in Chapter 7]. This way I can create a sacred space where clients can explore their sexual relationship or personal dilemma and find their own solution at the end. I am their guide through this, not telling them what to do, but asking where on the Wheel they need to be. I utilize Gestalt, Jungian, Ogden, movement, a type of Re-Membering (EMDR), and a client's in-the-moment experience to help bring forth the information that the client and I need in order to create forward movement. My clients have expressed repeatedly through the years how much common sense the Wheel makes to them and how they heal and grow through it. As both a therapist and a sex therapist, I find it an invaluable tool. My only warning is that you will have a lot of clients getting "cured," so marketing for new clients could become a much-needed skill!

USING THE WHEEL WITH ERECTILE DYSFUNCTION
A CASE NARRATIVE WITH ACCOMPANYING CASE SUPERVISION AND INTERACTIVE COMMENTS

Chapter 9 demonstrates how an MFT/sex therapist uses the Wheel to help a military officer who presents with erectile dysfunction (ED), an issue that holds potential for vast complexity. Though physicians routinely prescribe medication for ED without engaging in a deeper conversation with these men, there is a 50% dropout rate for using vasodilatation medications such as Viagra. The truth is, each man has his own story about how erectile problems affect his sense of sexuality, self, manhood, intimate relationships, agency in the world, and also his pocketbook. Until these are addressed, therapy may be incomplete. As Kamara relates Steve's case, note the creative use of objects, and the part they play. This is an example of a 4-D Wheel application for clients who can benefit from concretizing abstract concepts to gain the initiative and power to engage actively with their own healing process.

Kamara's case narrative is accompanied by my running commentary in shaded boxes, and by spaces that invite your observations. At the end of the chapter Steve's case is revisited so that you can see it described via the Wheel. Note that the purpose of this chapter is not to describe traditional sex-therapy practices for erectile dysfunction, but to illustrate how a practitioner uses the Wheel to expand these to include body, mind, heart, and spirit.

STEVE: THE PRESENTING ISSUE: ED, PERFORMANCE ANXIETY, AND MORE . . .

Kamara's Case Narrative: Steve was in his early 30s, a lieutenant from the nearby military base—a big guy, over six feet, muscular, and fit. His presenting issue was that he would lose his erection very soon after penetration. He was engaged to "the woman of my dreams," but with complications. According to Steve, his dream-woman thought the reason he couldn't hold an erection was because she wasn't pretty enough, and she constantly questioned his love for her. Steve's situation was further complicated by lack of proximity. He got to see her only every other weekend. He felt mega-pressured to perform sexually when he was with her, and his performance anxiety triggered his inability to hold an erection. Pressure was on the therapy, as well. Steve was going to be relocated out of state in three months, so treatment had to work fast.

> **Gina's Supervisory Comments:** An overriding factor is that this therapy needs to work so quickly—an interesting irony in that treatment for ED usually includes training the client to s-l-o-w down. Further, the most effective treatments for ED typically involve participation of a willing partner, and Steve has no regular physical access to his fiancée. It also appears that she might have self-esteem issues that compound Steve's performance anxiety, and that both she and Steve could uses some basic communication work. So this therapy needs to be creative and focused as well as fast, and expectations of success need to be limited accordingly.

[Your comments:]
What do you notice at this point?_____
What would you do at this point?_____
If you were Steve's therapist or counselor, what countertransference issues do you imagine might arise with this case?_____

STEVE: THE FIRST FOUR SESSIONS:
FOCUS ON MINDFULNESS AND "WIZARD BRAIN-LIZARD BRAIN"

K: During the initial session with Steve, I considered using the classic sex-therapy techniques for ED, but realized they are all goal-oriented, so determined to use the 4-D approach I've developed since discovering the Wheel. This approach involves systematically addressing negative thoughts, emotions, body image, and belief systems, and helping men transform these into positive attributes for pleasure, power, and relational satisfaction for themselves and their partners.

> **G:** Steve's is a complex situation without much time to resolve it. Kamara needs to be selective, and give him practical tools to recognize his anxiety and what to do about it. Do you think she'd be better off just suggesting Viagra to help him ensure his erections? What are other possible choice points you see looming in this therapy?

What do you notice at this point?_____

What would you do at this point?_____

K: I framed Steve's ED to him as an inability to hold onto pleasure, and normalized it as a form of pleasure anxiety, which is true of many men in this achievement-oriented culture. I affirmed to Steve that he could use medication, but that medication wouldn't address the relationship between himself and his fiancée. I said the overall treatment plan was to offer him awareness exercises: physical homework for helping him hold his erections longer, and in-the-office exercises to help him regulate his anxiety. We began with his sex history, focusing on his anxiety issues, to help him determine the factors that contribute to his inability to hold onto pleasure. He related a history of chronic childhood sexual abuse by multiple males in his neighborhood—and the shame that he still carried about that. He also related a history of substance abuse in his late teens and early twenties—mostly pot and alcohol, and watching gay male porn when he was drunk. He said he'd been clean and sober for seven years, and that he was clear he was straight, not gay.

> **G:** Steve has revealed a background of sexual abuse, substance abuse, porn use, and possible interest in gay sex. How much would you delve into this background? Would you find ways to relate it to his present dysfunction with his fiancée? Would you ignore his early experiences and focus on the sexual disappointments he experiences now with his fiancée?

What do you notice at this point?_____

What would you do at this point?_____

K: At the end of our first session, I explained the physiology of blood flow as "wizard brain/lizard brain" (prefrontal cortex/limbic system) and how anxiety triggers the limbic fight-or-flight response and draws blood away from the extremities, including the penis. I also gave Steve a diagram of the Wheel to show him that sexual response is more than just blood flow, and that his sexual response was more than just physical—it was also emotional, mental, and even spiritual, affected by his abusive past as well as his love for his fiancée and anxiety about pleasing her.

For homework, I gave him a hypnosis CD on calming anxiety (created by my colleagues Neil Cannon and Elaina McMillan), and asked him to listen to it each night until our next session. I also asked him to masturbate a few times a week to ejaculation, by using the Stop-Start technique: He was to start masturbating until he felt he was about to ejaculate, then stop and hold the sensation until his erection decreased, then start masturbating again. When he allowed himself to ejaculate, I asked him to imagine himself having intercourse and holding the pleasure. This exercise was to help him develop comfort with his flaccid penis and gain ability to back off and get erect again by himself, before having to muster the courage to do it with his partner.

> G: Kamara has done a lot of the work in this therapy so far, including assigning specific homework and providing a hypnosis CD. I wonder what her 4-D approach is, and how she's going to engage Steve in the process of his therapy.

What do you notice at this point?_____

What would you do at this point?_____

K: Right away, I could see that Steve was an active kind of guy, so by session two it felt important to give him something to do in addition to just talking about his issues. We used mindfulness breathing and meditation with two aims: to lower his anxiety and to increase his self-esteem. We worked on his being able to manifest his desires, and I assigned him some reading in the *Law of Attraction* by Michael Losier. Also, he happened to be going to yoga on base and that really helped to dovetail the connections that I was making for him. I always look for crossover strengths that the client already has to leverage my teachings.

Basically, I felt that Steve needed to move beyond thinking of himself as a wimp, so I suggested he think about someone with a lot of mojo that he would like to emulate. He chose Steve McQueen. So we now had some common language. We could move between Steve-*Wimp* and Steve-*King-of-Cool*.

> G: Kamara recognizes that Steve has a huge motivation to change, but little practice in self-revelation. She also recognizes his needs to be active in his therapy sessions. His choice of Steve McQueen is almost as if he's chosen an action figure avatar. He could become that action figure! Note that Kamara starts with asking Steve to identify with a positive power image before he further explores his anxieties and weaknesses (as in the Re-Membering activities in Chapter 5).

What do you notice at this point?_____

What would you do at this point?_____

STEVE: SESSION FIVE: WORKING WITH OBJECTS

K: We were ready for the Wheel. At the end of the fourth session, in addition to his usual homework assignment—the hypnosis CD and masturbation—I'd asked Steve to choose two objects and bring them to our next session: one object was to represent confidence—something in his sexual life to move toward; and the other to represent fear and/or something from his sexual past to move beyond.

Steve showed up to the session with four objects!

- Tight underpants—to represent the feeling of fear and restriction of his self, body, and spirit
- *Victims No Longer*—a book to represent his abuse history and how he wants to move beyond feeling defined by his abuse
- A bar of soap—to clear himself of all his automatic negative thoughts, and the shame from his abuse
- The hypnosis CD I had given him to help him stay calm and positive about maintaining his erections

As he placed his objects in the Wheel, he giggled at how silly and self-conscious he felt choosing these objects. I did not reassure him. Instead, I asked him what the giggling was about. He said, "I don't know." So I asked, "Where is 'I don't know'? Where in the Wheel would you locate it?"

> **G:** That Steve brought four objects is a powerful "Yes!" response—testimony to his enthusiasm for this therapy and his respect for Kamara. Yet his self-conscious reaction is testimony to how much work he still needs to do in order to follow through with his enthusiasms. The giggling is spontaneous and useful information—his body expressing a disconnection that's out of his control, similar in that way to what happens when he loses his erection during intercourse.
>
> Steve's giggling is also typical of clients for whom working with objects pushes them beyond their comfort zones. A big point is that Kamara does not bite the hook by trying to lessen his anxiety. Inviting him to locate and explore his "I don't know" shows respect for him. It recognizes his courage and willingness to explore the unknown—the lacuna in his emotional story that may hold the key to helping him lower his own anxiety levels, in the bedroom and beyond.
>
> The notion of the emotional lacuna in Steve's past reminds me of Fritz Perls's thumbnail definition of anxiety as "the gap between the Now and the Then."

What do you notice at this point?_____

What would you do at this point?_____

K: Steve stepped into the Wheel putting one foot into the middle and teetered there, fidgeting with his fingers and looking down. I noted to him that he was so unbalanced that it would be easy to push him over if I tried. He said that this is the place of "I don't know." His weak place—where he feels unworthy of his beautiful fiancée. While teetering there, he said he was like his tight underwear and the victims' book.

> **G:** Here, Kamara reflects back to Steve how she observes powerlessness reflected in his body language, and she does so in a non-judgmental way that he can hear. Beyond that, she is simply tracking and following Steve (as in the technique used in Zahira's story in Chapter 3). In effect, Kamara is trusting the Wheel process rather than trying to make something happen. As a result, Steve begins to make his own connections without Kamara pointing them out or offering interpretations. In a lightbulb moment, he links "I don't know" with his powerless body, and both of these with his tight underwear and the abuse book—the objects he wants to get rid of.

What do you notice at this point?_____

What would you do at this point?_____

K: I asked him how much longer in his life he wanted to be in this position. He said, 'Never again!'

> **G:** Bingo! This is the kind of exchange that makes all those hours of therapy worthwhile! Steve has made a giant step toward awareness. Now the issue is to help him gain even more awareness and connect it with maintaining his erections during penetration.

What do you notice at this point?_____

What would you do at this point?_____

K: So I asked him to "be" his powerful objects (the hypnosis CD and the soap)—to pick them up and walk into each quadrant, beginning wherever he wanted. He began by moving back and forth between Spirit and Mind. In the spiritual quadrant he found his centered and calm/strong self—where his body was aligned and his voice was strong. He spoke of his faith in a merciful God. Then he moved to Mind, where he was able to tell himself to connect with God and pray for confidence (here he was straddling Mind and Spirit). Then he took a deep breath, stabilized both feet, and stepped into Body. Here, too, he appeared solid and aligned. Finally, he stepped into Emotion where he put his objects down on the floor and placed both hands on his heart, and said he was opening his heart first to himself, then to his fiancée.

> **G:** Steve's actively walking the Wheel is clearly a powerful move in terms of the therapy. It's also powerful as a metaphor for his ability to hold onto pleasure and maintain his erections. I wonder if he has fully incorporated this power for himself, or if he's just saying the words he thinks the therapist wants to hear? Hopefully more Wheel work will help him fully integrate the positive messages.

What do you notice at this point?_____

What would you do at this point?_____

K: We ended the session with my suggesting that we continue with the Wheel next time—with any objects he would like to bring in. His assignment was to continue listening to the hypnosis CD followed by his Stop–Start masturbation practice. Additionally, I asked him to take his four objects home with him and put them mindfully in his apartment where he could see them, and where they could continue to act as his teachers.

> **G:** Kamara's assignments are specific, yet they also give Steve power and leeway in carrying them through ... a good preamble to ending the therapy, which must occur in a couple of weeks, per Steve's reassignment orders.

What do you notice at this point?_____

What would you do at this point?_____

STEVE, SESSION SIX: WORKING WITH OBJECTS, PART II

K: This time, Steve brought in only two objects. The first was a Steve McQueen DVD—the ultimate cool guy, who also had a troubled background as a kid. This object was to represent the ultimate confidence Steve (client) had in his own manhood. The other object represented what Steve wanted to move past. It was a Viagra prescription, with a story that he said represented his "lowest point of humiliation and shame." In a fit of anxiety before one weekend of being with his fiancée, he'd been too embarrassed to go to the doctor on the base. So he'd gone to his mother, to ask her to ask her present husband, who is a doctor, to get him this prescription.

> **G:** Interesting objects. Let's see which one proves to have the most mojo for Steve.

What do you notice at this point?_____

What would you do at this point?_____

K: I had Steve "be" the physical representation of his Viagra scrip as we walked each quadrant. What was particularly interesting to see was this 6 foot 2 man in full fatigues with combat boots crouching in a ball away from me on his tippy toes in the corner of my office to describe how he felt physically, emotionally, and spiritually. By the time he got to Mental, he said he was done feeling like this. He no longer wanted to feel small and ashamed and could no longer bring himself to be the Viagra scrip.

At this point he was happy to be the Steve McQueen DVD. All his shame and silliness had gone—and he was fully inhabiting his own presence. To be Steve McQueen, he marched out of the Wheel, and sat in *my* chair, which he saw as the power seat in the room. His left foot was firmly planted on the floor and his right ankle rested cockily on his left knee. His arms draped on the arms of the chair. He looked calm, confident, and completely in control. He looked me square in the eyes and said, "In this position the ladies come to me. And I can sit back and relax."

> **G:** What we see Steve enacting here is kind of a reprise of the previous session with his four objects. But now he has much more purpose and confidence. His body language fits his intentions. His final assumption of the Power Seat is a preview of his hoped-for "potency" during intercourse. It is important that he be able to "Re-Member" that sense of potency so that he can be in that place during intercourse—heart, mind, and spirit, as well as penis. Note that very little of this therapy is directly focused on his penis, and yet it's all about maintaining his erection.

What do you notice at this point?_____

What would you do at this point?_____

In your estimation, what does the use of concrete objects add to this therapy with Steve?

_____

STEVE, FINAL SESSION

K: Because this therapy was time-limited, we both knew it would end with this session. It felt important to say a definitive goodbye, yet also to leave the door open in case he wanted to return. In the event that Steve experiences future difficulties with sexual self-esteem or with his erections during intercourse, we discussed how he could continue to use the hypnosis CD and other practices to help him remember all that we worked on so successfully during his therapy. I wished him well, and a life filled with adventures.

> **G:** Kamara has demonstrated an effective short-term use of the Wheel as she incorporates it into her own approach for men with erectile difficulties. Her suggestions about follow-up work are invitational, without a tone of warning. She sends him off with confidence, practical tools, and an open door if he wants to return. We should all have such benevolent therapists, educators, and coaches.

What do you notice at this point?_____

What would you do at this point?_____

How would you close this session?_____

RESULTS

K: One month after Steve was relocated, he e-mailed me from his new station and said that not only has he had no ED but that he could control when, where, and how he ejaculated. To top that, he said his life-long social anxiety had also been cured! He had been able to go to parties and talk to everyone there and had even led some party games. He was very grateful and said he no longer had to use Viagra or pretend to be Steve McQueen.

G: This happy ending for Steve points to an important direction in treating some kinds of ED for some men: that is, to see the ED in a larger frame and give it context—not only by using all the dimensions of the Wheel, but also by framing ED in terms of time—and the ability to recover lost memories and make them conscious so they don't sabotage sex. For some men, it's crucial for them to move beyond pharmaceutical approaches to erection difficulties and be able to update all they bring into sexual relationship.

Noted sex therapist Bernie Zilbergeld used Gestalt techniques, which parallel some of the Wheel work Kamara used with Steve. Zilbergeld's work predates March 1998 and the birth of Viagra. In *The New Male Sex Therapy* he asks questions that get clients to think outside of the goal-oriented sex model and examine their deeper intentions: "When do you decide to stop having sex?" or "What would your penis say if it could talk?"

With Steve, Kamara uses her own version of Gestalt technique, and combines it with embodiment on the Wheel. Many practitioners intensify their Wheel sessions by asking clients to speak as their objects. In Chapter 10, Chelsea Wakefield offers a variation on this technique by asking her client Deborah to speak from each quadrant as her archetype.

How do you think the outcome might have been different for Steve if Kamara had used only sex-therapy techniques without the Wheel?_____

_____

How do you think using the Wheel enhanced sex therapy for Steve?_____

_____

Are there any ways you see that the Wheel and sex therapy limited each other?_____

_____

How do you think using objects enhanced sex therapy for Steve?_____

_____

Are there any ways you see that using objects limited the effectiveness of sex therapy for Steve?

_____

How do you think using movement enhanced sex therapy for Steve?_____

_____

Are there any ways you see that movement limited the effectiveness of sex therapy for Steve?__

_____

How do you think using the Re-Membering activity enhanced sex therapy for Steve?_____

_____

Are there any ways you see that using the Re-Membering activity limited sex therapy for Steve?

_____

What kernels of Kamara's wisdom or skill can you incorporate into your practice?_____

_____

STEVE'S 4-D WHEEL SESSION AT A GLANCE . . .

On the following pages, you'll find a two-page form: "Inviting Clients Into the 4-D Wheel." On it are jotted details of the sessions with Steve on the Wheel, so that you can see them at a glance as well as reading through the linear narrative. Recording these details in this way also demonstrates how you might record your own 4-D-Wheel sessions with your clients—as outlined in Chapter 13.

INVITING CLIENTS INTO THE 4-D WHEEL

Name of Client: Steve   **Date:** xxx
CASE NARRATIVE: Describe client's issues that led you to suggest exploring the Wheel

Army guy with erectile problems (won't take Viagra). Bkgrnd of abuse
also substance abuse (now sober). Therapy has to work fast as he's being
transferred in 2 mos. No couples therapy possible as fiancée lives out of
town.
Major issues: Anxiety and low self-esteem, plus lack of sex ed.
Hopefully the Wheel plus objects can provide an efficient way to get him
started and give him take-home tools.

ISSUES FOR THERAPIST: Describe what occurred for you during work with client, including any countertransference

My own performance anxiety due to time constraints—will I be able to help
him substantially?

4-D WHEEL DYNAMICS USED: Describe what you did (and how) during session(s) on the Wheel

Created safe space: Normalized his ED, gave him an overall plan, used combo of
mindfulness and sex ed to address his anxiety issues
Invited movement: Session 2, began Re-Membering (Steve McQueen = his
model). Sessions 5–7 Powerful Re-Membering ex. and walked Wheel w/
objects
Introduced ritual: Practiced Re-Membering; find objects; move objects into each
dimension

Suggested concretizing abstract concepts with tangible objects:
4 objects (Pos =Soap/hypnosis CD; Neg = tight undies/abuse bk)
Then 2 objects (Pos = Steve McQueen DVD; Neg = Viagra scrip)
Other: Work w/ objects = primary for Steve: engaged him, and gave him
take-home tools.

Name of Client: Steve   **Date:** xxx

PROGRESS OF THE SESSION(S): List client's movement from quadrant to quadrant, from beginning to end of your session(s) with the Wheel, also where objects were placed, if they were used. Add another sheet if necessary.

SESSION #5 (4 objects)

1. CENTER Teetered / a "pushover"
2. SPIRIT: w/ soap & book: strong/aligned
3. MIND: Pray for confidence
4. MIND-SPIRIT: Straddle
5. BODY Solid
6. HEART: Hands on heart for self &fiancée
7. Releases objects

SESSION #6 (2 objects)

1. BODY: crouch as Viagra scrip
2. HEART: crouch as Viagra scrip
3. SPIRIT: crouch as Viagra scrip
4. MIND: "done w/ that"
5. IN MY CHAIR . . .
    Embodies Steve McQueen—
    . . . . "The ladies come to me!"

MOVEMENT OF CLIENT: List the major issues and transformations in each quadrant

Lack of confidence
→ Faith

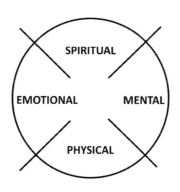

Fearful →
Open-hearted to
self and fiancée

Prayerful →
Confident/decisive

"Impotent"
→ "Cocky!"

REFERENCES AND SUGGESTED RESOURCES FOR ERECTILE DYSFUNCTION, SEX THERAPY, AND MORE

Annon, J.S. (1976, April 1). The PLISSIT model: A proposed conceptual scheme for the behavioral treatment of sexual problems. *Journal of Sex Education and Therapy*, 2(1): 1–15.

Cannon, N., and McMillan, E. (2013, April 30). Erectile difficulties. http://audiocounseling.com/.

Chopra, D. (2015). *Quantum healing: Exploring the frontiers of mind/body medicine* (rev. ed.). New York: Bantam.

Hartman, W., and Fithian M. (1972). *Treatment of sexual dysfunction: A bio-psycho-social approach*. Long Beach, CA: The Center for Marital and Sexual Studies.

Joannides, P. (2015). *The guide to getting it on* (8th ed.). Waldport, OR: Goofyfoot Press.

Kaplan, H.S. (1988). *The illustrated manual of sex therapy* (2nd ed.). New York: Routledge.

Kerner, I. (2010.) *She comes first: The thinking man's guide to pleasuring a woman*. New York: William Morrow.

Lew, M. (2004). *Victims no longer: The classic guide for men recovering from sexual child abuse*. New York: Harper Perennial.

Loe, Meika (2004). *The rise of Viagra: How the little blue pill changed sex in America*. New York: New York University Press.

Losier, M. (2010). *The law of attraction: The science of attracting more of what you want and less of what you   don't*. New York: Grand Central Life & Style (Hachette Group).

Masters, W. and Johnson, V. (1970). *Human sexual inadequacy*. Boston: Little, Brown and Company.

McCarthy, B.W., and Metz, M.E. (2004). Coping with erectile dysfunction: How to regain confidence and enjoy great sex. Oakland, CA: New Harbinger.

Perls, F.S. (1969). *Gestalt therapy verbatim* (J.O. Stevens, Ed.). Lafayette, CA: Real People Press.

Savage, D. (1998). *Savage love: Straight answers from America's most popular sex columnist*. New York: Plume.

Zilbergeld, B. (1999). *The new male sexuality: The truth about men, sex, and pleasure* (rev. ed.). New York: Bantam, Doubleday, Dell.

10

Deborah and Danny

Confronting the Voices of Vaginismus

"Rise up, my love, my beautiful one, and come away.
For, behold, the winter is past. The rain is over and gone.
The flowers appear on the earth. The time of the singing has come,
and the voice of the turtledove is heard in our land."
—*Song of Solomon 2:10–12*

CHELSEA WAKEFIELD

Chelsea Wakefield, PhD, LCSW, is a certified sex therapist, Jungian-oriented psychotherapist, dream worker, retreat leader, and author of *Negotiating the Inner Peace Treaty* and *In Search of Aphrodite: Women, Archetypes, and Sex Therapy*. She draws from a depth of training in clinical and transpersonal methods to help people move beyond wounds of the past to access their archetypal potential and live more vibrant and meaningful lives. www.ChelseaWakefield.com.

USING THE WHEEL WITH ARCHETYPES

As a Jungian therapist, I pay close attention to my nighttime dreams. It was in response to a series of dreams that I became a sex therapist, and along that path I was fortunate enough to meet Gina Ogden. I was deeply moved by the first "ISIS-Wheel" weekend I attended, watching Gina work on the Wheel, with symbolic objects, stories, shifting states, mystery, fire, discovery, and a circle of women in support of each other's journeys. During that weekend, I saw how I could integrate Wheel work with the work I was already doing, exploring women's sexuality from an archetypal perspective, helping them open their sexual imaginations and explore the wondrous realm of Aphrodite.

I came home from that weekend and immediately incorporated the Wheel as the center of my "Luminous Woman" weekends. Over the quadrants of the Wheel, I overlaid four key archetypes of the feminine, so that as women moved around that Wheel, they could explore the felt sense of these archetypes and experience the shifts in their bodies as they moved from Mother (Heart), to Lover (Body), to Warrior (Mind), and Mystic (Spirit). I found the process of movement around the quadrants a profound way for women to explore a capacity that I call "shifting states."

Since 2010, I have found the Wheel to be one of the most helpful, adaptable, world-opening tools in my clinical kit. I use it in the therapy room to open insight and get people unstuck. I use it in workshops and in settings where co-workers are struggling to cooperate or understand one another. The two objects can carry any creative question you can come up with. For example, in a workshop I did with group of teachers, I had them bring objects to represent what inspired them about their work, and what they found most disheartening. As each teacher placed her or his objects onto the Wheel, they suddenly saw their shared humanity and how the things that disheartened them were similar. This opened up a conversation about how they had withdrawn from each other, believing they were alone in their struggles. Now the conversation shifted to how they could collaborate to solve their shared problems. When the conversation got stuck, people went to stand in the quadrant where they were stuck and then began to move around the Wheel. As they moved, they could witness their tangles unwind as new possibilities opened up in their hearts, minds, spirits, and bodies. They left having experienced a new way of solving problems and celebrating together.

In 2015, I flew to China to present a sexuality workshop to a group of clergy and spiritual directors. Moving around the Wheel, women revealed histories of childhood sexual abuse and experienced a spontaneous release from an identity as *Damaged Goods*. Men released life-long shame they felt for their longings and fantasies. All discovered a tool they could use in their pastoral counseling to help others move beyond the constraints of sex-negative religious teachings. The 4-D Wheel raises these unconscious debilitating scripts to awareness and opens up the possibility for people to rewrite them. It invites the freedom to explore a sexuality where the body is a sacred vessel, the heart can open, and a journey of self-discovery and mutual self-revelation can take place between partners.

USING THE WHEEL TO ADDRESS VAGINISMUS AND PAIN

A CASE NARRATIVE WITH ACCOMPANYING CASE SUPERVISION AND INTERACTIVE COMMENTS

Chapter 10 demonstrates how a physical dysfunction can be effectively treated through non-physical approaches and offers a 4-D Wheel application for clients who can benefit from using imagination and deeply engaged role playing. Here, a Jungian sex therapist incorporates her work with archetypes into the Wheel to help Deborah and Danny, who present with profound lack of information about sexuality and inability to perform intercourse, all of which has blossomed into pain and vaginismus for Deborah. Note how movement around the Wheel helps this couple clarify messages about sex, communicate their passionate feelings for each other, and begin to release physical tension.

Chelsea's case narrative is accompanied by my running commentary in shaded boxes, and by spaces that invite your observations. At the end of the chapter the case is revisited, so that you can see it described via the Wheel. Note that the purpose of this chapter is not to prescribe a cure for vaginismus or a method of assigning Jungian archetypes, but to illustrate how a practitioner uses the Wheel in her own creative way to expand sex-history taking and help the couple communicate with one another.

DEBORAH AND DANNY: SESSIONS ONE AND TWO—THE PRESENTING ISSUE

Chelsea's Case Narrative: Twenty-four-year-old Deborah was referred to me by a local gynecologist—the diagnosis: vaginismus and dyspareunia. In our first session, she revealed that the sexual difficulties during the four years of her marriage were particularly problematic because she wanted to become pregnant. She didn't know how that could happen if she kept avoiding sexual intercourse because of the pain. She said the doctor told her she could be helped by sex therapy. I affirmed her concern and echoed her gynecologist's assertion that sex therapy could most probably help her. I suggested that her husband Danny accompany her to our next session as we continued our detective work. In my cosmology, therapists carry an archetypal position as well as clients, and in this case, I am acting as *Collaborating Detective*, working with Deborah to discover clues to her difficulties.

> **Gina's Supervisory Comments:** Among the many questions I have about Deborah's sexual background: Why has it taken this couple four years to seek help for a condition that must be painful to Danny as well as Deborah—is it shame? What is their level of sexual desire? Is having a baby the only compelling reason for them to want sex? Hopefully, much more will be revealed when the couple comes in together. What strikes me about this initial encounter is the notion of placebo effect (see Chapter 2). Deborah's pain is physical and persistent, yet both gynecologist and sex therapist have spoken positively of sex therapy. In other words, they have implanted a suggestion of hope. Placebo studies show that positive suggestions from clinicians can increase possibilities of healing by counteracting negative messages lodged in both thought patterns and body memories. Perhaps for Deborah, healing has already begun.

[Your comments:]
What do you notice at this point? _____

What would you do at this point? _____

If you were Deborah's therapist or counselor, what countertransference issues do you imagine might arise with this case? _____

C: In meeting with the couple for the first time, it was clear that they loved each other deeply and that both were motivated to solve their sexual problems beyond the desire to become pregnant. I also understood that they both came from profoundly conservative religious backgrounds, which had circumscribed their early sex education. In cases such as this, I need to stay aware of my own countertransference issues related to my personal outrage at how much sexual suffering religion has caused. I do this by staying focused on solutions.

> G: Chelsea raises a central point here—about being aware exactly and intelligently where we are hooked by our clients' issues. The issue of religion is one that hooks many sex therapists, because of the pleasure-negative stances of many religions. It bears repeating that whatever hooks us, it's crucial to keep our focus on our clients, and not our personal outrage, fear, or whatever. While it can be useful to take our prejudices seriously, it's not useful to project them onto our clients.

What do you notice at this point? _____

What would you do at this point? _____

C: In delving more deeply into their sexual routines, I gathered that the most information or education Deborah and Danny had received about sexuality had been in the form of stern warnings against pre-marital sex. Their first attempt at sexual intercourse together was shy and inexperienced. Danny was unable to penetrate Deborah, and ended up ejaculating on her stomach. This had been painful and bewildering for Deborah, and confusing and alarming for Danny. Both had been dismayed by the chasm between this experience and their romantic expectations—and had never discussed these feelings with each other. As we continued to talk, they admitted shamefully that penetration seemed impossible and that they had given up on intercourse after repeated failures. In their thinking, this meant they'd given up on sex altogether, because to them "sex" meant "intercourse."

> G: Several classic themes lift Deborah and Danny's case beyond the strictly physical realm of sexual dysfunction. All of these themes clamor for prime importance and are ripe for expressing through the venue of archetypes.
> 1) The 4-D power of negative messages that inhabit Deborah's brain, heart, spirit, and even her genital mucosa, literally closing her vagina to block penile entry, and to replace any possibility of sexual pleasure with pain.
> 2) Religious proscription—which shapes Deborah and Danny's belief systems about sex: What is (and is not) permissible? Who (or what) is the ultimate authority?
> 3) The fantasy model of sex, and the Men-Are-Out-for-One-Thing myth, both so prevalent in the larger culture. Both of these help shape this couple's beliefs.
> 4) The storied role of women gaining power through withholding intercourse—as famously depicted in Aristophanes' comedy *Lysistrata*: the women refuse sexual favors until the men end the Peloponnesian War. Withholding can be a dangerous route to power, but in some cultures even today, this is the only one open to women.

What do you notice at this point? _____

What would you do at this point? _____

C: I surmised that many of Deborah's problems had developed out of bracing for Danny's attempts at penetration. She saw "being available" as her duty as Danny's wife, but the pain was overwhelming. To help this couple conceptualize their problem in a way that was both understandable and non-shaming, I suggested we might view their story through an archetypal lens, which would allow them to clarify the various parts they were unconsciously playing out. I explained that the archetype of the *Dutiful Wife* is a deadly identity when it comes to women's sexual pleasure. In Deborah's case, performing her "wifely duty" over and over with an expectation of pain had led her into full-blown vaginismus—involuntary and painful spasms of her pelvic-floor muscles and vaginal walls. Her body had taken on the role of *Gatekeeper*—so effectively that Danny could not enter her. I assured them both that we would work together to find other archetypes for her to embody.

> **G:** Chelsea is helping this couple see the large picture, beyond "What's wrong with us?" At the same time, I wonder if she's going to refer Deborah to a pelvic-floor therapist to help her deal directly with her vaginal spasms and pain. Also at the same time, I'm aware that Helen Singer Kaplan's classic treatment for vaginismus is hypnosis—she cites a remarkable cure rate. So perhaps therapeutic suggestion and Deborah's imagination will be enough.

What do you notice at this point? _____

What would you do at this point? _____

C: Once I was sure I had their attention, I began to educate Deborah and Danny about the physiology of sexual response, beginning with the Masters-and-Johnson sexual response cycle, and following with basic information about lubrication and the importance of self-pleasuring—for both of them. This was the first information of this kind that they had ever received. Aware of their strict religious backgrounds, I watched carefully to see how they responded to a conversation about pleasure. I noticed that they looked relieved and fascinated.

> **G:** Chelsea is still using non-physical routes to restoring physical coherence. She preempts all of my speculation and goes back to basics—listening, accepting the clients, not pushing her agenda. To engage their curiosity she offers some specific suggestions, which are the "SS" of the P-LI-SS-IT model for sex therapy introduced by Jack Annon in 1976: (P = Permission, LI = Limited Information, SS = Specific Suggestions, IT = Intensive Therapy).

What do you notice at this point? _____

What would you do at this point? _____

SESSION THREE: USING THE WHEEL TO OBTAIN A DYNAMIC SEX HISTORY

C: Taking a sex history is considered a foundational aspect of sex therapy. While many sex therapists utilize some adapted version of the formats introduced by Masters and Johnson, I have found that utilizing the Wheel can yield a much more profound revelation of the underlying factors that impact sexual functioning. This proves to be true in our next session.

> G: Chelsea adds archetypes to the variations on using the Wheel to deepen the 4-D process of taking a sex history, which are outlined in Chapter 1.

What do you notice at this point? _____
What would you do at this point? _____

C: In session three, I laid out a simple Wheel on the floor of my office (I use four printed cards with the words Heart, Mind, Body, and Spirit). I invited Deborah to step into the Wheel and invited Danny to observe, standing beside me. I assured him that his time to share on the Wheel would come.

We began to unpack her experience. In the quadrant of spirit, Deborah began to recite a number of fear-centered, pleasure-negative, body-negative scripts she had learned at church, such as "no sex before marriage" and "men only want one thing." I moved her into the quadrant of the mind and this movement helped her to separate out these religiously inspired scripts from her actual experience of herself as a spiritual being. I could see her strongly developed archetypal identity as a *Good Girl*, and I spent some time engaging with what I call this inner character. When we moved to the body quadrant of the Wheel, she tearfully expressed her experiences of pain. In the quadrant of the heart she related her experiences of love, and longing, and heartbreak.

> G: In using the Wheel as a medium through which to gather information, Chelsea is exploring archetypes as a unique approach for vaginismus. She broadens the concept beyond a lonely, isolating, shameful pain to one that joins Deborah with an infinite sisterhood of women with pelvic pain and scant sex education. Let's see if this approach has as successful an outcome as Kaplan's use of hypnosis. Two major advantages of using the Wheel and archetypes over hypnosis include 1) that Deborah is fully awake and aware during sessions, and 2) that Danny can be involved in witnessing Deborah's inner experience, something she has never expressed to him before. He also has opportunities to participate in the sessions.

What do you notice at this point? _____
What would you do at this point? _____

C: As Deborah entered the quadrant of the spirit for the second time, she quieted down and looked up. With determination she stated, "I believe that God wants me to be a Good Girl—but I am a woman now, and I believe that God would want me to have a good relationship and experience joy." Her voice faltered as she asked, "I wonder if that includes pleasure?" As we moved into the quadrant of the mind, she began to redefine what she wanted to believe about herself as a sexual being—"If I want to be a mother, that means sex has to be OK, right?" As she moved into the quadrant of the body, I watched her tilt her head seductively, smile at her husband, unlock her pelvis, wiggle her hips and then shyly giggle. It was only a moment, but I was aware that I was watching her begin to birth her connection to Aphrodite and a playful, celebrated *Sensual Self*.

> G: Here we see the power of getting clients out of their chairs. Movement is at work—Deborah is stepping into the Wheel, stepping into her body, accessing her body intelligence—and showing it to Chelsea and Danny as well as herself.

What do you notice at this point? _____

What would you do at this point? _____

C: Almost immediately, Deborah's smile froze and her hips went back into lock-up. When I asked what was happening, she said "I feel frightened." When we explored her fear in the emotional quadrant, she said she was hearing the voice of the *Fire-and-Brimstone Preacher* of her youth, scolding and admonishing her. I call these introjected figures from the past *Voices of Warning*. They block a woman's path to pleasure. I reassured her that once we'd identified these voices echoing from the past, and fully "outed" them, she would be able to find her own voice, and dialogue convincingly with them.

> G: A palpable power of using archetypes includes the ability to name them, embody them, give them voice, and locate them via the dimensions of the Wheel. All of this offers Deborah the opportunity to feel and express distinctive and shifting states in her body, mind, heart, and spirit—past present, and future. In terms of her "freezing," I often observe to clients that after an expansion there can be a concomitant closing down as old defense systems attempt to maintain old habits and prevent change. The automatic sliding back into the comfort of the familiar, even the painful familiar, can be insidious.

What do you notice at this point? _____

What would you do at this point? _____

C: I asked Deborah to move back into the mind quadrant and speak with the voice of this *Inner Preacher*—to let him have his say. In articulating his voice so clearly, she was able to identify his words as part of her sexual script that she wanted to rewrite. When she then stepped into the heart quadrant, she found courage to talk back to this voice. She spoke her feelings of passionate love for Danny and even quoted some scriptural justification for sexual joy in their marriage. As she stepped again into the quadrant of the spirit, she remembered a sensual passage from the *Song of Solomon*, and began to cry softly as she recited the verse about the voice of the turtledove. With the biblical passage, Deborah invoked the call of that turtledove to her own heart and body with an attentiveness that made it a true *Invitation to Pleasure*.

Here, I felt Deborah could benefit from some spiritual and religious affirmation as well as sex education. I mentioned that views of sexual pleasure varied in different conservative traditions. For instance, in the Jewish traditions of the Sabbath, there is to be no labor, but making love is one of the activities that is blessed by God, and a woman's sexual pleasure is considered of primary importance. At this point, still in the spiritual quadrant, Deborah turned to the *Fire and Brimstone Preacher*, and with an *Aphrodite* hand on her once-again mobile hip, she dismissed him, stating, "You are clearly clueless and no longer an authority in my life!"

> **G:** A new spin on sex-history taking! Chelsea is asking Deborah to literally write a new script for her sexual self by stepping into her archetypes and speaking their stories out loud. I wonder what's happening with Danny? Will he be able to name his own *Voices of Warning*? Is he also opening to expanded sex education and the lyrical passion of the *Song of Solomon*?

What do you notice at this point? _____

What would you do at this point? _____

Danny had been observing all of this, and as Deborah sat down the couple beamed at each other. I asked them to talk about sexual messages that each of them had brought into their marriage—and to continue the conversation at home, along with anything they felt like saying to their *Voices of Warning*.

SESSION FOUR: DANNY ON THE WHEEL

C: In the next session, it was Danny's turn to explore each quadrant of the Wheel, and we engaged his *Voices of Warning*, the ones that shamed him regarding his "carnal" desires—his passion for Deborah's body, his fantasies about making love to every part of her. I invited them both into the Wheel to speak to each other. In the heart quadrant, especially, they both expressed their deep love, and their longing for a wonderful sex life. After only these initial sessions, they stated that they now understood certain triggers that shut them down and kept them from talking to each other. They could picture and describe these *Voices of Warning* as dark archetypal figures that had glowered and towered over their marital bed. Most importantly, they could invoke new voices to replace them. Empowered by this awareness, they were both rewriting their sexual scripts.

> **G:** To add to their sexual and spiritual remodeling, I might have suggested that Danny and Deborah create a specific ceremony to exorcise these *Voices of Warning* from their bedroom—as outlined in the section on the therapeutic role of ceremony in Chapter 2. This way, they would have a contingency plan to support their right to sexual pleasure at times when those voices attempt to reassert authority.

What do you notice at this point? _____

What would you do at this point? _____

How would you close this session? _____

SESSION FIVE AND BEYOND

C: In the next session I began to outline a process of body awareness and gentle re-engagement, including opportunities for communication and feedback. I engaged them in a modified version of sensate focus—asking them to invoke their pleasure-loving archetypes as they approached each other's bodies. We discussed lubrications that would make penetrative sex more comfortable for Deborah and more fun for them both. I sent them to vaginismus.com for resources and suggested they read Gina Ogden's *Return of Desire* and my book *In Search of Aphrodite*. Beyond that, I encouraged them to educate themselves by reading whatever books or articles appealed to them—and (most importantly) to underline passages they could discuss with each other. In terms of progressive exercises for penetration, I used an anatomical model to show Danny how to stimulate Deborah's vulva, then how to enter her vagina with one finger, then two, while Deborah tuned into her body and exercised her Aphrodite voice, giving progressive feedback (together, they discovered her G-spot). All of this was prior to his attempting to enter her again with his erect penis.

I continued to see Deborah and Danny more or less weekly for seven months—to answer their questions, help them tune into their own bodies, attune to each other, and reveal to each other what felt good in each moment. They continued to use the organizing principle of the Wheel as they explored and revealed themselves to each other. Patience became play. Deborah's physical rigidity and pain melted away along with her *Voices of Warning*, Danny transformed from *Clueless Clyde* into *Dashing Dan*, who now woos Deborah poetically, describing the wonders of her body rather than the shame of carnal lust. She took on the hopeful voice of the sensual Dove she discovered on the Wheel. As they became erotic partners, they continued to discover themselves and each other along with the joys of sexual love. When they felt challenged by their ongoing committed relationship with their church, we found spiritual language to help them justify their discovery of physical loving, which eventually led to experiences of union and ecstasy—and the birth of an adorable baby girl.

How do you think Deborah's and Danny's outcome might have been different if Chelsea had focused on vaginismus alone without using the Wheel? _____

_____

How do you think archetypes and the 4-D Wheel enhanced each other? _____

_____

Are there any ways you see that they limited each other? _____

_____

How do you think using movement enhanced sex therapy for Deborah and Danny? _____

_____

Are there any ways you see that movement limited the effectiveness of sex therapy for Deborah and Danny? _____

_____

What kernels of Chelsea's wisdom or skill can you incorporate into your practice? _____

_____

DEBORAH'S AND DANNY'S 4-D WHEEL SESSIONS AT A GLANCE

On the following pages, you'll find a two-page form: "Inviting Clients Into the 4-D Wheel." On it are jotted details of the session with Deborah and Danny on the Wheel so that you can see them at a glance as well as reading through the linear narrative. Recording these details in this way also demonstrates how you might record your own 4-D-Wheel sessions with your clients—as outlined in Chapter 13.

INVITING CLIENTS INTO THE 4-D WHEEL

Name of Client: Deborah (and Danny)   **Date:** xxx

CASE NARRATIVE: Describe client's issues that led you to suggest exploring the Wheel

Deborah—vaginismus and pain; avoids sex; old religious and societal proscriptions. They want a baby but can't perform intercourse.

Danny—ED triggered by Deb's pain plus religious and societal proscriptions

Using the Wheel to encourage D & D to see the large picture of sexual intimacy without directly confronting their church; also as a template for using archetypes.

ISSUES FOR THERAPIST: Describe what occurred for you during session(s), including any countertransference

Need to keep a close rein on my personal rage against a religious system that has caused so much pain for women, also men, for so many generations.

4-D WHEEL DYNAMICS USED: Describe what you did (and how) during session(s) on the Wheel

Created safe space: Introduced Wheel as a safe, nonjudgmental container for exploring their issues

Invited movement: Invited both (but mostly Deborah) to move to each dimension of the Wheel—stepping into archetypes

Introduced ritual: Asked her to address archetypes in each dimension: MIND (Fire and Brimstone Preacher) HEART (Good Girl) SPIRIT (Fire and Brimstone Preacher) BODY (Aphrodite—once she thaws)

Suggested concretizing abstract concepts with tangible objects: Used archetypes not objects; invited Deborah to step into all her Voices of Warning, and finally into her Aphrodite self

Other_____

Name of Client: Deborah (and Danny)   **Date:** xxx
PROGRESS OF THE SESSION(S): List client's movement from quadrant to quadrant, from beginning to end of your session(s) with the Wheel, also where objects were placed, if they were used. Add another sheet if necessary.

DEBORAH

1. SPIRIT: negative scripts
2. MIND: "What is a Good Girl?"
3. BODY: Pain/vaginismus
4. HEART: love/longing/heartbreak
5. SPIRIT: Quiet—"I am a woman!"
6. MIND: "Is pleasure really OK???"
7. BODY: Seductive wiggle, then lock-up
8. HEART: Fire & Brimstone Preacher
9. MIND: Talk back to Preacher

10. SPIRIT: Song of Solomon quote
11. SPIRIT: Preacher is "clueless!"

DANNY

1. SPIRIT: shame
2. BODY: "carnal desire" (hot for Deb)
3. MIND/HEART: love/sex fantasy

BOTH TOGETHER

1. HEART: love/longing/

MOVEMENT OF CLIENT: List the major issues and transformations in each quadrant

(Deborah)

Negative sexual scripts →
"You (Preacher) are clueless
and have no authority over my life!"

Heartbreak →
Love

Rigid judgments →
Curiosity and
discernment:
"Good = Pleasure"

Rigidity → Fluidity
Pain → Pleasure

REFERENCES AND SUGGESTED READING FOR SEX THERAPY FOR WOMEN, COUPLES COMMUNICATION, AND JUNGIAN THERAPY

Annon, J.S. (1976, April 1). The PLISSIT model: A proposed conceptual scheme for the behavioral treatment of sexual problems. *Journal of Sex Education and Therapy*, 2(1): 1–15.

Aristophanes (2009). *Lysistrata* (D. Parker Tr.). New York: Signet Classics.

Basson R. (2001). Female sexual response: The role of drugs in the management of sexual dysfunction. *Journal of Obstetrics and Gynecology*, 98: 350–353.

Beattie-Jung, P., Hunt, M.E., and Balakrishnan, R. (2001). *Good sex: Feminist perspectives from the world's religions*. New Brunswick, NJ: Rutgers University Press.

Bonheim, J. (1997). *Aphrodite's daughters: Women's sexual stories and the journey of the soul*. New York: Fireside.

Boston Women's Health Book Collective. (2011). *Our bodies, ourselves* (40th anniv. rev. ed.). New York: Touchstone.

Chalker, R. (2000). *The clitoral truth: The secret world at our fingertips*. New York: Seven Stories Press.

Ensler, E. (2000). *The vagina monologues: The V-day edition*. New York: Villard.

Erikson, M.A. (1980). *The nature of hypnosis and suggestion*. New York: Irvington Publishers.

Fisher, H.E. (2004). *Why we love: The nature and chemistry of romantic love*. New York: Holt.

Foley S., Kope, S., and Sugrue, D. (2012). *Sex matters for women: A complete guide to taking care of your sexual self* (rev. ed.). Binghamton, NY: Guilford Press.

Gottman, J.M. (2011). *The science of trust: Emotional attunement for couples*. New York: W.W. Norton.

Heiman, J., and LoPiccolo, J. (1987). *Becoming orgasmic: A sexual and personal growth program for women* (rev. ed.). New York: Fireside.

Johnson, S.M. (2008). *Hold me tight: Seven conversations for a lifetime of love*. Boston: Little, Brown.

Jung, C.G. (1959). *The archetypes and the collective unconscious* (R.F.C. Hall, Tr.). New York: Pantheon Books.

Jung, C.G. (1970). Civilization in transition. In *The collected works of Carl G. Jung* (Volume 10). New York: Bollingen.

Leavitt, J. (2012). *The sexual alarm system: Women's unwanted response to sexual intimacy and how to overcome it*. Northvale, NJ: Jason Aronson.

Kaplan, H.S. (1988). *The illustrated manual of sex therapy* (2nd ed.). New York: Routledge.

Masters, W., and Johnson, V. (1970). *Human sexual inadequacy*. Boston: Little, Brown and Company.

Northrup, Christiane (1995). *Women's bodies, women's wisdom: Creating physical and emotional health and healing*. New York: Bantam.

Ogden, G. (2007). *Women who love sex: Ordinary women describe their paths to pleasure, intimacy, and ecstasy* (3rd ed.). Boston, Trumpeter.

Ogden, G. (2008). *The return of desire: A guide to rediscovering your sexual passion*. Boston: Trumpeter.

Ogden, G. (2009). It's not just a headache dear: Why some women say no to connecting sex and spirit. In A. Mahoney and O. Espin (Eds.) *Sin or salvation: Implications for psychotherapy*. New York: Routledge, pp. 105–125.

Rosenbaum, T.Y. (2009). Physical therapy evaluation of dyspareunia. In A. Goldstein, C. Pukall, and I. Goldstein (Eds.) *Female sexual pain disorders: Evaluation and management*. Oxford: Wiley-Blackwell Publishing.

Solot, D., and Miller, M. (2007). *I love female orgasm: An extraordinary orgasm guide*. Boston: DaCapo Press

Stone, S.L., and Stone, H. (2012). *The Voice Dialogue anthology: Explorations of the psychology of selves and the aware ego process*. Albion, CA: Delos.

Wakefield, C. (2012). *Negotiating the inner peace treaty*. Carlsbad, CA: Balboa Press.

Wakefield, C. (2014, February). In search of Aphrodite: Working with archetypes and an inner cast of characters in women with low sexual desire. *Sexual and Relationship Therapy*, 29(1): 31–41.

Wakefield, C. (2015). *In search of Aphrodite: Women, archetypes and sex therapy*. New York: Routledge.

Winston, S. (2009). *Women's anatomy of arousal*. Kingston, NY: Mango Garden Press.

Young-Eisendrath, P. (1997). *The resilient spirit: Transforming suffering into insight and renewal*. Boston: Da Capo Press.

11

Ben

From Porn Addiction to Conversations with God

"How exactly does one become a butterfly?
You must want to fly so badly that you are
willing to give up being a caterpillar."
—*Trina Paulus*

KRISTIN HODSON

Kristin Hodson, MSW, LCSW, is founder and executive director of The Healing Group in Salt Lake City, Utah. She teaches human sexuality as an adjunct professor at the University of Utah in the Master of Social Work program, is a regular contributor to Salt Lake City radio and TV news, and is co-author of *Real Intimacy: A Couples Guide for Genuine, Healthy Sexuality*. Her mission is to contribute to the conversations happening in our culture around sex and intimacy to empower women and men to take charge of their own growth and healing. She is a mom to three active kids, partner to a wonderful man, and tries to live life passionately out loud. www.TheHealingGroup.com.

USING THE WHEEL WITH DIAGNOSED
AND SELF-DIAGNOSED PORN ADDICTION

As a therapist working with a religiously conservative population, I find a sadly common scenario: men of all ages are self-diagnosed as pornography addicts, and diagnosed by those they love and trust as well. Many clinicians label and treat these men as addicts and focus therapy on shaming them (not always intentionally), stopping the behavior, and recommending they seek recovery through 12-Step programs. These men have only two options: addict or not. But between those options I see a spectrum of relationships and stories. I want to help these men explore more than just their compulsive behaviors and limited thinking. I want to help them understand their emotional world—their anxieties, insecurities, sadness, and loneliness; their excitement, commitment, and desire. I want to see through the lens each of them uses, to know their thoughts about who they are and what they are doing sexually. I want to know their body sensations beyond only the urge to masturbate—what is going on in their chest, their fingertips, and beyond? How do they relate to their partners and family members? What was their sex education growing up? Who is their God? What is their relationship with God—and with their Church? Do they differentiate between spirituality and religion?

An overall theme that emerges for these men is that sex is something they "do" for a moment in the bedroom—versus sexuality being an integral part of who they are. For these men, sensual desire is a source of shame. They attempt to suppress it in many ways, including taking antidepressants. As I help them recognize the full scope of their sexuality, I am helping them understand that everything is connected. I am helping them learn that suppressing sexual desire suppresses their basic energy. We focus on how they approach work, family, relationships, fun, play, pleasure, and even God. I help them find their personal connection to their spiritual practices and beliefs and how sexuality can be part of expressing all of that. The goal of sex therapy for these men shifts from changing "bad" behaviors to helping them find out who they are and what they truly want, and exploring ways to connect body, mind, heart, and soul.

I had no adequate ways to express this integrated view of sexual desire and intimacy until 2012, when I discovered Gina Ogden's 4-D Wheel of Sexual Experience and started using it to help men connect with the whole story of their sexuality and incorporate it into their lives. The Wheel has offered me an opportunity to create a space where these men can explore their sexuality without negative judgments and without having to perform (or stop performing) in some specified way. Using the Wheel, I can invite them to examine their internal world and inhabit it in ways they had never been able to before.

USING THE WHEEL TO ADDRESS BELIEFS ABOUT PORNOGRAPHY USE

A CASE NARRATIVE WITH ACCOMPANYING CASE SUPERVISION AND INTERACTIVE COMMENTS

Chapter 11 addresses pornography use, one of the most controversial and contentious subjects in the field of sex therapy. This chapter demonstrates how porn use can be reframed and explored rather than pathologized as a sexual deviation, diagnosed as an addiction, and treated through shaming, abstinence, and possible Church discipline. A psychotherapist and sex counselor invites her client Ben, 26, a devout Mormon husband and father, to step into all the dimensions of the Wheel to explore positive aspects of his desires as well as negative aspects so that he can make informed choices about if, and how, he uses pornography. Ben's story focuses on Mormon belief systems, but it has implications for any client whose issues involve religious, cultural, or ethnic constraints on sexual desire and intimacy. The lesson here is about respecting the inner struggles of these clients, staying with every step they take toward their therapeutic goals as they unfold, holding impeccably safe space, and listening closely and without judgment, as if you are a visitor in their land intent on learning the nuances of their language.

Kristin's case narrative is accompanied by my running commentary in shaded boxes, and by spaces that invite your observations. At the end of the chapter the case is revisited so that you can see it described via the Wheel. Note that the purpose of this chapter is not to offer treatment for pornography addiction, but to illustrate uses of the Wheel to help a client explore his particular dilemmas of sexual desire.

BEN: THE OPENING SESSIONS—"HELP ME STOP!"

Kristin's Case Narrative: "I can't stop looking at pornography. I think about it all the time. It could cost me my marriage and I still can't stop. I want to but I can't." Ben was describing with great shame what he, his ecclesiastical leader, and his wife had diagnosed as his problem: sex addiction. To him and those in his circle of trust, watching porn or even wanting to watch it means being addicted. My first question to Ben was, "How often are you looking at pornography?" "Well," he said, "it's been about four times this year." It was August, so that worked out to about once every two months.

> **Gina's Supervisory Comments:** Background questions about the terms "sexual addiction" and "porn addiction" make me wonder how Kristin's theoretical stance might affect the therapy with Ben.
> 1) In the sex field, there is major controversy about these terms that will doubtless influence Ben's case: What constitutes addictive or compulsive use of pornography? Is the concept of sexual addiction evidence based or morality based? Shame and abstinence are core to 12-Step treatment programs for sexual addiction and porn addiction—how will Kristin integrate these into her 4-D sessions with Ben?
> 2) True addiction involves a constellation of symptoms, including persistent, ingrained habits and distinct physiological indicators—does thinking about porn "all the time" and viewing porn every two months qualify Ben for a diagnosis of addiction?

[Your comments:]

What do you notice at this point? _____

What would you do at this point? _____

If you were Ben's therapist or counselor, what countertransference issues do you imagine might arise with this case? _____

K: Ben's history was typical of many men who grow up in the Mormon faith. He had no sex education beyond being taught that sex should be saved for marriage and expressed only as intercourse with his wife. Masturbation is a sin. Watching porn is clearly a sin, and Ben feared that doing it meant he was an intrinsically evil person. Ben admitted to me that he'd been masturbating since he was ten and that he'd first masturbated with pornography at 14. Instead of reinforcing Ben's recovery program on how to quit, I felt it crucial to invite him to view sexuality from more angles so that he could see his relationship to porn in a more complex way.

> G: Ben's concept of sexuality is shaped by religious doctrine rather than by sex education, or his own experience, which means he has little frame of reference for how to express his sexual desires. Kristin needs to keep this in mind as she provides both context and education for Ben so that therapy can gently open his world without directly opposing his religious faith, to which he is committed. In some ways, Ben's dilemma parallels that of Deborah's in Chapter 10, where Chelsea uses archetypes as an organizing principle.

What do you notice at this point? _____

What would you do at this point? _____

K: As I was taking his sex history in our first session, I showed him a diagram of the 4-D Wheel, and described how it could help him explore his thoughts, emotions, and physical sensations beyond what he thought he "should" be experiencing. My hope was that using it could help Ben move all the desire and shame he was holding inside and bring it to the outside where the two of us could investigate it together. I could see his eyes open wide as he looked at the Wheel.

> G: Offering clients a visual of the Wheel can be eye-opening in a number of ways. For some clients, seeing the four dimensions of sexual experience outlined simply and clearly can provide a breakthrough of insight. It can also provide relief, because the four dimensions express visually what clients may instinctively know, but have never been able to articulate. Will insight and relief occur for Ben? Stay tuned . . .

What do you notice at this point? _____

What would you do at this point? _____

K: At the end of our second session, I asked Ben to bring two objects to our next meeting: First, an object to represent how his pornography use has disrupted his life. He asked for examples. "It could be: *It takes up so much time.* You could bring a clock or a watch, etc. Or: *I've spent too much money.* You could bring a dollar bill, or a credit card. Or: *I've lost religious opportunities.* You could bring a Bible. Or: *My marriage is on the line*—you could bring a wedding picture or marriage certificate . . . but you decide."

Once I knew he understood, I asked him to bring in a second object as well: one to represent how his pornography use was working *for* him rather than *against* him. This question catches clients off guard if porn is only seen as bad. But I mention to Ben that it can't be all that bad, or he wouldn't keep turning to it, right? "Your second object could represent ideas like: *Pornography is so easy.* Or: *Guaranteed results.* Or: *Helps me with my anxiety.*" I stressed that he needn't feel limited by these suggestions, just use them as a springboard to explore these aspects of how he uses pornography.

> **G:** Concretizing with objects is especially effective with clients whose issues are stuck on the cusp of the mental/spiritual dimensions in the Wheel—which is the locus of religious tenets. Hopefully, the process of choosing objects and working with them will engage Ben's emotions as well as his imagination, get him out of his head, and bring him back to earth where he can begin to connect with his senses in a more interactive way.

What do you notice at this point? _____

What would you do at this point? _____

BEN: SESSION THREE—RE-MEMBERING HIMSELF

K: Ben arrived with his objects in a brown paper bag. To bring us both into the room, I started with a brief grounding exercise of diaphragmatic breathing [see Chapter 2 for a basic breathing and grounding exercise]. Then we checked in about his week. I asked what it was like for him to find objects that represented his pornography use. "A bit odd at first. But once I found them it made more sense."

> **G:** Part of Ben's problem is that he makes too much sense—and too little connection with his heart and body. Staying in his head keeps him locked in a moral frame for sexual desire and intimacy. His only release is to break out into forbidden activities.

What do you notice at this point? _____

What would you do at this point? _____

He pulled out a 30-day chip from his recovery group—this was to represent how much time his porn use was taking up. He explained that he was going to this group once a week, plus having multiple discussions with his wife Carrie and meetings with his religious leader, not to mention the time he spent going back and forth in his head about whether or not to look at pornography. His second object was an electric lighter. "It's like Internet porn—once you know how to use it, it works every time. It's easy. And you can find lighters almost anywhere. They're just really convenient."

> **G:** That Ben brings his two objects is a big indicator that he's engaged in this therapy, though note that he brings them in a brown bag, as if they're illicit goods. He's still in his head—looking for his objects to "make sense." I wonder how Kristin will help him work with his objects, and which of his objects holds the most energy for him? Will he be able to connect emotionally to his objects or will he keep them at arm's length?

What do you notice at this point? _____

What would you do at this point? _____

K: I set up my Wheel on the floor—it is basic and utilitarian, made of office supplies. Especially with male clients, I find there is less hesitation and fewer barriers to the process if the Wheel is straight-forward. I line up four marking pens to make the vertical axis and four more pens for the horizontal axis. Then I have Physical, Emotional, Mental, and Spiritual written on white note cards. I set the quadrants so that the emotional and mental are across from each other, and the physical and spiritual are across from each other. Ben was curious. I said, "Would you like to step in?"

> **G:** Aha! Kristin has engaged Ben's curiosity and invited a "Yes!" response! (See Chapter 3.) This is another indicator that Ben is engaged and ready to take some initiative with his therapy instead of just making confessions and waiting for reproach and penance.

What do you notice at this point? _____

What would you do at this point? _____

K: I oriented Ben to each part of the Wheel: Emotional, Physical, Mental, Spiritual. Once he felt clear, I asked him to place his objects, without giving him direction where to start. I encouraged him to walk around the Wheel to see which quadrant called to him. Ben placed his lighter in Emotional. From this place he shared that he'd been so stressed with work, marriage, and a new baby that he often felt overwhelmed. Pornography was a release that required little to no work—it could simply be about him and his pleasure. He then placed his recovery chip in the spiritual quadrant, and confessed that he had really disappointed his wife, his God, and his religious leader. He'd wasted valuable time he could have spent building a foundation for his future, as a father and as a solid member of his Church.

> **G:** Note that Kristin offers Ben open permission to walk the Wheel, place his objects wherever he wants, and talk about them however he likes. Yet the Wheel also offers a boundary to keep Ben's experience focused and contained—so important for a client with a history of any kind of conservatism who is not used to much freedom. Although the Wheel offers specific guidelines to follow, these guidelines never directly confront the teachings of the Church.

What do you notice at this point? _____

What would you do at this point? _____

K: In the spiritual quadrant, Ben also confessed something new to him: that the burden of feeling like a giant disappointment weighed him down so much that he didn't feel like carrying it around anymore. I invited him to move into the physical quadrant to show me with his body what holding that burden was like for him. He didn't understand what I meant because he had never thought about this burden having a physical size and shape. I modeled a bit of how my body might bow down under a heavy load.

> **G:** Notice how seamlessly Kristin invites Ben out of his head and into his body—never challenging his religious beliefs, but arousing his curiosity, using tangible objects to concretize his abstract ideas, offering specific directions, inviting movement, and modeling fluid body language. Here, I'm reminded of the science of mirror neurons, which reflect acceptance and inspire positive action (see Chapter 2).

What do you notice at this point? _____

What would you do at this point? _____

K: Ben perched on his right leg while his upper body curled over and tightened into a ball. His eyes were closed tightly, his lips pursed. After a minute or so, I asked him what it felt like to hold this position

("Really unstable and tiring"). I then asked him to show me how he would like to feel in his day-to-day life. He stood firmly on two feet and uncurled his body. He tilted his head backward, stretched out his arms, lifted his chest toward the ceiling and smiled—so different. I asked what this position felt like to him. He said, "Free! Honest! How I used to feel when I was a kid, before life became so complicated." We both took a few breaths to take in that moment. Then I invited him to go back to the "burden" position, tucking his head and tightening his body.

> **G:** Ben is moving. He practices an application of the Re-Membering activity from Chapter 5. Compare Ben's Re-Membering experience with Steve's, in Chapter 9.

What do you notice at this point? _____

What would you do at this point? _____

K: Then I asked, "How do you get back to your free position?" Ben snapped upright and flung out his arms. "How about we slow it down for just a minute," I said. "Let yourself notice each movement and notice specifically what you do to move out of your Burden position and into your sense of freedom. We have all the time you need."

> **G:** Ben is quick to please. Kristin now understands this, and seems confident that he'll follow her directions even if they are uncomfortable or seem strange to him. She is able to keep him focused with directions that guide him to slow down and inhabit his body. At this point, the focus is not on porn or sex. It's on self-awareness; reminding him to notice every breath, sensation, movement, thought.

What do you notice at this point? _____

What would you do at this point? _____

K: Movement by movement, Ben paid attention to releasing each finger, straightening each vertebra, turning his chest from floor to ceiling, opening his eyes. I invited him to move into the emotional quadrant with me to explore his two positions—burdened and free. This way, we connected his physical body to his emotional feelings as we processed through the emotional experience of the burden. "How do you get from here to there emotionally?"

> **G:** It's so important here that Kristin keeps the focus on Ben's awareness rather than on his pornography use or the Church's stance on it—either of which could plunge him back into his familiar spiral of negative judgment.

What do you notice at this point? _____

What would you do at this point? _____

K: We continued this exploration in each of the other quadrants, slowly having him share the two positions of Burden and Freedom, and how he moved from one to another. What was most remarkable was Ben's slow unfolding as he went around the Wheel. He noticed that he was not able to maintain his crouched Burden position when he took full, deep breaths. He also noticed that in the Burden position he was unable to look at the sky—the place in his mind where God resides.

I asked Ben if this was enough for now. He said "Yes." As he gathered his objects, I asked what he would like to do with them this week: "I think I will take my chip with me in my pocket every day. I'd like to be more aware of when I feel burdened and when I feel free. As for my lighter, I'm not sure yet."

BEN: SESSION FOUR—CONVERSATIONS WITH GOD

K: He arrived on time as usual, but now his objects were out of the bag. His lighter was in his hand and his chip was in his pocket. We talked about how things went with his objects. He said he was surprised by how often he felt stressed and burdened not just by his pornography use but by his whole life—as a dad, as a husband, serving in his Church, all of it. He said he'd started experiencing himself differently. He noticed his thoughts. He noticed his emotions. He noticed his physical body.

> **G:** Ben's work between sessions shows that he's waking up in some major ways. Kristin's patience, methodical approach, and trust in the process are beginning to pay off.

What do you notice at this point? _____
What would you do at this point? _____

K: I asked him if he would like to get into the Wheel again, and he said "Yes." He placed both his chip and his lighter in the emotional quadrant and said, "Remember last week how I didn't know what to do with my lighter? Well, since everything feels so heavy and hard in my life and I'm failing at it all, I wonder if pornography is what helps give me a break from feeling all of that?" I asked Ben to tell me more.

> **G:** "Tell me more" is such a revealing and elegant phrase in doing 4-D work. Beware of giving suggestions and making interpretations, however smart they might be. As therapists, we need to remember that what initiates deepest and most lasting change is what clients discover for themselves. How smart we are isn't what's important. Telling clients what we know often puts them right back into their heads.

What do you notice at this point? _____
What would you do at this point? _____

B: When I hold the lighter, I feel free. Just like that position I found last week, I feel how I want to feel in my everyday life. Even if it's for just a moment. As weird as it sounds, I feel watching porn and masturbating are things I am actually good at.

K: Help me understand what you mean by that, Ben? Your statement took me by surprise!

> **G:** Again, Kristin is urging "Tell me more." She refrains from judgment or interpretation, just encourages Ben to speak.

What do you notice at this point? _____
What would you do at this point? _____

B: Well, I have these fantasies that I am actually making that woman happy—you know, the woman on the computer screen. That I am enough for her and that I am actually doing a good job.

> G: Ben's description of his fantasies is a "Bingo" moment! He's been conditioned by his Church to stay in his head and out of his body. Ironically, that conditioning has trained him to do exactly what the Church prohibits: watch porn, where he can stay in his head and disengage from sexual activities that involve connection with a real-life partner. In terms of his masturbation, he'd become so adept at fantasizing that he wasn't really present—so he could rationalize that he wasn't doing anything "bad."

What do you notice at this point? _____
What would you do at this point? _____

B: And when I feel like *this* [he held up his Burden chip] constantly, I need a break. I need to feel that I am *enough*. I don't necessarily want to have to use pornography to feel that way. But I do like how it feels.

> G: More moral conditioning. Ben is so overwhelmed by duties and judgments that he needs relief—which he can find only a laptop away. But he's becoming aware. And possibly in touch with emotions. Is there some feistiness in that word "enough?"

What do you notice at this point? _____
What would you do at this point? _____

B: [Moving his lighter into the mental quadrant] I grew up thinking sex was bad and dirty, at least until I was married. I shouldn't get aroused and if I did, that I did something to create it. So it was really confusing, because when I first saw pornography, which was a *Playboy* at my friend's house, I really liked it, but I'd been told for so long it was bad. I didn't know who to tell or if I wanted to tell. I didn't know what to do.

K: I asked him to pick up his lighter and move with me into the spiritual quadrant. Our conversation went like this:

K: Tell me what you learned about sex from your Church.

B: That sex is sacred and to be shared only when you were married. That you were to never masturbate, and if you did, it was a sin.

K: What have you learned about sex from God? [Ben looked at me as if I hadn't been listening to him for these past ten minutes. But I had. Which was exactly why I asked him that question.] Ben, have you ever talked to God about what he thinks about sexuality?

B: Well, no—because how do you talk to God about sexuality?

K: If you believe that God created you, then is there a possibility that God also created desire and sexuality and understands all of it?

K: Ben said he wanted to think about that. As he opened the door to leave he said, "Through my 12-Step process, I leaned on my Higher Power or God to help me give up bad sex with porn. But I never actually thought about talking to God about it." I smiled at Ben as he left for another week.

> **G:** Ben is now confused. This is a positive sign for his therapy. It means his usual way of "figuring things out" is disrupted. He's discovering other ways of gaining information.

What do you notice at this point?_____

What would you do at this point?_____

BEN: SESSION FIVE AND BEYOND—BUILDING BRIDGES

K: Ben jumped right in. Our conversation went like this:

B: What a week! Can we set up the Wheel?

K: [I laid out my markers and note cards] Where would you like to start?

B: In the spiritual quadrant! [He put his chip on the left side of the quadrant (Emotions) and his lighter on the right side (Mental).]

K: Tell me about where you've placed your objects.

B: I realized that I never learned what healthy sexuality is. My first experience with sex was in a bathroom at my friend's house, and it was really confusing. I knew I liked it, but I felt really ashamed and that's where everything began to go wrong. I kept my sexuality a secret and something that I felt bad about. But this week I started to wonder if I just got off on the wrong foot—which is why I placed these two objects apart today, with me standing between them. Maybe they aren't completely opposite. Maybe they're opposite ends of a bridge. I never thought that sexuality and God could go together. I never realized how much I take on that isn't mine.

K: This fifth session began another phase in Ben's journey—a "bridge" phase. He considered that maybe he wasn't merely an addict, but that he had a whole story to share about his sexuality that included his life and his relationship with his wife Carrie—and a whole new chapter, including how he wanted to educate baby Jared.

Ben continued therapy with me for almost two years. He explored how his thoughts played into his emotions. He worked to better understand his relationship to spirituality not just religion. A breakthrough occurred when he invited Carrie for couples sessions to address his fears around sharing what he wants: More foreplay throughout the week. More touch. More spontaneity and connection during sex: "I want you to be a willing participant, not just a body beside me in bed."

Using the Wheel, Ben found clarity about his own part in their communication cycle. As he walked the Wheel, he described his cycle like this:

B: I start off in the physical quadrant noticing my body is aroused. I move to the emotional quadrant noticing my desire for easy sex (with computer porn) and my anxiety (sex with Carrie). These are split like a fork in the road. Then I move toward the desire and away from the anxiety which means I turn away from Carrie. Then I jump into the mental quadrant where I can justify my path to the computer. The conversation in my head goes: "She's rejected me so many times, why would this time be any different? She's too tired . . . she doesn't like sex with me . . ." Then when I'm in the spiritual quadrant I experience only guilt and shame. No connection with God or the Church—or Carrie. Just guilt and shame.

K: Ben decided that disrupting this cycle could help him start reconnecting with Carrie. He realized he didn't need to be defensive or attack her reaction to him. He needed to communicate (in his words) "from a place of solid self and empathy." During their sessions on the Wheel, Ben and Carrie were able to talk about sex in a real way for the first time. She had known about Ben's porn use, so communicating about sex had been a major sore spot. She had seen any of his requests for sex as "because of the pornography." With both of them walking the Wheel, however, they were each able to listen to each other, and find an authentic voice to let each other know what they wanted in their bodies and hearts as well as their minds and spirits, and to express their love and commitment to each other and to their growing family.

Ben remained in his Church, where he stayed on track to be what he felt was a worthy member. His journey hasn't been easy, but he's finally realizing that sexual pleasure is much more than a set of "bad" behaviors, and that true spiritual connection is much more than getting rid of "bad" behaviors. As he recognized the complexity of his story he also recognized the beauty of it. He's continually appreciated how the Wheel honored it all.

What differences to you see between Ben's sexual response cycle and the Masters and Johnson sexual response cycle? _____

How do you think the outcome might have been different for Ben if Kristin had used abstinence-only techniques without the Wheel? _____

How do you think using the Wheel enhanced sex therapy for Ben? _____

Are there any ways you see that the Wheel and Ben's sex education limited each other? _____

How do you think using objects enhanced sex therapy for Ben? _____

Are there any ways you see that using objects limited the effectiveness of sex therapy for Ben? _____

How do you think using movement enhanced sex therapy for Ben? _____

Are there any ways you see that movement limited the effectiveness of sex therapy for Ben? _____

How do you think using the particular adaptation of the Re-Membering activity enhanced sex therapy for Ben? _____

Are there any ways you see that using the Re-Membering activity limited sex therapy for Steve? _____

What kernels of Kristin's wisdom or skill can you incorporate into your practice? _____

BEN'S 4-D WHEEL SESSIONS AT A GLANCE

On the following pages, you'll find a two-page form: "Inviting Clients Into the 4-DWheel." On it, are jotted details of the sessions with Ben on the Wheel, so that you can see them at a glance as well as reading through the linear narrative. Recording these details in this way also demonstrates how you might record your own 4-D-Wheel sessions with your clients—as outlined in Chapter 13.

INVITING CLIENTS INTO THE 4-D WHEEL

Name of Client: Ben (and Carrie)   **Date:** xxx
CASE NARRATIVE: Describe client's issues that led you to suggest exploring the Wheel

Ben, 26, Mormon, diagnosed/self-diagnosed "porn addiction"—feels shamed and dysfunctional w/ wife/ 12-step program, reprimanded by Church.
Use Wheel to expand/explore his true desires, and walk through conflicts w/ religious ideology. Eventually work w/ wife to clarify communication re desire, intimacy.

ISSUES FOR THERAPIST: Describe what occurred for you during session(s), including any countertransference

Stay w/ Ben's story w/o trying to influence him or solve his problems.

4-D WHEEL DYNAMICS USED: Describe what you did (and how) during session(s) on the Wheel

Created safe space: created simple, straightforward Wheel to help him expand ideas re healthy sexuality
Invited movement: Walking and "Re-Membering" in each quadrant

Introduced ritual: Continuing use of Wheel—with and w/o objects

Suggested concretizing abstract concepts with tangible objects: Recovery chip and lighter both play very important roles in concretizing conflict between Spirit/ church and "freedom" (body/mind/heart/spirit integration)

Other_____

Name of Client: Ben   **Date:** xxx

PROGRESS OF THE SESSION(S): List client's movement from quadrant to quadrant, from beginning to end of your session(s) with the Wheel, also where objects were placed, if they were used. Add another sheet if necessary.

SESSION #3   SESSION #4

1. HEART: stress (lighter)   1. HEART: (lighter = Freedom)

2. SPIRIT: guilt is burden (chip)   NB fantasies re pleasing women

3. SPIRIT: Re-Membering (chip/lighter)   2. MIND: Sex = bad

4. MIND: "   "   "   3. SPIRIT: convo w/Church

5. BODY: "   4. SPIRIT: convo w/God

6. HEART: "   "   "   SESSION #5

                                              1. SPIRIT: (chip/lighter) "Bridge"

MOVEMENT OF CLIENT: List the major issues and transformations in each quadrant

Guilt/shame →
Embracing complexity of life,
sexual desire, church

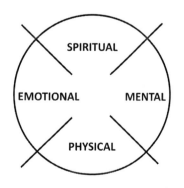

Desire for porn vs.
intimacy w/wife
→ Openness re desires

Justifying porn use
→ complexity &
understanding

Disconnected physical arousal →
body/mind/heart/spirit connection
and pleasure

REFERENCES AND SUGGESTED READING FOR PORNOGRAPHY, SEXUALITY AND RELIGION, SEXUALITY AND SPIRITUALITY, AND MORE

Coleman, E., Horvath, K.J., Miner, M., Ross, M., Oakes, M., and Rosser, B.R. (2010, October). Compulsive sexual behavior and risk for unsafe sex among internet using men who have sex with men. *Archives of Sexual Behavior*, 39(5): 1045–1053.

Elliott, D. (1993). *Spiritual marriage: Sexual abstinence in medieval wedlock*. Princeton, NJ: Princeton University Press.

Estrich, S. (2000). *Sex and power*. New York: Riverhead Books.

Feuerstein, G. (Ed.). (1989). *Enlightened sexuality: Essays on body-positive spirituality*. Freedom, CA: The Crossing Press.

Firestone, S. (1970). *The dialectic of sex*. New York: Bantam.

Fisher, H. (2000). Lust, attraction, attachment: Biology and evolution of the three primary emotion systems formating, reproduction, and parenting. *Journal of Sex Education and Therapy*, 25(1): 96–104.

Goudorf, C.E. (2000). The social construction of sexuality: Implications for churches. In K.M. Sands (Ed.). *God forbid: Religion and sex in American public life*. New York: Oxford University Press, pp. 42–59.

Griffin, S. (1981). *Pornography and silence*. New York: Harper & Row.

Guy, D. (1999). *The red thread of passion: Spirituality and the paradox of sex*. Boston: Shambhala.

Hall, P. (2013). *Understanding and treating sex addiction: A comprehensive guide for people who struggle with sex addiction and those who want to help them*. London; New York: Routledge.

Heyward, C. (1989). *Touching our strength: The erotic as power and the love of God*. New York: HarperCollins.

Hodson, K.B., Worthington, A.B., and Harrison, T.G. (2012). *Real intimacy: A couples guide for genuine, healthy sexuality*. Springville, UT: Cedar Fort, Inc.

Kerner, I. (2010). *She comes first: The thinking man's guide to pleasuring a woman*. New York: William Morrow.

Maltz, W., and Maltz, L. (2010). *The porn trap: The essential guide to overcoming problems caused by pornography*. New York: William Morrow.

Paulus, T. (1973). *Hope for the flowers*. Peabody, MA: Paulist Press.

Nelson, J.B. and Longfellow, S.P. (Eds.). (1994). *Sexuality and the sacred: Sources for theological reflection*. Louisville, KY: Westminster/John Knox Press.

Moore, T. (1998). *The soul of sex: Cultivating life as an act of love*. New York: HarperCollins.

Ogden, G. (1998, January–February). Sex as a path to the soul. *New Age*: 56–60.

Ogden, G. (1999, January–February). Sex and spirit: The healing connection. *New Age*: 78–81, 128–130.

Parrinder, G. (1980). *Sex in the world's religions*. New York: Oxford University Press.

Wilson, G. (2015). *Your brain on porn: Internet pornography and the emerging science of addiction* Margate, UK: Commonwealth Publishing.

12

Marnie

Low Libido, Trauma, and the Wheel

"The truth about our childhood is stored up in our body, and although we can repress it, we can never alter it . . . someday the body will present its bill, for it is as incorruptible as a child who, still whole in spirit, will accept no compromises or excuses, and it will not stop tormenting us until we stop evading the truth."

—*Alice Miller*

KEESHA EWERS

Keesha Ewers, PhD, ARNP-C, FNP, has been in the medical field for over 30 years; her research has focused primarily on female sexual desire. She is a board-certified functional and Ayurvedic medical practitioner, a psychotherapist, energy worker, yoga teacher, and an Andean mesa carrier and Huachumera (plant medicine healer) who works with sacred plant medicine during retreats with her students in various parts of the world. She is founder and host of the *Healthy YOU! Radio Network*. In 2015, she created the Academy for Integrative Medicine, which integrates various specialties of medicine, psychotherapy, and Eastern philosophy—"so women can stop falling through the cracks created by these separate domains in our current health care system." Her Integrative Medicine certification program is designed to help professionals use functional medicine, sexology, Ayurveda, energy work, and psychotherapy techniques to find and fix the root causes of clients' energetic depletion. Her pursuit of answers has taken her around the world, to learn from traditional healers and native cultures in Australia, India, Mexico, Peru, Africa, and Sri Lanka, as well as from the best of the innovative thinkers and scientists in the US. www.DrKeesha. com, www.healthyyouradio.com

THE 4-D WHEEL AS FOUNDATIONAL FOR TRAUMA WORK

Like many therapists and medical providers in the field of sex therapy, I work with clients who present with histories of trauma. When clients are dissociative and/or emotionally flooded, I've found that just identifying past trauma and talking about it does not engage the rich potential of the brain's neuroplasticity. By using EMDR and Brainspotting, I am able to facilitate trauma release from little-accessed reservoirs of the subconscious mind, help clients make connections between past events and current experiences, and aid in generating new functional neural pathways in the brain.

Using the 4-D Wheel has been a breakthrough in my practice, because it offers a practical and efficient way to help clients literally move the new connections and pathways they have created in their brains directly into their life experience. The model of treatment I use for women with diminished sexual desire is functional sexology. Within this model there are four root causes, plus the Libido Story and Libido Map to be explored in order to find and address the presenting problem. Those root causes are based on the four dimensions of the Wheel: physical, mental, emotional, and spiritual. The Wheel allows clients to actually experience the movement between all of the root causes and their stories that are being re-written and re-wired. Having the Wheel on the floor and using objects, walking, feeling, talking, and emoting has become akin to having a medicine wheel in my office. I can feel the healing power of medicine circles from all over the world and throughout time as my clients move through the sacred process of healing their bodies, minds, hearts, spirits, and stories. Each client has the opportunity to embody the transformation he or she is making by moving into each of the areas of herself or himself.

A note about when I use the Wheel in the course of therapy: With trauma clients, I usually introduce the Wheel after helping them release their trauma through EMDR or Brainspotting, each of which directly engages how we store the effects of trauma in our brains. My experience has been that clients are more likely to dissociate or shut down if I invite them into the Wheel before facilitating specific trauma release. This is how I decided to proceed with Marnie, who came to me with a hormone imbalance that she associated with low libido, among other symptoms.

COMBINING THE WHEEL WITH EMDR AND BRAINSPOTTING
A CASE NARRATIVE WITH ACCOMPANYING CASE SUPERVISION AND INTERACTIVE COMMENTS

Chapter 12 demonstrates how a functional medicine practitioner uses EMDR and Brainspotting with the 4-D Wheel to help a sexual abuse survivor with low libido and other issues. It offers a unique application of the Wheel for clients who can benefit from a protocol that helps them identify trauma and assists them in shifting to alternative neural pathways. This chapter is remarkable for two reasons. First, it moves beyond the paradigm of psychotherapy and sex therapy to document how a 4-D Wheel practitioner proceeds when the presenting problem is a medical one—in this case, hormone imbalance. Second, it offers a distinct preparatory structure for introducing clients to the Wheel. This can serve as a model for practitioners who focus on hormonal and neurological approaches to trauma and for those who may want to add other evidence-based methods to the improvisational nature of Wheel work

In Marnie's case, you'll see that the core dynamic of movement is key, especially her fluidity regarding past and present time as she unlocks stored memories, and her embodied movement around the Wheel as she reinforces new neurological pathways and incorporates behavioral changes into her life.

Keesha's case narrative is accompanied by my running commentary in shaded boxes, and by spaces that invite your observations. At the end of the chapter the case is revisited so that you can see it described via the Wheel. Note that the point of this chapter is not to describe hormone assays, EMDR, or Brainspotting in any detail, but to demonstrate how the Wheel can be used seamlessly and effectively with other modalities, and how a practitioner uses the Wheel as transition from physiological and neurological work to helping a client implement behavioral change—mental, emotional, physical, and spiritual.

MARNIE: SESSION ONE—THE PRESENTING ISSUE

Keesha's Case Narrative: Marnie, age 64, presented with a self-diagnosed hormone imbalance. She had been experiencing weight gain, poor sleep quality, low libido, fatigue, and irritability. Her stated reason for her visit to the clinic was to explore bio-identical hormone replacement therapy. I agreed to run a salivary adrenal and hormone test for her. She relaxed, seemingly happy that she was being heard.

Because I suspected that there was a complex story behind her hormone imbalance, I began casually asking questions to further explore the root causes of her symptoms. Marnie revealed that she had been sexually abused at age four by her older brother, had lost her father at age seven, had a high-stress job that required late-night hours, and had just learned that her mother had early-onset Alzheimer's. She reported her sexual satisfaction level at a 4 on a scale of 1–10, with 10 being the highest—a particular problem being her low libido with her life-partner, a woman who suddenly wanted sex "all the time."

I explained to her that hormone supplements might not be the only answer to her issues, as the symptoms she described might be affected by many factors. I suggested we meet for a few sessions while we waited the four weeks for her lab results to come back—then once we had those results, we would know much more about the context of her hormone levels, and she would be in a better position to implement the changes she wanted.

> **Gina's Supervisory Comments:** Keesha recognizes the potential complexities in Marnie's request for hormone therapy—then makes a convincing statement that pharmacological intervention is seldom the only effective approach to hormone imbalance, especially when relational issues are involved. Even when chemical analysis is exactly right, self-awareness and personal engagement are needed to manage and integrate life changes. During Keesha's conversation with Marnie, I'm thinking of the countless women who seek testosterone as a magic cure for low desire—without understanding that lasting change will doubtless mean that they also need to explore the full Wheel of their desire—physical, emotional, mental, spiritual, and relational.

What do you notice at this point? _____

What would you do at this point? _____

If you were Marnie's therapist or counselor, what countertransference issues do you imagine might arise with this case? _____

K: I further explained to Marnie that we'd begin these sessions with a genogram, a graphic form of sex-history taking. With this, we'd focus on helping her find some historical basis for her imbalances. Then we'd teach her specific tools to help her manage her life and hopefully increase her sexual desire.

> **G:** Such a smart preamble. Marnie came in imagining she'd receive a prescription for a pill or a patch. She's getting more than a medical-model quick fix, and Keesha needs to evoke a "Yes!" response so that Marnie will engage in the work. (Marnie says "Yes!" to Keesha's proposal.)

What do you notice at this point? _____

What would you do at this point? _____

K: I was sure I'd use the Wheel with Marnie, but not right away. My experience is that clients with early abuse issues tend to dissociate when they're in the Wheel, and then I have to wait for them to get back into their bodies. To prepare these clients, I resource them neurosynaptically, then use EMDR or Brainspotting. Marnie was new to self-awareness, and I felt she needed some kind of script to follow before she could get the most benefit from the Wheel. Following a set protocol can be like a lifeline for clients who are first learning to be aware of their health and sexual health. It's like doing scales on the piano; you learn the basics, then you can branch into creative applications.

> **G:** There's no one right way to use the Wheel, and Keesha is demonstrating that here. Her decision to defuse trauma and train Marnie to tap into her inner resources in preparation for the Wheel is interesting to me, as most Wheel practitioners do it the other way: use Wheel work to guide clients to find their inner resources. What's important is that Keesha finds an approach that works for her—because what works for her is most likely to work for Marnie, and Keesha's other clients.

What do you notice at this point? _____

What would you do at this point? _____

MARNIE: SESSION TWO—GENOGRAM AND INNER RESOURCES

K: The genogram process dramatized for Marnie that she had three particular points of shock: abuse by her brother (at age four), her father's death (at age seven), and, a newly emerged factor, her partner's lobbying to open up their longtime union into a poly relationship that included a male co-worker with whom she was having an affair. The genogram helped Marnie see how these events created thematic and cumulative triggers for her to freeze and shut down, as was her habitual response during relational conflicts and any kind of sexual intimacy. Like other clients in shock, Marnie can't retrieve information in a useful manner—it disappears into a part of the brain where the appropriate response is not stored.

> G: Keesha's description of clients in shock resonates with the polyvagal reactivity to stress, a primitive fight/flight response outlined in Chapter 5. It also resonates with the lacuna state, outlined in Chapter 3—in which clients may dissociate ("Where am I?") or shut down sexual response, as Zahira did in that chapter, until she explored—and thawed—the grief that had been frozen at age five, when her mother died.

What do you notice at this point? _____

What would you do at this point? _____

K: After the genogram, I taught Marnie a progressive practice for finding her inner resources, and let her know she could use this practice any time she feels her freeze state coming on. The resourcing practice began with Marnie finding a safe place in her mind—using all five senses plus her imagination to give it size, shape, color, sound, smell, taste, and texture (Marnie chose a meadow and wildflowers). We then created a cue word that would instantly evoke that safe place (Marnie chose *Meadow*).

Our progression followed like this, using the word *Meadow* to cue her feeling of calm:

- How do you feel when I say *Meadow* ...? Marnie said: *Calm.*
- *Meadow* . . . where in your body do you feel calm? Marnie said: *My heart and throat.*
- *Meadow* . . . what color do you associate with calm? Marnie said: *Purple.*
- And so forth, cuing Marnie to *Calm* in various neutral situations (physical, emotional, mental, and spiritual) then using a 0–10 scale for situations in which she experienced frustration—beginning with minor experiences and working up to her partner's affair, which caused panic.

During this resourcing process, Marnie discovered a primary spiritual connection, the archetype of the Earthmother, which she was able to connect to, and felt she could embody. Now we were ready to work with trauma release in the brain.

> G: Finding a safe place is absolutely consistent with the first core dynamic of 4-D Wheel practice: creating safe space. Here, Keesha names it as a "resource," and presents it as a separate practice so that Marnie can take it home with her. Note that the resourcing exercises with Marnie follow the pattern of the 4-D Wheel: physical, emotional, mental, and spiritual. Keesha chooses to offer these before she introduces Brainspotting or EMDR, with special emphasis on identifying trauma, releasing it, and finding an alternative place to be. (See "Re-Membering" in Chapter 5.)

What do you notice at this point? _____

What would you do at this point? _____

MARNIE: SESSION THREE—BRAINSPOTTING

K: With Marnie, I decided to use Brainspotting rather than EMDR, as Brainspotting offers a gentler opening into traumatic material. It's also more efficient—and I felt Marnie might be willing to come for only a limited number of sessions, as her test results were now due in just two weeks.

I explained to Marnie that until her trauma memories were released, her flight/fight mechanisms would remain deeply archived in her brain. She now understood that was why she automatically freezes during sex and intimacy. She also understood that she possessed numerous resources she could use to bring herself into *Calm*. Through the technique of Brainspotting, we were going to use those resources to take those trauma memories out of her hippocampus and bring them into her conscious mind. This way, she and I could take a look at them—like taking old boxes out of a storage vault or closet to discover what's in them. Then we could plan how to help her and her libido and general energy level—and let the process proceed at its own speed.

> **G:** Brainspotting was pioneered by David Grand as an offshoot of EMDR, without the pendulum finger movement—see www.brainspotting.pro. The short version of what will happen here is that Keesha will track Marnie's eye movements to identify Marnie's points of trauma, help her connect with where her brain stores those memories, then support her in releasing the memories.

What do you notice at this point? _____

What would you do at this point? _____

K: We began the Brainspotting method with what felt to Marnie like the major triggers: Dad dying; partner texting the male co-worker. Marnie experienced these in her throat and head at "10." I used a pointer to cross her line of vision, slowly followed her eyes, then stopped and spotted where her eyes were focused, linked to the place in her brain where that memory was stored. [See the Brainspotting website for more details on how this technique works.]

I directed Marnie to keep her eyes focused on that spot, be aware of her thoughts and feelings, and tell her story with whatever came up. She sobbed—"My father died on my seventh birthday." (She said she felt this in her heart, and I reminded her to stay aware.) "My mother and sister snuck me into the hospital, but I didn't know what it was about. My mother remarried. I hated my stepfather who had all sorts of rules and he'd lock me in my bedroom and wouldn't let me come out for supper. I had to be so careful to be good—or *else*." Then the big, big realization hit: "OMG! It's like I married my stepfather. My partner's having an affair and changing our lives and I'm walking on egg shells trying to be a perfect 'wife.' She never wanted that much sex before. I knew something was going on behind my back."

We stayed with Brainspotting for some 40 minutes, until her sobbing and big downloads were over. That's the point at which I feel clients are ready to use the Wheel—to help them integrate what they've downloaded.

> **G:** I notice that Brainspotting trauma release involves cognitive beliefs, story, behavior, plus all the dimensions of the Wheel. That is, Brainspotting reveals material similar to what the Wheel often reveals. The method is different, and it would be so interesting to find a way to determine how the levels of trauma release may differ—or be similar. Bottom line, it depends on the client, as always. But it also depends on the practitioner's training and expertise—and comfort level with the work.

What do you notice at this point? _____

What would you do at this point? _____

MARNIE: SESSION FOUR—THE WHEEL

K: After her sessions of genogram, resourcing, and Brainspotting, Marnie was able to acknowledge how traumatic events from her childhood connected with her turned-off desire as well as with the physical issues that had brought her to see me. She also understood that her fear response to her partner's new sexual interests had acted like a perfect storm to activate these connections. Further, she understood the concept of shock, and had now experienced how and where her responses had been frozen in time.

We were ready for the Wheel—as a tool to help bring Marnie into her body so she could take her new understanding home. I explained that working with the Wheel would be vital to her ability to translate the Brainspotting information into changes she wanted to make in her relationship.

Once Marnie began to walk the Wheel, I didn't have to say or do much. She already knew the way, because we'd done the intense trauma work in all four dimensions with resourcing and Brainspotting. She fluidly moved—immediately connecting with the little girl who had been traumatized. She was able to recreate the meanings she had made as an upset four-year-old and seven-year-old and translate them into here and now perceptions that could work for her as a 64-year-old. She was able to self-identify and take responsibility for her own emotions and the behaviors she had adopted. She honored them as survival strategies that had been very wise for a child, but which were not working for her as an adult in an intimate relationship that was being rocked by her partner's new sexual awakenings.

> **G:** Now that she's in the Wheel, Marnie is moving largely on her own volition instead of sitting in chair with a therapist initiating the moves. Physically stepping into the Wheel is a crucial transition away from trauma, which will hopefully help her take her new knowings she can apply in her life—by recreating her calm and empowered self at home.
>
> Here might be a prime moment to ask Marnie to practice the Re-Membering activity from Chapter 5, which is another tool she can take home to use in moments of stress.

What do you notice at this point? _____

What would you do at this point? _____

K: Marnie began in the mental dimension of the Wheel. Here she stated her new message: "I'm a woman of juice and power," and turned it into an affirmation—which she wrote on a card: "I have survived my own version of purgatory and hell. I am now powerful enough to do anything I choose."

In the emotional dimension, I suggested to her that she breathe light from her flower-filled Meadow into her heart center. She breathed the light in, and reported feeling calm and expanded.

With her calm, expanded self, Marnie then stepped into the physical dimension of the Wheel, and into the hormone imbalances which had originally brought her to seek help. She repeated a similarly empowered statement: "My hormones are a reflection of me. I can change my hormones by how I think and feel." This was a spontaneous statement, and I could see that it surprised her. I asked her to repeat it. This opened an opportunity for us to discuss that hormone levels are only part of the big picture of health and desire, and that it truly could be possible for her to change her hormones as she practices bringing more energy and light into her life.

In the spiritual dimension, Marnie met the Earthmother, the powerful archetype she had connected with during her resourcing. Here, in the Wheel, she named her as the Giver of Light— an image of a beautiful Being from the Dreamtime who used to come to comfort her after her father died. This session had the sense of an integrative peak experience, a touchstone Marnie could return to and hold in times of uncertainty.

G: So many processes come together in the Wheel: Empowerment messages, an enlightened heart, an explosion of body intelligence about a new relationship with her hormones— and finally, meeting the protective Earthmother who has been with Marnie since childhood. When she steps into all of these dimensions, Marnie physically steps into that new person she wants to be.

I am remembering Christiane Northrup's wise advice to women, especially to older women: "The greatest predictor of great sex is a new partner. So: Become that new partner yourself."

These four sessions may or may not generate permanent magic for Marnie, though perhaps they mark the beginning of ongoing change. Marnie has a lot on her plate at home, including repair and renewal of her relationship. Her partner has stated willingness to work on the question of whether they stay monogamous or open up to relational fluidity—or stay together at all.

What do you notice at this point? _____

What would you do at this point? _____

How would you close this session? _____

MARNIE'S LAB RESULTS AND BEYOND

K: Marnie's lab results revealed a stage-three level of adrenal fatigue, likely due to chronic stress and past trauma that had put her system into a hyper-vigilant survival mode. Her thyroid was hypoactive, common when the adrenals are burned out. She had low progesterone and estrogen dominance and almost no DHEA or pregnenolone (the raw materials needed for her to produce her own hormones). I started her on a protocol to heal her adrenals and thyroid, in addition to bio-identical topical DHEA, pregnenolone, and progesterone, with a re-test in five months. Marnie's adrenals should heal with proper replacement of nutrients and stress-reduction strategies. She will not need to be on hormones forever as she learns to patch the hole in the bottom of her boat through our work on the Wheel. I referred Marnie and her partner for couples sessions with a colleague. According to reports, their relationship now feels better for both of them.

How do you think Marnie's outcome might have differed if Keesha had used only the hormone tests that Marnie had requested? _____

_____

How do you think Keesha's doing the hormone tests affected the outcome for Marnie?_____

_____

How do you think the genogram affected the outcome for Marnie?_____

_____

How do you think the resourcing exercise affected the outcome for Marnie? _____

_____

How do you think the Brainspotting affected the outcome for Marnie? _____

_____

How do you think using 4-D Wheel affected the outcome for Marnie? _____

_____

What kernels of Keesha's wisdom or skill can you incorporate into your practice? _____

_____

MARNIE'S 4-D-WHEEL SESSION AT A GLANCE

On the following pages, you'll find a two-page form: "Inviting Clients Into the 4-D Wheel." On it, are jotted details of the session with Marnie on the Wheel, so that you can see them at a glance as well as reading through the linear narrative. Recording these details in this way also demonstrates how you might record your own 4-D-Wheel sessions with your clients—as outlined in Chapter 13.

INVITING CLIENTS INTO THE 4-D WHEEL

Name of Client: Marnie   **Date:** xxx

CASE NARRATIVE: Describe client's issues that led you to suggest exploring the Wheel

Marnie, 64, HSDD self-diagnosed hormone imbalance—depression, low libido while waiting 4 wks for labs, I suggest therapy sessions to address related emotional issues:

- Genogram: 3 major pockets of shock:
  - >4y.o. abuse by brother
  - >7 y.o. dad died
  - >Present: partner—affair w/man, plus opening to poly
- Resourcing and Brainspotting to release shock
- Wheel: to bring her back into body—take learning home

ISSUES FOR THERAPIST: Describe what occurred for you during session(s), including any countertransference

Need not to get hooked into trying to rescue Marnie—or do too much to make her feel better. Have to remember not to work harder than my clients :)

4-D WHEEL DYNAMICS USED: Describe what you did (and how) during session(s) on the Wheel

Created safe space: Listened to her story, validated her by doing hormone tests before suggesting therapy

Invited movement: After Brainspotting, asked her to walk Wheel—all dimensions—she moved fluidly in and out of each

Introduced ritual: Asked her to move into each dimension

Suggested concretizing abstract concepts with tangible objects: No

Other Neuro techniques for release meant that most of the trauma work was done by the time we used the Wheel—so Wheel work was for integration.

Name of Client: *Marnie*   **Date:** *xxx*

PROGRESS OF THE SESSION(S): List client's movement from quadrant to quadrant, from beginning to end of your session(s) with the Wheel, also where objects were placed, if they were used. Add another sheet if necessary.

Explores ea. dimension fluidly

1. MIND: "I'm a woman of juice & power"
2. HEART: Breathes in light
3. BODY: "I can change my hormones!"
4. SPIRIT: Earthmother archetype: "Giver of Light"

MOVEMENT OF CLIENT: List the major issues and transformations in each quadrant

Victim/Waif →
Earthmother

Depressed/
Constricted/
Anxious →
Open Heart

Shock →
"Woman of juice &
power"

HSDD/Hormone imbalance →
"I am in charge;
I can change my hormones"

REFERENCES AND SUGGESTED READING FOR WOMEN, TRAUMA, GENOGRAMS, EMDR, BRAINSPOTTING, AND MORE

Anapol, D. (1997). *Polyamory: The new love without limits: Secrets of sustainable intimate relationships* (rev. ed.). San Raphael CA: IntiNet Resource Center.

Bass, E., and Davis, L. (2008). *The courage to heal: A guide for women survivors of child sexual abuse* (4th rev ed.). New York: William Morrow.

Boston Women's Health Book Collective. (2011). *Our bodies, ourselves* (40th anniv. rev. ed.). New York: Touchstone.

Chopra, D. (2015). *Quantum healing: Exploring the frontiers of mind/body medicine* (rev. ed.). New York: Bantam.

Cohn, R. (2011). *Coming home to passion: Restoring loving sexuality in couples with histories of childhood trauma and neglect.* Santa Barbara, CA: Praeger.

Ewers, K. (2014, February). An integrative medicine approach to the treatment of HSDD: Introducing the HURT model. *Sexual and Relationship Therapy,* 29(1): 42–55.

Grand, D. (2013). *Brainspotting: The revolutionary new therapy for rapid and effective change.* Louisville, CO: Sounds True.

Haines, S. (1999). *The survivor's guide to sex: How to have an empowered sex life after child sexual abuse.* San Francisco: Cleis Press.

Herman, J.L. (1997). *Trauma and recovery* (rev. ed.). New York: Basic Books.

Kaptchuk, T.J. (2002, June 4). The placebo effect in alternative medicine: Can the performance of a healing ritual have clinical significance? *Annals of Internal Medicine,* 136(11): 817–825.

Kaptchuk, T.J., and Miller, F.G. (2015, July 2). Placebo effects in medicine. *New England Journal of Medicine,* 373: 8–9.

Leavitt, J. (2012). *The sexual alarm system: Women's unwanted response to sexual intimacy and how to overcome it.* Northvale, NJ: Jason Aronson.

Maltz, W. (2012). *The sexual healing journey: A guide for survivors of sexual abuse* (3rd ed.). New York: William Morrow.

McGoldrick, M. (2008). *Genograms: Assessment and intervention* (3rd ed.). New York: W.W. Norton.

Miller, A. (1994). *The drama of the gifted child: The search for the true self.* New York: Basic Books.

Nagoski, E. (2015). *Come as you are: The surprising new science that will transform your sex life.* New York: Simon & Schuster.

Nagoski, E., Janssen, E., Lohrmann, D., and Nichols, E.T. (2012). Risk, individual differences, and environment: An agent-based modeling approach to sexual risk-taking. *Archives of Sexual Behavior,* 41(4): 849–860.

Nelson, T. (2013). *The new monogamy: Redefining your relationship after infidelity.* Oakland, CA: New Harbinger.

Northrup, C. (2010). *Women's bodies, women's wisdom: Creating physical and emotional health and healing* (rev. ed.). New York: Bantam.

Northrup, C. (2012). *The wisdom of menopause: Creating physical and emotional health and healing during the change* (rev. ed.). New York: Bantam.

Ogden, G. (2007). *Women who love sex: Ordinary women describe their paths to pleasure, intimacy, and ecstasy* (3rd ed.). Boston, Trumpeter.

Perel, E. (2007). *Mating in captivity: Unlocking erotic intelligence.* New York, HarperPerennial.

Shapiro, F. (1997). *EMDR: The breakthrough therapy for overcoming anxiety, stress, and trauma.* New York: Basic Books.

Shapiro, F. (2012). *EMDR: Getting past your past: Take control of your life with self-help techniques from EMDR therapy.* Emmaus, PA: Rodale.

Siegel, D. (2010). *Mindsight: The new science of personal transformation.* New York: Bantam.

Spring, J.A. (2012) *After the affair: Healing the pain and rebuilding trust when a partner has been unfaithful* (2nd ed.). New York: William Morrow.

van der Kolk, B. (2015). *The body keeps the score: Brain, mind, and body in the healing of trauma.* New York: Penguin.

Winston, S. (2009). *Women's anatomy of arousal.* Kingston, NY: Mango Garden Press.

13

Making Your Own Practical Applications—And Providing Handouts for Your Clients

"Wisdom is not a product of thought.
The deep knowing that is wisdom arises
through the simple act of giving someone
or something your full attention."
—*Eckhart Tolle*

YOUR 4-D TAKE-HOME

It has been my pleasure to introduce you to some of the intricacies of using the 4-D Wheel—both the innovative approaches and the practical applications. As you review your own responses to the variety of activities in this book, what do you see as your major take-home messages? How do you envision using the Wheel with yourself and your clients? And what are the action steps you will take to incorporate the Wheel into your practice?

How I Envision Using the 4-D Wheel

My major take-home messages from the workbook

_____

_____

_____

_____

_____

_____

_____

_____

Steps I will take to incorporate the Wheel into my practice

_____

_____

_____

_____

_____

_____

_____

_____

WHAT'S BEYOND THIS BOOK?

If you resonate with what you've found here and would like to learn more about how you can use the Wheel to help your clients and grow your practice, please check out our practitioners' website: www.4-DNetwork.com. Here, you can learn how you can engage in supervision, become certified to work with the Wheel, take an online course, or participate in a personal enrichment retreat.

Please keep walking the Wheel yourself and with your clients. I'd so appreciate your sending me photos and videos of your Wheels. And write to let me know what happens as you explore desire and intimacy issues by stepping into the four dimensions—body, mind, heart, and spirit. The 4-D Wheel process is continually changing and growing, and I invite you to be part of our exciting transformations and to help us document them.

INVITING YOUR CLIENTS INTO THE WHEEL

The message at the close of this workbook is: Make it your own! From the innovative approaches in Part I, you can see that there are time-tested protocols involved in using the Wheel with clients. These include creating safe space, using ritual, encouraging movement, and concretizing abstract concepts. You can also see that 4-D Wheel protocols can encompass all the core knowledge areas required for certification as a sexuality professional. Further, these 4-D Wheel protocols introduce areas of skill and nuance that you can apply in a variety of therapeutic situations.

From the practical applications in Part II, you can see that the sky's the limit in terms of implementing these concepts and skills. You can adapt any or all of the ideas and processes in this book to address the concerns of your clients and students. Importantly, you can also adapt them for yourself as a curious, creative professional—incorporating into them any other skills you know.

RECORDING YOUR OWN WHEEL SESSIONS WITH CLIENTS

As the final exercise of the book, I invite you to begin to keep records of your own Wheel sessions with clients. On the following two pages, find a blank copy of the form: "Inviting Clients Into the 4-D Wheel." This is for you to use to chart the progress of your clients. You can make extra copies or download them from my websites.

> ☀ Hot Tip—You can adapt the form "Inviting Clients Into the 4-D Wheel" to fit specific issues and dynamics of your clients. You can create your own format by changing the form provided on the following two pages.

INVITING CLIENTS INTO THE 4-D WHEEL

Name of Client(s):   **Date:**

CASE NARRATIVE: Describe client's issues that led you to suggest exploring the Wheel

_____

_____

_____

_____

_____

ISSUES FOR THERAPIST: Describe what occurred for you during session(s), including any countertransference

_____

_____

_____

_____

_____

4-D WHEEL DYNAMICS USED: Describe what you did (and how) during session(s) with the Wheel

Created safe space/"Yes!" response:

_____

_____

Invited movement:

_____

_____

Introduced ritual:

_____

_____

Suggested concretizing abstract concepts with tangible objects:

_____

_____

Other _____

Name of Client: **Date:**

PROGRESS OF THE SESSION(S): List client's movement from quadrant to quadrant, from beginning to end of your session(s) with the Wheel, also where objects were placed, if they were used. Add another sheet if necessary.

1._____   11._____
2. _____   12._____
3._____   13._____
4._____   14._____
5. _____   15._____
6._____   16._____
7._____   17._____
8. _____   18._____
9. _____   19._____
10. _____   20._____

MOVEMENT OF CLIENT: List the major issues and transformations in each quadrant

Major issues   **Transformed to**

Major issues

Transformed to

Major issues

Transformed to

SPIRITUAL

EMOTIONAL   MENTAL

PHYSICAL

Major issues   **Transformed to**

© 2017, *Exploring Desire and Intimacy: A Workbook for Creative Clinicians*, Gina Ogden, Routledge

HANDOUTS AND DOWNLOADS FOR YOUR CLIENTS

The following handouts and downloads are addressed directly to clients, not to you as a practitioner. Please offer any of them to specific clients as it feels appropriate to you.

1. Four-Dimensional Wheel Handout (four-page informational handout to help you tell your own story of desire and intimacy)
2. Exploring Your Sexual Desire and Intimacy: What Do You Really Want? (one-page exercise to help you explore your own issues)
3. Your Sexual Rights (two-page handout from the World Association for Sexual Health)
4. A Brief Guide to some Hot-Button Issues (three-page handout that describes a range of sexual diversities—inviting you to research more on your own)
   - Enhancing Pleasure
   - Opening Communication
   - Erotic Communication
   - Fantasies
   - LGBTQ Issues
   - Growing Older
   - Injury and Illness
   - Using Porn
   - Affairs
   - Polyamory
   - Kinky Sex
   - Your Brain on Desire
   - The Pharmaceutical Revolution: Viagra, Addyi, etc.
   - And much more!

THE FOUR-DIMENSIONAL WHEEL OF SEXUAL EXPERIENCE: EXPLORING YOUR SEXUAL STORY FROM EACH DIMENSION— BODY, MIND, HEART, AND SPIRIT

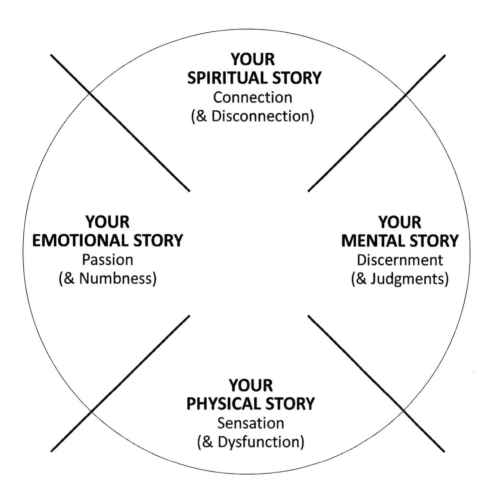

YOUR SPIRITUAL STORY
Connection
(& Disconnection)

YOUR MENTAL STORY
Discernment
(& Judgments)

YOUR EMOTIONAL STORY
Passion
(& Numbness)

YOUR PHYSICAL STORY
Sensation
(& Dysfunction)

For comprehensive guides to the Four-Dimensional Wheel, see Gina Ogden's books:
Expanding the Practice of Sex Therapy
The Heart & Soul of Sex
The Return of Desire

EXPLORING YOUR SEXUAL STORY: BODY, MIND, HEART, AND SPIRIT

The Four-Dimensional Wheel (4-D Wheel) is an invitation for you to describe your sexual story for yourself rather than comparing yourself to other people, or depending on an outside expert to tell you what's "normal." Think of it as an adventure in discovery—physical, mental, emotional, and also spiritual, in the sense of connection and meaning rather than organized religion.

4-D paths don't always follow the rigid boundaries shown in the Wheel diagram. As you probably know from your own sexual relationships, these paths are likely to twist and turn or detour, even come to dead ends. Following them can sometimes feel like slogging through a wilderness—because sex isn't always a straight shot to bliss. Sometimes sex triggers pain instead of pleasure. And sometimes painful experiences lead to positive outcomes. When you factor in other complexities such as age, social class, ethnicity, race, gender, gender identity, and sexual orientation, you may discover that any of these may affect all of your sexual desires and responses—past, present, and future. The notion may sound complicated, but it's really just about looking at the big picture of how sex relates to your whole life, not only seeing it in small bits and pieces. And it's about giving yourself permission to know what you want—body, mind, heart, and spirit.

You can use the 4-D Wheel to map all kinds of sexual responses. You can start anywhere, as long as you're willing to move beyond the idea that sex is only about performance, that is, intercourse with a goal of orgasm. The bottom line is that there's no one right way to experience sex. In the Wheel approach, you get to decide what's right for you, as long as it's consensual and doesn't hurt anyone else.

Using the 4-D Wheel: A Guide to Exploring the Quadrants

The physical path: How you experience your full range of sexual senses—touch, taste, sight, smell, and hearing. Movement and stillness. Comfort and safety. Arousal, orgasm, and other physical sensations. The optimal 4-D physical experience is characterized by heightened senses—brighter colors, increased sensitivity, exquisite awareness of all parts of your body. The shadow side of the 4-D physical experience includes pain, numbness, and dysfunction.

The emotional path: How you experience your full range of emotional feelings about sexuality—love, passion, longing. Empathy—the ability to feel what others feel. Compassion—the ability to love yourself and others even when you feel conflicted. Trust—the ability to let go of control. The optimal 4-D emotional experience includes self-esteem, open-heartedness, pleasure, and joy. The shadow side of the 4-D emotional experience includes disappointment, anger, fear, boredom, and a closed heart.

The mental path: How you experience your beliefs and messages about sexuality—including religious beliefs and messages. Imagination, intuition, memory, dreams, and fantasies. Wishes, intentions, and expectations. The optimal 4-D mental experience includes an open mind, increased understanding, and expanded beliefs. The shadow side of the 4-D mental experience includes negative messages and rigid judgments about what sex *should* be like; how and with whom you're supposed to experience it.

The spiritual path: What sex means to you and how you experience a sense of sexual connection with yourself, your partner, and also a "higher power"—if you believe that sex can be a path to the soul. The optimal 4-D spiritual experience is characterized by ecstasy, increased energy, lasting satisfaction, and transcendence. The shadow side of the 4-D spiritual experience includes a profound sense of disconnection, isolation, and loss.

The center: How you experience the realm of mystery and paradox, when all the 4-D paths meet and merge in the center. This is the uncharted territory of the sexual mysteries. Each journey to the center is totally subjective, so it's yours to define for yourself. You may experience oneness and integration, shape shifting, and timelessness. You may experience extraordinary light and lightness of being. You may find yourself communing profoundly with your partner and with yourself. It's a place of clarity and vision, magic, and unconditional love. The shadow side of the center includes hopelessness and utter despair.

USING THE 4-D WHEEL TO MOVE FROM SEXUAL DISCONNECTION AND PAIN TO CONNECTION AND PLEASURE

Checklist for Your 4-D Wheel Practice
- Carve out protected time when your attention won't be focused on your job, friends, or family.
- Turn off your phone, computer, and other electronic devices.
- Create space—clear your room, close doors, remove distractions, or be outside in nature.
- Clear yourself—wash your hands, breathe deeply, and use any other energy-clearing techniques.
- Set a clear intention for your own sense of adventure, discovery, and well-being.
- If it's appropriate for you, light a candle—to reflect your willingness to "light your own fire."
- If it's appropriate for you, call in the energies of body, mind, heart, and spirit, along with any other energies you know to be helpful.

Opening Your Session for Yourself
- Place the 4-D diagram on the floor, draw it or imagine it on the ground, or set up a more elaborate 4-D Wheel (you can find suggestions on www.4-DNetwork.com).
- Stand in front of the Wheel and say your name out loud
- Blow your breath into the center of the Wheel—to establish a personal connection with the Wheel.

Exploring the Wheel for Yourself
- Say out loud what part of your sexual story you want to explore.
- Walk around the Wheel to locate the quadrant where you feel that part of your story begins—body, mind, heart, or spirit.
- Stand in that quadrant and describe your issue or problem—out loud—and take time to notice how it feels to do that.
- Now move to each of the other quadrants to describe your story from these other places. For instance, if you have entered the physical quadrant to tell a story of physical pain—now move to the emotional quadrant to tell that story from the point of view of your emotions. Then move to the mental quadrant to tell that story from the point of view of messages and judgments. Then move to the spiritual quadrant to tell that story from the point of view of connection and meaning. (You can move in any order.)
- As your story evolves, allow yourself to move back and forth to whatever quadrant calls to you—as many times as you like.
- Notice how you experience your story in each quadrant. Are there differences?

Bringing Your Session to a Close
- Stand outside the Wheel and state out loud what you have learned about yourself.
- You can begin with the phrase: "I learned that I …"
- If it's appropriate for you, clearly state your commitment to change.
- Say your name again.
- Express gratitude to the Wheel.
- Blow your breath into the center.
- If you have lit a candle, blow it out.
- Place your 4-D Wheel in a safe place where you can find it again.

Creating Rituals for Growth and Change
- Reflect on your situation in terms of the 4-D Wheel template.
- Feel, think about, and meditate on any changes you notice after you explore the Wheel.
- Talk about your experiences with your partner(s) and/or others who can encourage the unfolding of potentially sensitive and subtle material rather than shutting it down.
- Trust in the process—surprising results may manifest during or after your 4-D session.

THE 4-D WHEEL OF SEXUAL EXPERIENCE: FAQS

What Is the 4-D Wheel of Sexual Experience?
- A template for sexual awareness and growth—based on the Medicine Wheel, an ancient template for exploring our life journeys: physical, emotional, mental, and spiritual.
- A cognitive frame to help you organize your sexual story, including desire, fantasies, function, dysfunction, body image, cultural messages, gender, partner preference, affairs, polyamory, and other issues you may experience.

What Does the 4-D Wheel Uniquely Offer?
- A representation of four dimensions of sexual experience: physical, emotional, mental, and spiritual.
- An invitation for you to explore these four dimensions—past, present, and future.
- An invitation for you to range between the perimeter and center of the Wheel—to explore your deepest desires, sensations, fears, and longings.

For Whom Might Using the 4-D Wheel Be Especially Beneficial?
- Anyone seeking increased awareness about sexual issues and dynamics.
- Individuals and/or couples with sexual dysfunctions—to maximize your options by clarifying which of your physical issues may have significant emotional, mental, or spiritual components.
- Individuals and/or couples with low self-esteem—to explore options for a fuller sense of self.
- Partners with difficulties fully understanding one another's sexual desires—to have the space to speak and listen.
- Individuals and/or couples questioning gender and orientation—to safely explore sexual fluidity.
- Individuals and couples who are "stuck": rigid, defensive, resistant to change, attuned to past experience rather than the present—to expand their stories by moving into each quadrant.
- Couples torn apart by an affair—to enter a safe forum for expressing feelings, hearing each other, and negotiating what each of them truly wants.
- Individuals who hold the perception of never receiving enough love—to rehearse multiple ways of entering into the center of the Wheel, the meeting of body, mind, heart, and spirit.

How Might Using the 4-D Wheel Help You?
- As a context for you to understand your own sexual sensations, feelings, meanings, messages, desires, decision-making, relationships, and other issues—so that you can make distinctions, clarify confusion, and rehearse new options for connection and pleasure.
- As a dynamic way to expand your sexual story beyond cultural, religious, or medical models—to factor in family history, race, class, culture, and myth—including abuse issues if they are part of your story.
- As an arena for change in which you can map out new behaviors such as self-responsibility, ownership of feelings, motivations, and actions—as distinct from co-dependent responses, violence, shame, blame, etc.
- For many individuals and couples, the invitation to enter the Wheel provides a sense of safety, initiation, and transformation (with or without using the language of spiritual ceremony).

Why Is It Important to Move around the Wheel?
- Moving to and speaking from different quadrants helps you literally "step into" new ways to describe—and experience—your desires, problems ... and also solutions.
- For couples: movement around and within the Wheel shows where your partner locates himself/herself when you are speaking from each of the quadrants—physical, emotional, mental, or spiritual.

EXPLORING YOUR SEXUAL DESIRE AND INTIMACY: WHAT DO YOU REALLY WANT?

This is an exercise to help you know yourself better—and be better able to communicate what you want and don't want. In the blanks next to each quadrant below, write a word (or more) about the kinds of sex, love, and intimacy you want, and the kinds you don't want. Notice if what your body wants is the same or different from what you want in your heart, or your mind, or in the spiritual aspects of you that yearn for connection and meaning.

How are your desires now the same or different from your desires in the past? Beneath each statement, explore the past vs. the present: Use additional paper if you need more space.

What I Want

What I Don't Want

What I Want

What I Want

What I Don't Want

SPIRITUAL

EMOTIONAL   MENTAL

PHYSICAL

What I Don't Want

What I Want

What I Don't Want

Declaration of Sexual Rights from the World Association for Sexual Health

Revised, 2014, by the WAS Special Task Force and Expert Consultation. Reprinted with permission.

This declaration affirms that sexual rights are human rights pertaining to sexuality . . .

1. The right to equality and non-discrimination
Everyone is entitled to enjoy all sexual rights set forth in this Declaration without distinction of any kind such as race, ethnicity, color, sex, language, religion, political or other opinion, national or social origin, place of residence, property, birth, disability, age, nationality, marital and family status, sexual orientation, gender identity and expression, health status, economic and social situation and other status.

2. The right to life, liberty, and security of the person
Everyone has the right to life, liberty, and security that cannot be arbitrarily threatened, limited, or taken away for reasons related to sexuality. These include: sexual orientation, consensual sexual behavior and practices, gender identity and expression, or because of accessing or providing services related to sexual and reproductive health.

3. The right to autonomy and bodily integrity
Everyone has the right to control and decide freely on matters related to their sexuality and their body. This includes the choice of sexual behaviors, practices, partners and relationships with due regard to the rights of others. Free and informed decision making requires free and informed consent prior to any sexually related testing, interventions, therapies, surgeries, or research.

4. The right to be free from torture and cruel, inhuman, or degrading treatment or punishment
Everyone shall be free from torture and cruel, inhuman, or degrading treatment or punishment related to sexuality, including: harmful traditional practices; forced sterilization, contraception, or abortion; and other forms of torture, cruel, inhuman, or degrading treatment perpetrated for reasons related to someone's sex, gender, sexual orientation, gender identity and expression, and bodily diversity.

5. The right to be free from all forms of violence and coercion
Everyone shall be free from sexuality related violence and coercion, including: rape, sexual abuse, sexual harassment, bullying, sexual exploitation and slavery, trafficking for purposes of sexual exploitation, virginity testing, and violence committed because of real or perceived sexual practices, sexual orientation, gender identity and expression, and bodily diversity.

6. The right to privacy
Everyone has the right to privacy related to sexuality, sexual life, and choices regarding their own body and consensual sexual relations and practices without arbitrary interference and intrusion. This includes the right to control the disclosure of sexuality-related personal information to others.

7. The right to the highest attainable standard of health, including sexual health with the possibility of pleasurable, satisfying, and safe sexual experiences
Everyone has the right to the highest attainable level of health and wellbeing in relation to sexuality, including the possibility of pleasurable, satisfying, and safe sexual experiences. This requires the availability, accessibility, acceptability of quality health services and access to the conditions that influence and determine health including sexual health.

8. The right to enjoy the benefits of scientific progress and its application
Everyone has the right to enjoy the benefits of scientific progress and its applications in relation to sexuality and sexual health.

9. The right to information
Everyone shall have access to scientifically accurate and understandable information related to sexuality, sexual health, and sexual rights through diverse sources. Such information should not be arbitrarily censored, withheld, or intentionally misrepresented.

10. The right to education and the right to comprehensive sexuality education
Everyone has the right to education and comprehensive sexuality education. Comprehensive sexuality education must be age appropriate, scientifically accurate, culturally competent, and grounded in human rights, gender equality, and a positive approach to sexuality and pleasure.

11. The right to enter, form, and dissolve marriage and other similar types of relationships based on equality and full and free consent
Everyone has the right to choose whether or not to marry and to enter freely and with full and free consent into marriage, partnership or other similar relationships. All persons are entitled to equal rights entering into, during, and at dissolution of marriage, partnership and other similar relationships, without discrimination and exclusion of any kind. This right includes equal entitlements to social welfare and other benefits regardless of the form of such relationships.

12. The right to decide whether to have children, the number and spacing of children, and to have the information and the means to do so
Everyone has the right to decide whether to have children and the number and spacing of children. To exercise this right requires access to the conditions that influence and determine health and wellbeing, including sexual and reproductive health services related to pregnancy, contraception, fertility, pregnancy termination, and adoption.

13. The right to freedom of thought, opinion, and expression
Everyone has the right to freedom of thought, opinion, and expression regarding sexuality and has the right to express their own sexuality through, for example, appearance, communication, and behavior, with due respect to the rights of others.

14. The right to freedom of association and peaceful assembly
Everyone has the right to peacefully organize, associate, assemble, demonstrate, and advocate including about sexuality, sexual health, and sexual rights.

15. The right to participation in public and political life
Everyone is entitled to an environment that enables active, free, and meaningful participation in and contribution to the civil, economic, social, cultural, political, and other aspects of human life at local, national, regional, and international levels. In particular, all persons are entitled to participate in the development and implementation of policies that determine their welfare, including their sexuality and sexual health.

16. The right to access justice, remedies, and redress
Everyone has the right to access justice, remedies, and redress for violations of their sexual rights. This requires effective, adequate, accessible, and appropriate educative, legislative, judicial, and other measures. Remedies include redress through restitution, compensation, rehabilitation, satisfaction, and guarantee of non-repetition.

DESIRE AND INTIMACY: A BRIEF GUIDE TO SOME HOT-BUTTON ISSUES

Here are 13 short descriptions of issues I'm often asked about. You can find more info on any of these issues online or in books. There's much more you might want to explore—sex toys, safe sex, talking with kids about sex and intimacy, and on and on. There's space at the bottom for you to add your own issues.

Enhancing Pleasure

Pleasure is a quality that can get lost when we focus on the serious work of health, healing, recovery issues, and more. A primary question I repeatedly ask clients about desire and intimacy is "What do you really want?" Too many of us have never explored this question—which is where the 4-D Wheel can be so effective, especially if you step fully into every dimension: physical, emotional, mental, and spiritual—allowing yourself to breathe, feel, remember. It's crucial to know that what we want may change as our lives and relationships become more or less complex. Finding ways to update what feels really good *right now* can feel like coming home to yourself.

Opening Communication

Whether the issue is pleasure or pain, a vital part of intimate relationship is being able to transmit our views and feelings to our partners. Some basic communication guidelines may help: 1) Create safe, private space from kids, work, electronic devices. 2) Vow confidentiality, so you know your conversation won't go beyond the room. 3) Use "I" statements, so each of you takes responsibility for what you share (no blaming or shaming permitted). 4) Listen to your partner, even when you feel like interrupting (try setting a time limit for each of you to speak). 5) Make eye contact. 6) Find ways to express gratitude to each other at the end of the conversation, even if it's difficult.

Erotic Communication

Adapting the basic guidelines above, focus on what each of you wants—and allow yourself to communicate with your body language and movements as well as words. Use the language of all your senses—smell, touch, taste, seeing, and hearing. See how much you can learn about yourself and each other, especially if you can let go of goals and outcomes—those bugaboos of performance-oriented sex.

Fantasies

Using the imagination to enhance desire means activating the mental dimension of the 4-D Wheel. Fantasies may range from memories of peak experiences to taboo subjects: same-sex encounters, kinky sex, and even unspeakable violence. We can actively call forth our fantasies, or they may be spontaneous, sometimes through dreams. Fantasies can be potent enough to generate orgasm with no touch involved (numerous women have spoken to me about the pleasures of "thinking off"). Sharing fantasies with a partner can be a powerful aphrodisiac; some fantasies are best kept to one's self. Either way, our fantasies are a barometer to our desires, as well as a potential enhancement.

LGBTQ Issues

Some of us know early in life that we're sexually attracted to people of the same sex, or wishing we could change our biological sex from male to female, or female to male. For others, such discoveries may happen over time. The point is, most human beings are innately gender fluid to some degree, yet almost all of us are socialized to identify as only male or female—and as solidly heterosexual. Stepping into identities of lesbian, gay, bisexual, transgender, queer, questioning, and other diversities can run the gamut from joyous and freeing to fraught with angst and prejudice. It often requires a coming-out process—a time to practice new roles, truths, and sensations, and build new communities of love and support.

Growing Older

Media stereotypes of late life sex depict dirty (if dysfunctional) old men lusting after titillating (if brain-dead) sex kittens. They also depict women beyond reproductive age as asexual, and therefore invisible. Actor Julie Harris summed up this notion trenchantly in an interview on National Public Radio (8/3/00): "After the age of fifty, we become women of glass. Men look right through us." Yet many in their 60s, 70s, and 80s speak of a sexual confidence and fullness of expression that's informed by many years of life experience rather than eroded by it. In my national survey on sexuality and spirituality, respondents spoke of finally outgrowing cultural constraints, moving beyond personal negativity, and appreciating the richness of their relationships. So take heart. To paraphrase Yogi Berra: "It's never over till it's over."

Injury and Illness

Surviving a serious injury or illness, or living with a chronic condition, brings physical changes, emotional responses, and relationship challenges. Often you are left feeling like less of a man or woman, defective, undeserving of love, fearing rejection, and avoiding sex. However, injury or illness doesn't have to end your sex life. These words are from Dr. Mitchell Tipper's website, which offers a video series and much more about sexual health: drmitchelltepper.com.

Using Pornography

Porn use didn't start with the Internet. Erotic images adorn the walls of ancient caves, and have appeared in just about every civilization since. The Internet can take credit for the widespread availability of explicit sexual imagery today. Sexual liberals point out that these images are educational and liberating in our pleasure-repressive society. Others point out that these images are mostly sexist, often violent, and always unrealistic, featuring flawless bodies and on-cue orgasms—not good education for real people, or for loving relationships. Frequent porn use may condition users to prefer easy mechanical sex rather than relational sex where partners take time and energy to respond to each other. The blanket terms "porn addiction" and "sexual addiction" have been used to label porn users. These terms present their own problems because "addiction" is seldom a truly accurate label, and most addiction recovery methods stress shame and abstinence, which are arguably ineffective approaches for promoting the kinds of desire and intimacy that engage body, mind, heart, and spirit.

Affairs

Extramarital affairs occur worldwide; more than 20% of both men and women engage in sexual infidelity (with little emotional involvement), romantic infidelity (no sex), or a combination of both. An affair may arise from an unsatisfying marriage, but not always. Other contributing factors include genetics, and complex brain structure, which makes it possible for some people to feel deep attachment for one partner, plus romantic love for another, plus lust for even more partners. That said, the result of an affair is often shame-based pain and chaos for the couple. Effective therapy involves calming the crisis and helping the couple know and communicate their deep desires. At this point, there are various ways for helping couples discover or re-discover the flame of passion. For guides in this beyond the 4-D Wheel, see Esther Perel's *Mating in Captivity* and Tammy Nelson's *The New Monogamy*.

Polyamory

Polyamory means openly engaging in sexual intimacy with more than one partner, as distinct from monogamy, where the contract is fidelity with only one partner, or one partner at a time. Poly relationships differ from affairs, in that they involve honesty rather than cheating. Most importantly they involve the capacity to enjoy your partner's joy of sexual connection with somebody else. Exploring a poly lifestyle starts with acknowledging your desires for opening your relationship, and engaging your partner in the process of discovery. This requires continual openness with yourself, and the energy to negotiate with all your partners about logistics as well as feelings.

Kinky Sex

"Kink" is a catch phrase for consensual sexual variations like non-monogamy, and BDSM (bondage/discipline/sadism/masochism), which includes erotic bondage, power exchange, sensation play, and experimenting with erotic toys, roles, costumes, and/or fetishes. Consensual non-monogamy includes agreements to open long-term relationships to multiple sexual or romantic partners. Polyamory and swinging are examples. Some people like to dabble in these occasionally. Others make them the centerpieces of their sexual lifestyles. For an overview of hundreds of these variations see: www.kinkacademy.com.

Your Brain on Desire

Our brains are interactive, and during desire and intimacy (or during turn-off and rejection) different areas of our brains connect with each other. For an opportunity to zoom inside an animated brain to highlight brain structures as you inquire about exactly what happens during desire and intimacy see: www.TheAnatomyoflove.com. To watch a short animation of your brain on orgasm see: www.thevisualmd.com/read_videoguide/?idu=1033607627&q=orgasm%20brain.

The Pharmaceutical Revolution: Viagra, "Pink Viagra," etc.

Some say that the real sexual revolution wasn't the social movement of the 1960s, 1970s, and 1980s, but the pharmaceutical events that sparked changes in how women and men experience intercourse: the birth control pill (1960) and Viagra (1998). Pharmaceutical companies are now seeking a "pink Viagra" that will spark desire in women who feel bored, turned off, or numb. But low desire most often has multiple roots—physical, emotional, mental, and spiritual. And pharmaceutical companies are most often focused on monetizing rather than sexual healing. Bottom line to a complex and often contentious issue: pharmaceutical intervention may be helpful in certain circumstances. But sexual desire cannot be created and sustained by a pill. Desire arises from body, mind, heart, and spirit. Its care and feeding begins with knowing what we want, when to assert our will, and when to let go in blissful surrender. This is the ultimate secret to great sex and to a great life. If we could figure out how to package this understanding, we could all be billionaires.

ADD YOUR OWN HOT-BUTTON ISSUES HERE:

_____
_____
_____
_____
_____
_____
_____
_____
_____
_____
_____
_____
_____
_____

REFERENCES AND SUGGESTED READING FOR HOT-BUTTON ISSUES

Anand, M. (1989). *The art of sexual ecstasy: The path of sacred sexuality for western lovers.* Los Angeles: Jeremy Tarcher.

Anapol, D. (1997). *Polyamory: The new love without limits: Secrets of sustainable intimate relationships* (rev. ed.). San Raphael, CA: IntiNet Resource Center.

Bornstein, K. (2010) *Gender outlaws: The next generation.* New York: Seal Press.

Bornstein, K. (2013). *My new gender workbook: A step-by-step guide to achieving world peace through gender anarchy and sex positivity* (2nd ed.). New York: Routledge.

Carellas, B. (2007). *Urban tantra: Sacred sex for the 21st century.* Berkeley, CA: Celestial Arts.

Diamond, L. (2009). *Sexual fluidity: Understanding women's love and desire.* Cambridge, MA: Harvard University Press.

Easton, D., and Hardy, J.W. (2009). *The ethical slut: A practical guide to polyamory, open relationships, & other adventures.* Berkeley, CA: Celestial Arts.

Feinberg, L. (1997). *Transgender warriors: Making history from Joan of Arc to RuPaul.* Boston: Beacon Press.

Gromko, L (2015). *Where's my book: A guide for transgender and gender non-conforming youth, their parents, & everyone else.* Bainbridge Books.

Hall, K., and Graham, K. (Eds.). (2012). *The cultural context of sexual pleasure and problems: Psychotherapy with diverse clients.* New York: Routledge.

Joannides, P. (2015). *The guide to getting it on* (8th ed.). Waldport, OR: Goofyfoot Press.

Kleinplatz, P.J, and Mosher, C. (2006). *Sadomasochism: Powerful pleasures.* New York: Routledge.

Kort, J. (2003). *Ten smart things gay men can do to improve their lives.* New York: Alyson Books.

Loe, Meika (2004). *The rise of Viagra: How the little blue pill changed sex in America.* New York: New York University Press.

Michaels, M., and Johnson, P. (2012). *Great sex made simple: Tantric tips to deepen intimacy & heighten pleasure.* St Paul, MN: Llewellan Publications.

Nelson, T. (2013). *The new monogamy: Redefining your relationship after infidelity.* Oakland, CA: New Harbinger.

Nin, A. (1969). *Delta of Venus.* New York: Bantam.

Northrup, C. (2001). *The wisdom of menopause: Creating physical and emotional health and healing during the change.* New York: Bantam.

Northrup, C. (2010). *Women's bodies, women's wisdom: Creating physical and emotional health and healing* (rev. ed.). New York: Bantam.

Perel, E. (2007). *Mating in captivity: Unlocking erotic intelligence.* New York: Harper.

Queen, C. (1995). *Exhibitionism for the shy.* San Francisco, CA: Down There Press

Rich, A. (1980, Summer). Compulsory heterosexuality and lesbian existence. *Signs: Journal of Women in Culture and Society,* 5(4): 631–660.

Savage, D. (2012). *It gets better: Coming out, overcoming bullying, and creating a life worth living.* New York: Plume.

Sprinkle, A. (2005) *Dr. Sprinkle's spectacular sex: Make over your love life with one of the world's great sex experts.* New York: Tarcher.

Taormino, T. (2008). *Opening up: A guide to creating and sustaining open relationships.* San Francisco: Cleis Press.

Taormino, T. (2012). *The ultimate guide to kink: BDSM, role play and the erotic edge.* San Francisco: Cleis Press.

Tiefer, L., and Kaschak, E. (Eds.) (2001). *A new view of women's sexual problems.* Binghamton, NY: Haworth Press.

Tolle, E. (2003). *Stillness speaks.* Novato, CA: New World Library.

INFORMATIONAL WEBSITES

TheAnatomyOfLove.com (your brain on love). KinkAcademy.com (videos and info on kink). Newviewcampaign. org (challenging the medicalization of sex). Iflscience.com/editors-blog/how-do-surgeons-turn-penis-vagina. Drmitchelltepper.com (sexual pleasure after injury and illness).

Appreciations

It takes a village to write a book, and I've found myself drawing often from the village well. I would not have begun this adventure without the loving encouragement and editorial genius of my life partner, Jo Chaffee. Your mark is imprinted on every page as well as in my heart. Collaboration with two Routledge editors helped shape and shepherd the manuscript: Marta Moldvai, who supported the idea from the beginning, and Elizabeth Graber who guided this book through the potentially daunting production process. Graphic designer Belinda Morse created the original Wheel in 2004 and has refined and updated it here. Web designer Michele Stohen created the inspirational cover design.

Profound gratitude to the colleagues whose chapters in Part II exemplify their creativity and expertise in working the 4-D Wheel: Keesha Ewers, Kristin Hodson, Lindsay Jernigan, Kamara McAndrews, and Chelsea Wakefield. Your healing spirits shine in how deeply you practice your craft and how sensitively you collaborate with your clients. Thanks also to other practitioners whose Wheels and unique approaches contribute to this book: Sherri Aiken, Elliott Kronenfeld, Tina Nevin, Claudia Thompson, and Debra Wickman. To many more in our professional network and beyond who made suggestions, proofread, and otherwise supported me in the process of writing and editing, especially Patti Britton, Valeria Chuba, Katherine Ellin, Magdalena Fosse, Katherine Golub, Kimberly Jackson, Jacqui Mendez, Tammy Nelson, Yara Perez, Tina Sellers, and Russell Stambaugh. Appreciation to the organizations who support 4-D work and who have offered me space to teach, especially AASECT, AAMFT, COSRT, Esalen Institute, Rowe Conference Center, and the Casa de los Artistas.

Gratitude to the thousands of clients, supervisees, trainees, and retreat participants who have stepped into the Wheel to expand their lives. You bring to life the practices outlined in this book. Particular gratitude to the growing family of professionals who are incorporating the 4-D Wheel into your practices. You are the heart and soul of this approach to exploring desire and intimacy. As the 4-D Network, you are also the future of this work as you make it your own and introduce it to others.

To the colleagues and mentors present and past who have inspired me and shaped my personal and professional focus for this workbook: Lucy Brown, Emilie Conrad, Riane Eisler, Oscar Miro-Quesada, Judy Norsigian and other founders of *Our Bodies, Ourselves*, Christiane Northrup, Esther Perel, Wilhelm Reich, Virginia Satir, Reva Seybolt, Leonore Tiefer and other members of the New View Campaign. You are shape-shifters in the fields of medicine, neuroscience, family therapy, sex education, bodywork, energy healing, bioenergetics, movement, cultural anthropology, shamanism, and activism—all of which impact our capacity for desire and intimacy: body, mind, heart, and spirit. I stand humbly on your shoulders.

To you the reader, on whom the effectiveness of this book depends: In true workbook style, I invite you to acknowledge yourself here. Give yourself heartfelt congratulations for the gifts you bring to your practice _____

_____

Index

Note: Page numbers in *italics* indicate figures.